FEMINIST REREADINGS
OF
MODERN AMERICAN DRAMA

FEMINIST REREADINGS OF MODERN AMERICAN DRAMA

Edited by
JUNE SCHLUETER

Rutherford • Madison • Teaneck
Fairleigh Dickinson University Press
London and Toronto: Associated University Presses

© 1989 by Associated University Presses, Inc.

All rights reserved. Authorization to photocopy items for internal or personal use, or the internal or personal use of specific clients, is granted by the copyright owner, provided that a base fee of $10.00, plus eight cents per page, per copy is paid directly to the Copyright Clearance Center, 27 Congress Street, Salem, Massachusetts 01970. [0-8386-3359-5/89 $10.00 + 8¢ pp, pc.]

Associated University Presses
440 Forsgate Drive
Cranbury, NJ 08512

Associated University Presses
25 Sicilian Avenue
London WC1A 2QH, England

Associated University Presses
P.O. Box 488, Port Credit
Mississauga, Ontario
Canada L5G 4M2

The paper used in this publication meets the requirements of the American National Standard for Permanence of Paper for Printed Library Materials Z39.48-1984.

Library of Congress Cataloging-in-Publication Data

Feminist rereadings of modern American drama / edited by June Schlueter.
   p.   cm.
Includes index.
ISBN 0-8386-3359-5 (alk. paper)
  1. American drama—20th century—History and criticism.
  2. Feminism and literature—United States. I. Schlueter, June.
PS338.F45F46 1989
812'.509352042—dc20   88-46149
                                                                            CIP

PRINTED IN THE UNITED STATES OF AMERICA

To the memory of my father,
Alex Mayer
1912–1985

CONTENTS

Acknowledgments · 9
Introduction · 11
JUNE SCHLUETER

PART 1: EUGENE O'NEILL

"A Monster of Perfection": O'Neill's "Stella" · 25
ANNE FLÈCHE

O'Neill's Ghostly Women · 37
SUZANNE BURR

Theatricality and Otherness in *All God's Chillun Got Wings* · 48
BETTE MANDL

PART 2: ARTHUR MILLER

The Exchange of Women and Male Homosocial Desire in Arthur Miller's *Death of a Salesman* and Lillian Hellman's *Another Part of the Forest* · 59
GAYLE AUSTIN

Women and the American Dream of *Death of a Salesman* · 67
KAY STANTON

Paper Dolls: Melodrama and Sexual Politics in Arthur Miller's Early Plays · 103
JEFFREY D. MASON

Betrayal and Blessedness: Explorations of Feminine Power in *The Crucible*, *A View from the Bridge*, and *After the Fall* · 116
ISKA ALTER

PART 3: TENNESSEE WILLIAMS

Authorizing History: Victimization in *A Streetcar Named Desire* · 149
ANCA VLASOPOLOS

"Weak and Divided People": Tennessee Williams and
the Written Woman   171
   JOHN TIMPANE

PART 4: EDWARD ALBEE

What's New at the Zoo?: Rereading Edward Albee's
American Dream(s) and Nightmares   183
   MICKEY PEARLMAN

Magnified and Sanctified: *Tiny Alice* Reconsidered   192
   NAOMI CONN LIEBLER

PART 5: SAM SHEPARD

Sam Shepard's Spectacle of Impossible
Heterosexuality: *Fool for Love*   213
   LYNDA HART

Self as Other: Sam Shepard's *Fool for Love* and *A Lie of
the Mind*   227
   ROSEMARIE BANK

Notes on Contributors   241
Index   245

ACKNOWLEDGMENTS

Thanks to Harry Keyishian, Director of Fairleigh Dickinson University Press, for his encouragement and guidance; to Bernard F. Dick of Fairleigh Dickinson University for his helpful suggestions; to Richard Everett and Evangeline Bicknell of Skillman Library, Lafayette College, for their interlibrary loan assistance; and to Lafayette College for its financial support. Special and ongoing thanks to Paul Schlueter for his support, advice, and love.

Permission for the following is gratefully acknowledged:

Excerpt from "The Waste Land" in *Collected Poems 1909–1962* by T. S. Eliot, copyright 1936 by Harcourt Brace Jovanovich, Inc., copyright © 1963, 1964 by T. S. Eliot, reprinted by permission of the publisher.

Excerpt from Julian Wasserman, "The Idea of Language in the Plays of Edward Albee," from *Edward Albee: An Interview and Essays*. Houston: The University of St. Thomas Press, 1983.

From *A View From the Bridge* by Arthur Miller. Copyright © 1960, renewed © 1988 by Arthur Miller. All rights reserved. Reprinted by permission of Viking Penguin, Inc.

From *The Crucible* by Arthur Miller. Copyright 1953, renewed © 1981 by Arthur Miller. All rights reserved. Reprinted by permission of Viking Penguin, Inc.

From *After the Fall* by Arthur Miller. Copyright © 1964 by Arthur Miller. All rights reserved. Reprinted by permission of Viking Penguin, Inc.

Anca Vlasopolos, "Authorizing History: Victimization in A Streetcar Named Desire," *Theatre Journal* 3, no. 8 (October 1986): 322–38. Permission to reprint granted by the Johns Hopkins University Press.

Jacket photo: Kim Hunter as Linda Loman and Nehemiah Persoff as Willy Loman in Stratford (Ontario) Festival's 1983 production of Arthur Miller's *Death of a Salesman*. Photo by Robert C. Ragsdale. Courtesy of the Stratford Festival Archives.

INTRODUCTION
June Schlueter

In what may be the most consistently valorized of modern American plays, Linda Loman, wife to the literary world's famous salesman, pleads with her sons that they not neglect their father. He is, after all, a "human being," to whom "attention must be paid." Although herself unsuspecting, Linda Loman has provided a silent subtitle for this collection, registering a similar plea by feminist critics that attention be paid, not to the has-been drummer who seems to have found a permanent place in American culture, but to the gender constructs of that culture and of its literature. Indeed, Linda herself wins attention from three of the critics in this volume, who are engaged with others in the enterprise of rereading male literary texts and in examining and revising the process of the critical enterprise.

Such rereading of canonical literary texts is, of course, not restricted to feminist criticism, but the work of feminist critics has contributed significantly to displacing the complacency that, until recently, assumed the literary canon was closed. For many feminist critics, the "Revisionary Imperative," as Sandra M. Gilbert describes it,[1] insists that attention be paid to texts by the "other" half of society, who, for the most part, have not been graced with canonical regard. Such criticism—essentially a recovery mission—is an important part of the feminist agenda and the principle of a second collection I am preparing called *Modern American Drama: The Female Canon*.

For this volume, however, I have collected rereadings of canonical male plays—plays by the five American playwrights who, during this century, seem to have the most persistent claim to a permanent place in dramatic history. That such a claim is intact was affirmed by the submissions I received when I first announced in *PMLA* that I would be editing this collection: a few on female playwrights, who immediately joined the competition for a place in the companion volume, and all the rest on these five male playwrights: Eugene O'Neill, Arthur Miller, Tennessee Williams, Edward Albee, and Sam Shepard.

The plea of this collection, then, is not that attention be paid to female playwrights but that the work of male playwrights be looked at again, this time differently. As Annette Kolodny puts it in "Dancing Through the Minefield: Some Observations on the Theory, Practice, and Politics of a Feminist Literary Criticism":

> what is attended to in a literary work is often determined not so much by the work itself as by the critical technique or aesthetic criteria through which it is filtered or, rather, read and decoded.[2]

The feminist critic, attending to questions of gender in canonical texts, offers perceptions that encourage a fuller understanding of the assumptions of both literature and culture. Again, Kolodny notes that feminist criticism offers "an acute and impassioned *attentiveness* to the ways in which primarily male structures of power are inscribed (or encoded) within our literary inheritance. . . ."[3]

Attentiveness to gender in male texts, like feminist criticism in general, takes a variety of forms. The one with the "longest" history, the "images-of-women-in-literature" approach, dates back to 1949, when Simone de Beauvoir's *The Second Sex*, accounting for the historical and contemporary place of women in Western culture, provided a chapter on "The Myth of Woman in Five [Male] Authors": Henry Montherlant, D. H. Lawrence, Paul Claudel, André Breton, and Stendhal.[4] Mary Ellmann's *Thinking About Women* (1968) reactivated the discussion of the "second" sex in literature by identifying an array of stereotypes of woman that appear and reappear in literature by both men and women.[5] Kate Millett's *Sexual Politics* (1969), while taking a broader cultural view, devoted a section to "The Literary Reflection," which spoke not only of the programmatic degradation of women in literature by men but also of how writers such as D. H. Lawrence, Henry Miller, and Norman Mailer—but not Jean Genet—insist on phallic privilege.[6]

The "images-of-women" approach, which several contributors to this volume pursue, remains valuable as an expository device, designed to reveal the extent to which male-authorized fictional worlds portray mythical or stereotypical female characters and to which both author and reader, in failing to question those worlds, have endorsed the prevailing gender paradigm. As Gilbert describes it, we are a "masculinist culture," evolving into a "masculinist-feminist culture."[7] Bringing attention to ways in which women are portrayed in literature may provide an important part of that evolution.

But in the twenty years since Ellmann's book, feminist criticism has moved into more sophisticated—and riskier—territory, coming into contact with more established critical methods as well as contemporary theoretical modes: archetypal, anthropological, and psychoanalytical criticism, deconstruction, semiotics, and reader response, for example. Indeed, part of the attraction of feminist criticism is what might be called a kind of critical intertextuality, an interaction with other approaches that provide a point of entry and a critical paradigm but in no way neutralize the feminist focus. Feminist criticism, in its plurality, remains resistant to categorization, connecting, at will, with any number of formalist, structuralist, or poststructuralist methodologies. In this collection, it becomes singular only in its effort to generate awareness of the gender inscriptions that inform and shape the canon so that it might offer a new way of seeing what we once thought we saw.

The thirteen essays in this collection are arranged not by literary approach but by playwright, with two to four essays devoted to each. In "'A Monster of Perfection': O'Neill's 'Stella,'" the first essay in this volume, Anne Flèche proposes that "the dominant architectural feature" of O'Neill's writing is the "unstable female character who is nevertheless structurally central to the competing male narratives around her." The dilemma confronting the feminist critic is how to read O'Neill's female characters without de-contextualizing character, without, that is, removing the character from its narrative context. Focusing on act 4 of *A Long Day's Journey Into Night*, Flèche explores the character of Mary Tyrone in this Oedipal narrative, which, in its struggle for origins and for the end of desire, reveals its nature through the woman who motivates yet is herself unmotivated. Flèche claims that the play's Oedipal structure is revealed through the elusive, seductive "jouissance" of the mother and that Mary's central significance, which seems indisputable yet indescribable, relies on her elusiveness.

Suzanne Burr's "O'Neill's Ghostly Women" offers a reassessment of O'Neill's treatment of women, rejecting claims of misogyny and replacing them with the proposal that O'Neill's work reflects what today would be called a "feminist consciousness." Noting, with Louis Shaeffer, the "legion of dead wives and mothers" in O'Neill's plays, Burr explores how, through portraits of dislocated, trapped, and silenced women—and particularly through Mrs. Keeney in *Ile* and Mary Tyrone in *A Long Day's Journey Into Night*—O'Neill expresses a remarkable empathy with women's psychic and social entrapment and disenfranchisement.

In "Theatricality and Otherness in *All God's Chillun Got Wings*," Bette Mandl explores the complicated conceptual space of this O'Neill play, noting social and aesthetic dictates that impose themselves on race and gender. O'Neill's insistence on the universality of human experience prevents the play from becoming the commentary on otherness that the playwright envisioned. The coexistence of race and gender polarities complicates dramatic movement and impact, as does a vertical pull between the "diabolic" represented by the African mask and the "heaven" suggested by the play's title. Mandl concludes that it was easier for O'Neill to renounce cultural biases than to create a dramatic structure that does not implicitly reinforce those conditions.

Four contributors offer rereadings of plays in the Arthur Miller corpus. Gayle Austin's point of departure in "The Exchange of Women and Male Homosocial Desire in Arthur Miller's *Death of a Salesman* and Lillian Hellman's *Another Part of the Forest*" is Gayle Rubin's study, "The Traffic in Women" (1975), an essay that synthesizes theories of Marx, Lévi-Strauss, and Freud (via Lacan) to offer a model of feminist anthropology. It is a model adopted and modified by Eve Kosofsky Sedgwick to propose that the principle of exchange—designed to facilitate men's relationships with each other—may be found in literary works as well as in particular cultures. Austin argues that modern American drama, "informed as it is by capitalist, psychoanalytic social conditions," provides an opportunity for exploring this theory. Focusing on *Death of a Salesman*, she points out how women in this play are "exchanged among men" and how they are represented as "objects to be so exchanged," a condition that eliminates women as active subjects in the play. She then moves on to a text of the same period by a female playwright, Lillian Hellman's *Another Part of the Forest*, suggesting that although the women in this play function within socially-prescribed rules, they are active agents. Austin sees *Death of a Salesman*, a play that is central to modern drama, as an obstacle to the inclusion of women's experience in serious drama; she sees Hellman's play, which provides an understanding portrait of women, as a signal that serious drama in which women can be "subjects acting on their own behalf" is possible.

Kay Stanton's "Women and the American Dream of *Death of a Salesman*" scrutinizes Miller's depiction of the American Dream as personified in Willy Loman and finds it to be "male-oriented" but requiring "unacknowledged dependence upon women as well as women's subjugation and exploitation." She determines the Dream to have three competing dimensions: the Green World, the Business World, and the Home, all with "ascendant male figure heads and submerged female presences." Willy tries to make an all-male (patriarchal-fraternal) community in each, but his efforts are doomed to self-destruction, partly because of the complexities of exploiting women without acknowledging dependence on their value and partly because of the obsession of the masculine mythos of competition. Because the dream can only be realized if one is "number-one man," it puts men (especially Willy and Biff) into phallic rivalry, such that they must "castrate" one another or be "castrated." The men all agree that women must be kept ignorant of male failures, but Linda, The Woman, and other female characters witness these failures, and the women's emergence unleashes, without acknowledgment, the truth of the Loman men from the sham of the Dream. To Stanton, the tragedy of the play hinges on Willy's choice of the dead, aggressive, fantasy male mythos epitomized by Ben over Linda's living, loving realistic female value system.

Jeffrey D. Mason's "Paper Dolls: Melodrama and Sexual Politics in Arthur Miller's Early Plays" surveys four of the early works, proposing that, in contrived penultimate scenes, Miller "borrows the methods and espouses the sexual politics of melodrama." In *All My Sons, Death of a Salesman,* and *A View from the Bridge,* he separates the male protagonist from his wife and family in the penultimate scene, requiring him to choose in isolation. In *The Crucible,* although he grants Elizabeth Proctor presence, she refuses to counsel her husband in his decision. Mason argues that the conventions of mid-nineteenth-century American melodrama inform Miller's early plays, enforcing a "devastating separation" of men and women and "distributing situations, options, and agony along gender lines."

Iska Alter's "Betrayal and Blessedness: Explorations of Feminine Power in *The Crucible, A View from the Bridge,* and *After the Fall*" claims that critics, intent on exploring the dimensions of male identity and authority that are patent in Miller's playworlds, have simplified the position of Miller's women. Using three of the canonical plays to make her point, Alter suggests how Miller evokes an "elaborate palimpsest of feminine authority, derived from presumptive archetypes representing modes of generalized human behavior, social forms enclosing individual action, and psychoanalytic explanations of personal response." In each of these plays, Miller's men, bundles of "unresolved Oedipal paradoxes," turn first to duty and responsibility and then to female sexuality—despite its anarchic potential—as a redemptive, even sanctifying force.

Anca Vlasopolos's essay on Tennessee Williams, "Authorizing History: Victimization in *A Streetcar Named Desire*," brings together literary applications of anthropology as well as deconstructionist and feminist methods to reread *Streetcar*. Noting the inadequacies of generic or ethical measures of the play, Vlasopolos examines the conflict over narrative authority in the play and the extent to which gender determination excludes Blanche from the larger historical discourse. Both historical revisionists, Blanche and Stanley tell different stories of Blanche's past, with Blanche casting herself as a priestess of Aphrodite and Stanley casting her as a "male joke about insatiable fallen women." Extending her analysis to audience response, Vlasopolos registers the audience's role in a hierarchical historical discourse that sees Blanche as a deviant, whose actions subvert social order. Stanley's version of history wins authority not only within the conflict of the play but within the dynamic of theater as well. Vlasopolos's essay holds a special place in the collection. In 1986, *Theatre Journal* asked me to evaluate the piece: my recommendation that the journal publish the essay, however, was not the end of my association with it. The essay introduced me to a reading of this canonical text that immediately found its way into my own thinking and teaching and eventually inspired this collection. The only essay in this volume that has been published previously, it deserves repeating because of its insights and influence.

John Timpane's "'Weak and Divided People': Tennessee Williams and the Written Woman" uses Williams's characterization of women to point to the limits and possibilities of feminist readings. Ranging through the canon of Williams's plays, Timpane proposes that the women in those plays are "destroyed not by male dominance, patriarchy, or misogyny but by their own predeliction for destruction" and "by their own desires." Noting Williams's repeated defenses of ambiguity of character, he argues

Introduction   17

that attributing gender expectations to Williams's female characters can "idealize, stylize, trivialize," making the written woman consumable and exhaustible. Both misogynist and advocate readings, he suggests, eliminate "competing ways of reading the written woman." For Timpane, rereading Williams with gender expectations obscures the ambiguity and ambivalence that should mark the truly feminist depiction of women. In his creation of female characters, Williams may well have provided "an authentic and authoritative depiction of female foolishness, limitations, and error."

Mickey Pearlman's "What's New at the Zoo?: Rereading Edward Albee's *American Dream*(s) and Nightmares" places both *The Zoo Story* and *The American Dream* in the context of the American eighties. For Pearlman, a contemporary feminist rereading reveals the caustic and cryptic vision of Albee's anti-female dramatic worlds. Women in *The Zoo Story* are "powerful and pathetic, damaging or deranged, vulgar and vicious, impinging on the spaces of men with damaging regularity." This two-(male) character play, she contends, invites its audience to "agonize over the predicaments of men by further diminishing the emotional, sexual, and spiritual needs of women." Similarly, an audience re-experiencing *The American Dream* in the eighties cannot blithely accept the "odious [matriarchal] triumvirate" of Mommy, Mrs. Barker, and Grandma or the stereotypes of American females they epitomize. From the perspective of the eighties, Albee's view of women as "enemies of the Dream" is "empty bombast."

Naomi Conn Liebler looks at one of the "absent" women in Albee's plays: Tiny Alice. In "Magnified and Sanctified: *Tiny Alice* Reconsidered," she reviews critical attempts to understand this puzzling play. Liebler focuses on its feminization of the spiritual and powerful variables—or abstractions—to which people attach themselves and on the possibility and responsibility of individual choice in such matters. In her view, the play balances the questions of choice and commitment against those of assumption and certainty. By locating these questions in a female presence provocatively and arbitrarily called "Tiny," Albee has confounded readers, who, like the protagonist Julian, cannot accept a feminine locus of power without a contextual and evaluative label such as "maternal" or "sexual"—what Albee called in *The Zoo Story* "the old pigeonhole bit." Combining feminist, structural, and response criticism, Liebler considers how the audience shares Julian's perplexity about the play's elusive subject, rendered in terms of female identity that will not submit to meaningful, i.e., limiting labels.

The two essays on Shepard, the most recent playwright to join the canon, suggest that the "Revisionary Imperative" extends to contemporary American drama as well. Lynda Hart begins her essay, "Sam Shepard's Spectacle of Impossible Heterosexuality: *Fool for Love*," with a discussion of the coincidence between Shepard's public image and the dramatic roles he both creates and plays. She concedes a growing awareness in Shepard's plays of the relationship between "male disorders," such as violence and obsessive authoritarian control, and patriarchy. She also acknowledges Shepard's experience with the transformational principles of the Open Theater. But, she argues, Shepard regresses into "a naive realism," failing to use the strategies of transformation to disrupt sexual difference. Attentive especially to *Fool for Love*, Shepard's first effort to create a "fully autonomous female character," Hart concludes that the play perpetuates the fantasies of male (hommo)sexual desire and power, dramatizing the impossibility (as Shepard himself once claimed) of heterosexual relationships.

Rosemarie Bank's "Self as Other: Sam Shepard's *Fool for Love* and *A Lie of the Mind*" also re-examines, with different results, this allegedly transitional play, adding *A Lie of the Mind* to her analysis. Bank's approach is by way of Foucault, whose notion of the heterotopic, she argues, signals a shift in dramatic discourse away from binary critical constructs. The relationships within these two playworlds are "all the real sites in a culture, 'simultaneously represented, contested, and inverted.'" Bank sees the heterotopic world of Shepard's plays as a locus for exploring doubling and transformations of gender that challenge and confound received traditions.

Individually, the essays in this volume represent rereadings, in feminist terms, of major texts in American drama. Collectively, they propose a reappraisal of the dramatic canon that renews and revitalizes the interest in these plays that originally secured them canonical stature. None of the essays strikes me as an argument for decanonization, but all insist that ways of reading these documents of modern American drama and culture have not been exhausted. As Kolodny points out, "readers as diverse as Adrienne Rich and Harold Bloom have arrived by various routes at the conclusion that *re-vision* constitutes the key to an ongoing literary history."[8]

Introduction

Notes

1. Sandra M. Gilbert, "What Do Feminist Critics Want?: Or a Postcard from the Volcano," *ADE Bulletin* 66 (1980); reprinted in *The New Feminist Criticism: Essays on Women, Literature, Theory*, ed. Elaine Showalter (New York: Pantheon Books, 1985), p. 29.
2. Annette Kolodny, "Dancing Through the Minefield: Some Observations on the Theory, Practice, and Politics of a Feminist Literary Criticism," *Feminist Studies* 6 (1980); reprinted in *The New Feminist Criticism*, ed. Elaine Showalter, p. 160.
3. Ibid., p. 162.
4. Simone de Beauvoir, *Le Deuxième Sex: I. Les Faits et les Mythes; II. L'Experience Vecue* (Paris: Librairie Gallimard, 1949); *The Second Sex*, trans. and ed. H. M. Parshley (New York: Knopf, 1953).
5. Mary Ellmann, *Thinking About Women* (New York: Harcourt, Brace and World, 1968).
6. Kate Millett, *Sexual Politics* (Garden City: Doubleday and Company, 1969).
7. Gilbert, "What Do Feminist Critics Want?," p. 43.
8. Annette Kolodny, "A Map for Misreading: Or, Gender and the Interpretation of Literary Texts." *New Literary History* (1980); reprinted in *The New Feminist Criticism*, ed. Elaine Showalter, p. 59.

FEMINIST REREADINGS
OF
MODERN AMERICAN DRAMA

PART 1
EUGENE O'NEILL

"A MONSTER OF PERFECTION"
O'Neill's "Stella"

Anne Flèche

There has always been far too much to say about Eugene O'Neill, and the feminist critic in particular finds herself staring at an Everest of possibilities. For O'Neill, important innovations in the drama—reactions against the prevailing naturalism he called "'holding the family Kodak up to ill-nature'"[1]—were almost always Oedipal structures, built around an embattled female character. Such plays as *Anna Christie, Desire Under the Elms, Strange Interlude, Mourning Becomes Electra,* and, of course, *A Moon for the Misbegotten,* are constructed around women whose relationship to their men is ambivalent: alternately nurturing and, especially in their sexual role, threatening. The mother betrays the son by acquiring sex, and her redemption seems possible only when the reverse process occurs, as in *A Moon for the Misbegotten*. The woman hovers unsteadily between contradictory poles, each determined by her relationship to men; the limitations placed on her by these roles enter her in an endless dialectics of betrayal. These women are always mothers—i.e., symbolic "women." They can never be quite *solid* as a result. Their sexuality is dependent on "jouissance," on the hiddenness and seductiveness of their very *lack* of being.[2]

The unstable female character who is nevertheless structurally central to the competing male narratives around her is perhaps the dominant architectural feature of O'Neill's writing. It has been noted by John Henry Raleigh, who associates feminine centrality with O'Neill's "great" achievements: "All the late, great plays are in great part about feminine suffering." But Raleigh quickly sets this female presence in its narrative (male) context:

> Men—sons, husbands, lovers—and whiskey, these are the sources of feminine sorrow in O'Neill's world. And at the end of the long, dark tunnel of the long day's journey into night stands a wounded woman,

grieving at what time has done to her, at her present sorrows or lost felicities, of life's general impossibilities.[3]

What Raleigh—and even some women readers of O'Neill, who decry his use of biologically-driven female "stereotypes"[4]—have read "in context," however, has tended to privilege male narrativity[5] in these plays. That is, they have read the plays from the point of view that locates the woman in that realm of indefinability that excludes her from feminist analysis. But the alternative seems equally frustrating: a reading that de-contextualizes "character," though "character" appears to be inseparable from the idea of "context." Teresa de Lauretis argues persuasively that a feminist reading must perform the impossible, must read a "text" that does not (yet) exist, speaking from within a language it is speaking against. Speaking a contradiction may seem specious reasoning, but de Lauretis is compelling on this point. Feminist readings must deny the very terms of the argument in which they find themselves. As she observes, quoting Anthony Wilden,

"Whoever defines the code or the context, has control . . . and all answers which accept that context abdicate the possibility of redefining it."[6]

To move back to "character" is thus to "rediscover" the context, to act as if it had not existed previously, and so to question the conditions it makes for "character." Character that does not meet these conditions will be etherealized, rendered invisible. It will be seen to obviate the obvious—to withstand and avoid the pressures of "context" or "reality." Consequently, this character will appear both weaker and more threatening than the "reality" it detours; it will be "other." As other it is not hard to find but is hard to name; and it will be easiest to find where the process of naming breaks down.

Raleigh's statement, then, seems a good place to begin. He suggests a text for discussion, *Long Day's Journey into Night*, as well as a feminine "text," Mary Tyrone. Mary's seeming centrality to the play ("at the end of the long, dark tunnel of the long day's journey into night stands a wounded woman") is contradicted by her objectification as a product of male narrative ("Men . . . are the sources").[7] The woman's *action*, apparently, is to suffer. Raleigh's thematic summary is made negative by a self-contradiction into a celebration of pathos, a lack—a "wound"—with and through which the feminine is identified. The feminine is produced by a dark passage, generated by men—not just husbands,

"A Monster of Perfection"

but men in all their relations with women ("sons, husbands, lovers"—he might have added, fathers); she is visible as the product of this passage, its end result and its visible pole, which points back to the male source. The image is female here, threatening and restrictive; yet it places Mary in an indefinable position as an abstraction that, produced vaguely at some distant point by men, nevertheless seems to give birth to itself. Mysteriously, monstrously self-engendering, the feminine epitomizes the absence of the male, his loss and fear of loss. This "long, dark tunnel" is surely a passage toward the indefinite, into night, and away from the specificity implied by "Men . . . and whiskey." By the end of this "passage," Raleigh has transformed woman's grief into a transcendent problem of absence: "life's general impossibilities." The attempt to name Mary's central function in the drama keeps pointing away from its ostensible goal. Perfect pathos can be circumscribed, perhaps, but not described.

As a character, Mary represents a space for "men's dream," a "text," an "unattainable goal" that narrative inscribes.[8] This is the way Mary's prototype, *Strange Interlude*'s Nina Leeds,[9] describes herself:

> My three men! . . . I feel their desires converge in me! . . . to form one complete beautiful male desire which I absorb . . . and am whole . . . they dissolve in me, their life is my life . . .[10]

Nina is "pregnant" with these narratives, and this gives her an aura of power. (The frightening, threatening side of this power, for men, was recently illuminated by one reviewer's Strindbergian reading of Mary Tyrone as witch-mother in Jonathan Miller's revival of *Long Day's Journey*.[11] But woman's "mystery" need not threaten for long, because as the convergence of male desires she is automatically not a speaking subject. As man is "the sole term of reference,"

> . . . the position of woman in language . . . is one of non-coherence; she finds herself only in a void of meaning, the empty space between the signs . . . a place not represented, not symbolized, and thus preempted to subject (or self) representation.[12]

Woman, then, provides exactly that space in which narrativity lives and achieves its biologically-inspired coherence. Conflicts appear to take place across and around her,[13] but she is the condition of narrativity, pregnant with narrative yet outside the community it generates. As the space, lack, wound, and pathos, she cannot well be defined by the language of inclusion.[14]

Mary Tyrone, however, does have the only bonafide monologues in *Long Day's Journey*, in 2.2 and act 3 (106–8). In these speeches, she expresses her frustration at being constantly "spied upon" by the men, her need to be alone, and her deep feelings of loneliness. Similarly, Nina Leeds, like the other characters in *Strange Interlude*, speaks interior monologues. Are these, then, moments of female "self-representation"? Mary seems to find some relief in talking to the serving girl, Cathleen. But the long speeches in act 3 are directly occasioned by morphine, which changes her into a spirit trapped in a body, a platonic idea dreamed up by the plot that relies on a transcendent other. What is implied by each feminine solus in these plays is the grip of narrativity and language and cultural definitions that distance woman from the immediacy of the speaking and acting subject. Nina, pondering her father's death in act 2, becomes increasingly absorbed into it:

> There is only his end living—his death. It lives now to draw nearer me, to draw me nearer, to become my end! (*Then with a strange twisted smile*) How we poor monkeys hide from ourselves behind the sounds called words! (315–16)

Left to herself by Cathleen's exit, Mary starts to recite the "Hail, Mary": "You expect the Blessed Virgin to be fooled by a lying dope fiend reciting words! You can't hide from her!" (107) Language is a given, constructed reality each woman tries to hide behind; and the realization of her doubleness is a *guilty alienation* from herself. *Strange Interlude's* interior monologues might be read as O'Neill's move (necessarily unsuccessful) to expose language as a cultural product that reproduces its own meaning in narrative. But he cannot get around language, spoken or "(*unspoken*)," as the silent ellipses of the speeches suggest. Language keeps implicating itself in a context that entraps the woman—it makes her aware of her entrapment. There are no representable women here, just a representative "woman"; "to know inauthenticity is not the same as to be authentic."[15]

What are the terms of Mary's representation? Mary's negativity is epitomized and materialized (in Artaudian terms) by her morphine addiction, which increasingly removes her from the men in the play and suspends her as an image, a floating reminder of repressed guilt. She is the focus of strong Oedipal associations

"A Monster of Perfection"

and, as woman, of the logic Oedipal narrative weaves around her. The search for origins is a major structural motif in *Long Day's Journey* (who did what? when?). The play is composed of a tissue of narratives (including Mary's) that circle the Oedipal conundrum of woman as haven/lure. She represents both the "paradisal" past with its illusions of stasis and origin and its consequence: time as seduction, betrayal, loss. All the characters are caught in the logic of narrativity, whose self-effacing trace is Mary Tyrone.

> All narrative, in its movement forward toward resolution and backward to an initial moment, a paradise lost, is overlaid with what has been called an Oedipal logic—the inner necessity or drive of the drama—its "sense of an ending" inseparable from the memory of loss and the recapturing of time.[16]

In *Long Day's Journey*, the paradisal reflections of Edmund and his father in act 4 are anticipated by Mary's speeches to Cathleen in act 3 and reprised by her in the last moments of the play. The happy past is perceived as a moment outside of time that threatens to smash and betray happiness. Tyrone recalls Edwin Booth's praise as "the high spot in my career. I had life where I wanted it!" But like Mary's spring romance with the young James Tyrone, the high point only lasts "for a time" (150). Jamie, whose Oedipal story is the subject of another play, explicitly links Mary's morphine addiction with Oedipal narrative and identifies the origin of time with her transformation, through morphine, from idealized mother to degraded "whore."

> Never forget the first time I got wise. Caught her in the act with a hypo. Christ, I'd never dreamed before that any women but whores took dope! (163)

Jamie's association of dope with whores and dreams is remembered in the context of a primal scene ("the first time I got wise"; "caught her in the act"). Moreover, Mary's injections take place upstairs, away from the "living room" of family collectivity, and require her to leave her husband's bed and sleep in the spare room. In her drugged state, Mary speaks the telling lines of the Proustian/Oedipal narrative of recapturing and loss. She becomes the symbol and origin of time, the lure of narrativity—the measure of retrogression.

> The past is the present, isn't it? (87)

> . . . at last everything comes between you and what you'd like to be, and you've lost your true self forever. (61)

Judith E. Barlow has shown that, in revisions, O'Neill works Mary's addiction more subtly by postponing her first injection, limiting references to morphine, and softening Mary's antagonistic outbursts.[17] Barlow points out that one effect of the revisions is to make Mary's surrender to the morphine seem unique and final (80–81). Thus, it is through Mary that O'Neill gives the play its "sense of an ending," just as, through her, he epitomizes its disruptive vision. By act 4, Mary has become almost wholly symbolic, functioning as the unseen presence that keeps the men guiltily downstairs because they are fearful of meeting her "ghost," as they do at the end of the play. For someone so withdrawn and helpless, she seems to produce an unexpected awe and dread in the other characters, who carefully avoid seeing her, even as they keep conjuring her in the conversation. The men rehearse their idyllic past, trying to keep the conversation afloat and avoiding an ending. But it is as if they are waiting for Mary to appear. She is also searching for something she has lost, but she cannot remember what it is or where to look for it— "What is it I'm looking for? I know it's something I lost" (172). Mary's arrival halts the play on an eery plane of indecisive longing. Her lost something is indefinable, more lost than a scrap of paper with Edwin Booth's words on it or a shipboard experience that is past. She has abstracted loss from its existential moorings. In our last glimpse of her, she looks as if she, too, could slip away, sitting by the windows, speaking a speech that keeps slipping further into the past tense. Her gradual disintegration, the play's only real gesture toward closure, underscores the problem of presence in drama, in which what is lost can only become more lost if it is to be representable *as* lost.

Mary is the symbol of this chaos and its borderline. Her association with the increasing fog and the windows through which it is visible is emphasized by her position at the play's end. Outside is the chaos where "Nothing was what it is," "where truth is untrue" (131), a ghostly indeterminacy to which Mary's ghostliness has a special affinity. Yet as woman and mother she is also a rarefied being who stands between the men and that chaotic, changeable, untruthful world. Mary can be at once the negativity and its representation—the edifice against loss that male narrative needs in order not to lose itself. The mutuality of these apparently contradictory roles has been explained by Toril

"A Monster of Perfection" 31

Moi, who sees woman's inside-outside, threat-and-protector split as a condition of her marginal position in male representation:

> In the first instance the borderline is seen as part of the chaotic wilderness outside, and in the second it is seen as an inherent part of the inside: the part that protects and shields the symbolic order from the imaginary chaos.[18]

The morphine addiction that connects Mary with the fog and enables her representation through the phallocentric vision Moi describes also transforms her own powers of vision: she really does see the invisible, the ineffable. De Lauretis reminds us that in the legends of Perseus and Oedipus, Medusa and the Sphinx—the female monsters—are threats "to man's vision, and their power consists in their enigma, . . . their luring of man's gaze into the 'dark continent,' as Freud put it, the enigma of femininity." "Medusa's power," she writes,

> to cast the spell which in many cultures is actually called "the evil eye," is directly represented in her horribly "staring eyes," which are a constant feature of her figurative and literary representations. . . .[19]

Mary's function as a central illuminating figure can be traced in the light imagery of act 4. In her absence, the men light the room artificially. But when she enters, Mary over-illuminates the parlor, so that her glow is visible before she enters the men's field of vision, spilling over into the living room. Her eyes seem to glow with their own vision, and for once she seems unconcerned about her mislaid spectacles. Like Medusa and the Sphinx, she is the monster of this story, the creature whose name means "portent" or "warning," a vision of something terrible and one whose visions terrify. In act 4, Mary's disappearance upstairs turns the living room into a place of fearful waiting, and what the men fear both is and is not Mary herself. She now represents a measure of value betrayed, a warning of self-dissolution and chaos to come. The paradisal stories of Edmund and Tyrone are of loss and disillusionment; Mary's loss of her "true self forever" is their destiny and truth. The men measure themselves consciously against her. "I'd begun to hope," Jamie says, "if she'd beaten the game, I could, too" (162).

The mother of Oedipal narrativity is thus whore and betrayer; yet her betrayal is an inevitable consequence of her position as the ultimate object of narrative desire. She is the standard of value, "an equivalent more universal than money," as de Lauretis describes her, translating Lea Melandri, "the most abstract measure ever invented by patriarchal ideology."[20] As the propulsion of narrative movement, the mother's dialectics of expectation and betrayal is an inexhaustible, self-perpetuating conflict of repression and disclosure. She is continually giving birth to herself, moving backwards toward her own birth out of male narrative that then pushes her off into a dreamy world of objectified desire or lack, leading back seductively toward the "paradise lost," the presumed "existence" before symbolization, and so on. The mother thus accrues value and status only as her role, her "character," expends itself and disintegrates, receding to the seductive, mysterious realm of loss and pre-Oedipal existence. Yet her symbolic role as mother-wound is not existence, either, because she never becomes a speaking subject, just a spokesperson for male repressed desire and fear. She discloses the dread at the center of the Oedipal drama, and her prophetic power to pronounce doom condemns her to a "dramatic" life outside, beyond, or transcending the drama—the "reality"—in which she is located. Its narrativity demands its sacrifice.

Mary's role as prophetess is thus inescapably linked to her role as mother. De Lauretis, citing Vladimir Propp, notes that the prophet enters folklore only with the advent of the patriarchal state. Then the terms of succession become patricidal, and the son's wish to kill (depose) his father must be wished for him by an outside source.[21] Edmund and Jamie attack and undermine their father in *Long Day's Journey*, particularly in act 4, in which God, Shakespeare, Mammon, and Edwin Booth are pulled out from under him like so many rugs. Edmund replaces the paternal verities and values with the poetry of modernism and the dreamy isolated unbelonging of the newer age. *The Waste Land* stands behind this act with its references to Baudelaire, fog, cards, drowning, and *The Tempest*. "'We are such stuff as manure is made on,'" Edmund says, ". . . so let's drink up and forget it" (131). Edmund's revisions of Tyrone are part of the passing of the old order, the erosion of time, which Mary's absent presence foretells with divine detachment:

> Yes, she moves above and beyond us, a ghost haunting the past, and here we sit pretending to forget, but straining our ears listening for the slightest sound, hearing the fog drip from the eaves like the uneven tick of a rundown, crazy clock . . . (152)

Mary's monstrousness, her paradoxical vision, and the double function it implies (inside and outside the action, vision and visionary, mother and whore) are perhaps closer to *The Waste Land*'s Tiresias than to either Medusa or the Sphinx. Like her vision in act 4, Tiresias's vision is double; like hers, his character has been universalized into a function of seeing. His vision *is* the poem, as Eliot's notes to the poem point out.

> I Tiresias, though blind, throbbing between two lives,
> Old man with wrinkled female breasts, can see
> At the violet hour, the evening hour that strives
> Homeward, and brings the sailor home from sea.[22]

The androgynous "phallic" mother is a goddess who holds the double power of life and death over man.[23] A double-sexed creature, Tiresias epitomizes the prophet's link between the two ages, matriarchal and patriarchal, the past and the future. The past and future are "now" for Mary as well, not caught in the temporal causality others find so reassuring: "The past is the present, isn't it? It's the future, too" (87). Her visionary powers, which increase at "the violet hour," as the play moves into night, become more disturbing, more threatening to the notion of presence in the drama. Tiresias's gift of prophecy, according to legend, is coincidental with his blindness, as if to emphasize the paradoxical nature of vision as blessing and curse. Causality is the ordering principle of narrative time and so of mimetic drama. But Mary's double vision relativizes and undermines this order. The mother represents the point at which "(social and biological) identity recedes,"[24] in other words, where the biological and dialogical structures of narrative originate and disappear. The narrative or realistic structure of the drama is a *family* structure; as de Lauretis, quoting Roland Barthes, points out, "the pleasure of the text" is "an Oedipal pleasure (to denude, to know, to learn the origin and end)."[25] The desire for this knowledge is both centered in and frustrated by Mary, who is the unknowable and its symbolic presence. Her disappearance in act 4 cannot really be accounted for in a realistic, contextual reading, which seeks echoes and reinforcements between the text and the stage image, language and reality. She is gone, but the text goes on, beneath and around her. She is "above and beyond" the text, having become the text to be played out, the object of the language's desire.

The elusive feminine in *Long Day's Journey* is still hard to name, and the effect of her analysis has been and only can be to make her elusiveness more evident. O'Neill also found her difficult to name. Barlow has pointed out that O'Neill at one time considered calling Mary "Stella" (69). Besides more closely resembling the chosen name of his own mother, Ella (Sheaffer notes that her full name was Mary Ellen), the name would have gone even further toward abstracting the character's presence. Stella, as the star that determines destiny and worth, is an image of woman "as the real, as Truth,"[26] as a transcendent source of value. In literature, she is the poet's beloved, constructed out of literature, the subject as well as the impulse of poetry. Ironically, Mary Tyrone, whose failure to win the struggle with morphine addiction represents the central motivation for the (in-)action of *Long Day's Journey*, is all these things. But she is also theatrical, as "Stella" implies, the "leading lady," the "star," whose role it is to objectify male desire, to lure and seduce men. It is a role Mary self-consciously (and naïvely) rejects: "I've never had the slightest desire to be an actress" (102). But her role is perceptible only within a desire that is not her own. The home to which the evening hour strives is an unfamiliar place in which she finds no rest or identity except as outcast, monster, prophetess—"I've never felt at home in the theater" (102). She is indeed, in the seventeenth-century phrase, a "monster of perfection," whose presence is uncongenial to the very form that produces and requires her.

Long Day's Journey can be seen as a culmination of realistic domestic drama. Oedipal narrative, its struggle for origins, is revealed through the character of the woman who, motivating these things, is herself unmotivated, thrust into a role that is neither character nor narrator but both: the subject and impulse of the narrative. She exists because Oedipal narrativity demands its mother, its monster, its prophet; and it seems natural to overlook the troubled quality of her existence. But the narrativity she makes possible demands an origin and an ending, of either redress or atonement, that seem impossible here.[27] The sense of an ending O'Neill labored to achieve through Mary had made her, like Tiresias, impervious to time. She remains in her state of morphine transformation, inaccessible and untransformable. Closing the play, she defies closure, and her words emphasize how fleeting, inadequate, and misleading language's attempt is to reconcile reality with imagination. "I fell in love with James Tyrone and was so happy for a time" (176).

Notes

1. Louis Sheaffer, *O'Neill: Son and Artist* (Boston: Little, Brown, 1973), p. 124.

2. ". . . the lost-unrepresentable-forbidden jouissance of a hidden mother, seducing the child through a lack of being" (Julia Kristeva, *Desire in Language: A Semiotic Approach to Literature and Art*, ed. Leon S. Roudiez, trans. Thomas Gora, Alice Jardine, and Leon S. Roudiez [New York: Columbia University Press, 1980], p. 248). "Jouissance" includes a complex of meanings (see, e.g., "introduction," pp. 15–16), and I use it here to stress the indefinite—and the infinite—quality of O'Neill's feminine characters. Josie Hogan's difference from these other women seems to be that she is a lover first and only becomes a mother in the process of an explicit Oedipal exorcism. Jamie transfers his guilty feelings for his mother to Josie, who then becomes his mother, with all the sexuality this implies, and absolves him. The play ends on a static image of death, as there seems to be nothing left to dramatize once the Oedipal plot has been exposed and disposed of, creating a coherent "I" that cannot participate in dialectic. The end of narrative desire is the beginning and end of the self.

3. John Henry Raleigh, *The Plays of Eugene O'Neill* (Carbondale: Southern Illinois University Press, 1965), p. 142.

4. See, for example, Doris Nelson, "O'Neill's Women," and Bette Mandl, "Absence as Presence: The Second Sex in *The Iceman Cometh*," *The Eugene O'Neill Newsletter* 6, no. 2 (1982): 3–7, 10–15.

5. ". . . by 'narrativity' I mean both the making and the working of narrative, its construction and its effects of meaning" (Teresa de Lauretis, *Alice Doesn't: Feminism, Semiotics, Cinema* [Bloomington: Indiana University Press, 1984], p. 10). On the Oedipal logic of narrative, see chapter 5, "Desire in Narrative."

6. Ibid., p. 3 (Anthony Wilden, *System and Structure: Essays in Communication and Exchange* [London: Tavistock, 1972], p. 294).

7. Mary's centrality is recognized by Judith E. Barlow, *Final Acts: The Creation of Three Late O'Neill Plays* (Athens: The University of Georgia Press, 1985) and Leonard Chabrowe, *Ritual and Pathos—The Theater of O'Neill* (Lewisburg: Bucknell University Press, 1976), p. 171, and implicitly by Timo Tiusanen, *O'Neill's Scenic Images* (Princeton: Princeton University Press, 1968), who devotes to Mary much of his argument on *Long Day's Journey*. Quotations from Raleigh are from p. 142.

8. De Lauretis, *Alice Doesn't*, p. 13.

9. For comparisons of Nina Leeds and Mary Tyrone, see Tiusanen, *O'Neill's Scenic Images*, pp. 223–24, who suggests that Nina is an earlier version of Mary, and Barlow, *Final Acts*, p. 70.

10. Eugene O'Neill, *Strange Interlude*, in *Selected Plays of Eugene O'Neill* (New York: Random House, 1967), p. 395. Subsequent references are cited parenthetically by page number within the text.

11. Brendan Gill, "Unhappy Tyrones," *The New Yorker* 62 (12 May 1986): 93–94.

12. De Lauretis, *Alice Doesn't*, p. 8.

13. Barlow, *Final Acts*, describes an interesting note for *Long Day's Journey* in which O'Neill, who was "glued to the radio for war news" (p. 72), sets up the play as shifting lines of battle: "O'Neill carried through this military motif, the family as battleground, in two of his proposed titles: 'The Long Day's Insurrection' and 'The Long Day's Retreat'" (p. 75). The image of the family at war with itself is supported by the notion of woman as instigator, pawn and prize, especially in Greek tragedy, to which O'Neill had turned for the model of *Mourning Becomes Electra* (1931). Of Aeschylus's trilogy, Sheaffer reports, O'Neill said it "'has greater possibilities of revealing all the deep hidden relationships in the family'" than other Greek tragedies (p. 336).

14. The notion that Mary is a space, a point of connection, a womb, is further suggested by the name O'Neill chooses for her. Kristeva, *Desire in Language*, traces Mary's development in the writings of the Catholic Church and finds an Orthodox version of her as "a *union, a contact without gap, without separation,*" derived from images of her as "privileged *space,* living *area, ladder* (of Jacob), or *door* (of the Temple, in Ezekiel's vision)—*dwelling*" (pp. 250–51, italics Kristeva's).

15. Paul de Man, *Blindness and Insight: Essays in the Rhetoric of Contemporary Criticism*, 2d ed., rev. (Minneapolis: University of Minnesota Press, 1983), p. 214.

16. De Lauretis, *Alice Doesn't*, p. 125.

17. Barlow, *Final Acts*, p. 76 passim.

18. Toril Moi, *Sexual/Textual Politics: Feminist Literary Theory* (New York: Methuen, 1985), p. 167.

19. De Lauretis, *Alice Doesn't*, p. 110.

20. Ibid., p. 30.

21. Ibid., p. 114 (Vladimir Propp, "Edip v svete fol'klora," *Serija filologičeskich nauk*, 9, no. 72 [1944]: 138–75).

22. T. S. Eliot, *The Complete Poems and Plays, 1909–1950* (New York: Harcourt, Brace and World, 1971), p. 52, lines 218–21.

23. Sarah Kofman, *The Enigma of Woman: Woman in Freud's Writings*, trans. Catherine Porter (Ithaca: Cornell University Press, 1985), p. 72.

24. Kristeva, *Desire in Language*, p. 242.

25. De Lauretis, *Alice Doesn't*, pp. 107–8 (Roland Barthes, *The Pleasure of the Text*, trans. Richard Miller [New York: Hill and Wang, 1975], p. 10).

26. Ibid., p. 16.

27. This is the finale of realistic dramas that dramatize and then dispose of woman's need to rebel. In *The Second Mrs. Tanqueray* and *Margaret Fleming*, for example, the woman who is in some socially-defined sense guilty and/or wronged is punished/saved at the end. Her maternal role conflicts with her personal desire, and the woman is forced to sacrifice one or the other. Paula Tanqueray commits suicide because she cannot see herself as a wife and mother; Margaret Fleming accepts both her unfaithful husband and his illegitimate child by the woman he ruined. What Ibsen makes of this choice in *A Doll House* reveals his rejection of the "realistic" woman's play's traditional closure.

O'NEILL'S GHOSTLY WOMEN

Suzanne Burr

It has become fashionable to highlight the misogynistic strain in Eugene O'Neill's work and to stress his inability to imagine women as realistic, sympathetic and, above all, *human* beings. Louis Sheaffer, whose comprehensive biography offers some very interesting ideas about O'Neill and his emotional experience but who stresses O'Neill's particular blindness towards women, has asserted that,

> paralleling his mentor Strindberg, O'Neill created in the majority of his leading female characters either bitches and other agents of misfortune or impossibly noble souls. He could praise Woman only in exaggerated, unrealistic terms.[1]

Sheaffer argues that O'Neill's misogynistic strain is so pronounced that women are continually presented as agents of men's destruction, as threatening and ultimately negative characters. A complicating factor, in Sheaffer's opinion, is O'Neill's desire and need for a mother, a being who would nurture him and shelter him from the world. The combination of the desire for protection and the resulting hatred that arises from his dependency on women makes O'Neill a hotbed of rage, resentment, and terror, the kind of man who romanticizes women to rid them of their terrifying power over him.[2]

Although Strindberg's influence is considerable in O'Neill's work, there is an important difference between the two writers in their portrayal of women, particularly when these women are presented as ghosts, haunting their lives instead of living them, alienated from self and others. Writing about female ghosts in O'Neill's plays, James Robinson has noted the pattern of female "absence as presence" (using Bette Mandl's words) that runs throughout O'Neill's work, illustrating the connection between *The Iceman Cometh* and *Long Day's Journey into Night* and asserting that all O'Neill's ghostly women are experimental figures who anticipate the ultimate female ghost, Mary Tyrone.[3] While Robinson focuses on O'Neill's ambivalent stance toward his mother expressed by these spectral women, Sheaffer himself takes a more negative position, noting

> a legion of dead wives and mothers in O'Neill's writings, a clan larger than one may realize, since many of its ghostly members died before the plays begin and are referred to only fleetingly.[4]

It is this ghostly tribe that is, for Sheaffer, a "sinister fact" of O'Neill's misogyny: in this view, they represent another piece of evidence supporting O'Neill's apparently negative and oppressive view of women, as if O'Neill had invented women as ghosts to keep them as outsiders, to obstruct their "fellowship" as sympathetic characters in his work.

I propose another view of this ghostly collection: namely, that their ghostliness does not constitute an expression of O'Neill's misogyny but reflects his remarkable empathy with women, with their psychic and social imprisonment, with their painful and oftentimes confusing disenfranchisement. This expression of empathy divorces O'Neill, in my view, from a strict imitation of Strindberg and aligns him more closely with Ibsen, whose incipient feminist stance is echoed in O'Neill's presentation of women. Ibsen, above all, perceived and wrote passionately about women's disenfranchisement and isolation. Plays such as *Pillars of Society*, *Ghosts*, *Hedda Gabler*, and *The Master Builder* illuminate the many shades of anguish and rage women experience as a result of their ghostliness, as well as the shock men experience when they realize the truth of women's repressed status in society: as Consul Bernick comes to realize, women simply are invisible to men—they are ghosts. (". . . it seems as if all these years I've never really seen you," Bernick says to his sister at the end of the play; and Lona, the moral center of the drama, responds: "I can well believe it. This society of yours is a bachelors' club. You don't see women."[5]) Like Ibsen, O'Neill confirms women's displacement in a society that values maleness and male authority and denigrates women's personal and political power. Although this is not the context for an exhaustive study, I will examine several plays in which the presentation of female ghostliness reveals O'Neill's empathy with, rather than hatred for, women.

O'Neill's sense of women's isolation, particularly the recurring image of a woman imprisoned in a male structure, derives from his experience with his mother's misery. (I do agree with Sheaffer's premise that O'Neill is an autobiographical writer.) Dion Anthony in *The Great God Brown* voices O'Neill's own words when he says: "'And my mother? I remember a sweet, strange girl, with affectionate, bewildered eyes as if God had locked her in a dark closet without any explanation.'"[6] Arthur and Barbara Gelb insightfully draw our attention to O'Neill's fantasy of his mother as a girl locked in a dark closet and note the influence on O'Neill of Strindberg's *The Ghost Sonata*, in which the Mummy does, indeed, live locked in a dark closet. The Gelbs point out that, soon after his mother's death, O'Neill told a friend that "she had lived in a room from which she had seldom ventured—that, in a way, she was like the Mummy."[7] So a powerful force behind O'Neill's image of the imprisoned woman grew out of his personal experience with a mother who was locked in, trapped, and isolated, as well as the dramatic example supplied by Strindberg's closet-bound Mummy. Yet O'Neill transforms the Strindbergian motif of the trapped woman to represent not her baseness but her martyrdom, not her lack of worth but the unjust quality of her imprisonment and subjugation.

The ghostly mother in *Desire Under the Elms*, for example, suggests O'Neill's sympathetic stance toward women's isolation and their wasted powers. Many writers have commented on the importance of the elms as symbols of maternal suffering, for these "enormous elms" are "like exhausted women resting their sagging breasts and hands and hair" on the roof of the house, "and when it rains their tears trickle down monotonously and rot on the shingles."[8] These exhausted, sexless remnants of life parallel the exhaustion Eben recalls that his mother felt, as she was worked to death by her iron-willed husband. Now Eben is haunted by her ghost, who, interestingly, has schooled him in the harshness and deprivation of her life, a life he had ignored when she was alive. "It was on'y arter she died I come to think o' it," he says,

> Me cookin'—doin' her work—that made me know her, suffer her sufferin'—she'd come back t' help—come back t' bile potatoes—come back t' fry bacon—come back t' bake biscuits—come back all cramped up t' shake the fire, an' carry ashes, her eyes weepin' an' bloody with smoke an' cinders same's they used t' be. She still comes back—stands by the stove thar in the evenin'—she can't find it natural sleepin' an' restin' in peace. She can't git used t' bein' free—even in her grave. (143)

Once again, O'Neill underscores women's physical and psychic imprisonment, and here the idea is more striking because even death itself cannot provide peace or freedom. It is as if O'Neill wants us to see a direct connection between the mother's exploitation in life and her ghostly unrest after death: trained to be a slave to her husband, she remains in perpetual bondage as a restless ghost.

Anna Christie also reveals a similar pattern of bondage, although in Anna's case her deprivation led to prostitution instead of death. Here is another portrait of a woman ruined and trapped by men. As Anna tells the story of her moral collapse, she stresses that her early life as a governess provided only entrapment and servitude: "I was caged in, I tell you—yust like in yail—taking care of other people's kids—listening to 'em bawling and crying day and night—when I wanted to be out—and I was lonesome—lonesome as hell! [*With a sudden weariness in her voice*] So I give up finally. What was the use?"[9] It is clear that prostitution, for Anna, seemed to offer an escape from this life of bondage. As she says emphatically, "I never could stand being caged up nowheres" (76). Yet at the end of the play, it is unclear whether Anna, through her marriage to Mat Burke, will find redemption or only another trap: certainly it is suggested that fate will prevail regardless of the wishes and needs of these paltry human beings. Like the mass of humanity the characters represent, Anna, Mat, and her father are adrift on an uncertain sea, prey to life's ironies, accompanied only by the "muffled, mournful wail of steamers' whistles" (160), ghostly and subdued sounds of woe.

The crepuscular quality surrounding O'Neill's portrayal of Anna and her kin illustrates another feature of O'Neill's ghostly women, one that also derives from his experience with his mother. Speaking of his mother's drug addiction, O'Neill once referred to her morphine-induced withdrawal as "a kind of twilight zone," a phrase that calls to mind all the woeful, wandering women under discussion here. When we think of Anna Christie losing herself in the sea's disguising fog or Mary Tyrone wandering like an unhappy spectre through her prison-home, we see the same crepuscular dreaminess. The state of being "in between," emblematized by twilight, is the condition of these lonely ghost-women, never fully at home, like the "fog people" Edmund refers to in his long speech about his own alienation. It is typical of all O'Neill's ghostly characters that they can never belong and must

O'Neill's Ghostly Women

always feel like outsiders caught in the twilight zone of their own alienation.[10]

We see this most clearly in *Ile* and *Long Day's Journey into Night*, plays from the beginning and end of O'Neill's writing career that highlight the most significant features of his ghostly women and that deserve close attention. In the sea play, *Ile*, O'Neill initiates his portraits of spectral women in the characterization of Mrs. Keeney, Captain Keeney's haunted and hauntingly deranged wife. Her situation resembles that of the later doomed Mary Tyrone: like Mary, Mrs. Keeney dreamed of a romantic life of pleasure and adventure, which she thought her husband could provide. She has joined her husband on a whaling expedition to the Arctic, fantasizing that they will share the excitement of the sea. But when the play opens, Mrs. Keeney is on the verge of madness, unhinged by the ship's isolation in a wilderness of ice and silence. She is pitted against her husband in a battle of wills and desires: his ambition to find and bring home the "ile" drives him ever onward, while Mrs. Keeney pleads with him to return home, back to the comforts she had previously taken for granted. Most of all, Mrs. Keeney longs for contact with other women. But, like a prisoner inside her husband's floating jail cell, she is the victim of his egotism and pride, attributes that O'Neill will later write about as singularly masculine qualities.

Mrs. Keeney thus initiates the type of trapped woman that O'Neill returns to in his later portraits: she is the prototype of feminine ghostliness, dislocated and unhappy but unable to change her lot. Although the play focuses on Captain Keeney's search for his precious "ile," the central dramatic tension emerges from the conflict between what he wants and what will save his wife's sanity. At the outset, Captain Keeney is presented to the audience as an inflexible, brutally obsessive man whose longing for achievement is driving his wife mad. An opening conversation between the Steward and Ben, the cabin boy, establishes the main dramatic problem and conditions our understanding of the husband/wife conflict. The Steward bemoans the Captain's actions and asks who but a madman "would take his woman—and as sweet a woman as ever was—on a stinkin' whalin' ship to the Arctic seas," where she may "lose her senses forever—for it's sure she'll never be the same again." Echoing the Steward's memory of Mrs. Keeney before her madness, Ben pathetically recalls: "[*Sadly*] She useter be awful nice to me be-

fore—[*His eyes grow wide and frightened*] she got—like she is."
Both characters thus help us picture Mrs. Keeney before her ruin,
as if they were holding up a picture of her earlier, "alive" self, so
that we may perceive the contrast when the ghostly Mrs. Keeney
appears. And their empathy indicates she has justification for her
rage and fear, for, as the Steward says, "'Tis a God's wonder we're
not a ship full of crazed people—with the damned ice all the
time, and the quiet so thick you're afraid to hear your own
voice."[11]

When we meet Mrs. Keeney, we realize the truth of the previous description and are prepared to accept the fact that her present state is one that has been developing over time; we are catching her in crisis, at the breaking point. Although her description bears traces of the woman she once was ("*She is a slight, sweet-faced little woman primly dressed in black*"), we also see the signs of evident strain, with her "*eyes red from weeping and her face drawn and pale*" (117). More importantly, she seems caught in the grip of "*some nameless dread*" and stands immobilized, "*clasping and unclasping her hands nervously*" (118). At this point, we cannot avoid seeing her resemblance to Mary Tyrone, whose nervous hands O'Neill made a point of highlighting in his stage directions:

> *What strikes one immediately is her extreme nervousness. Her hands are never still. They were once beautiful hands, with long, tapering fingers, but rheumatism has knotted the joints and warped the fingers, so that now they have an ugly crippled look. One avoids looking at them, the more so because one is conscious she is sensitive about their appearance and humiliated by her inability to control the nervousness which draws attention to them.* (12)

We can see the similarity of vision: two women, both bewildered and bruised and trapped in circumstances they do not understand, traumatized by life, whose restless, tremulous hands express the life force that has been squeezed brutally out of them. Both women are afraid, all the more so because their dread is "nameless," something they cannot control by using their voice to master their anxiety. Their spiritual condition—the fact that they've lost their souls—is related to this inability to use language to make meaning.

In Mrs. Keeney's case, the forfeiture of authentic life is signalled by her continual complaints against the ice and cold, but, most of all, against the terrible, deafening silence. Her remarks bring up the same images so often that we can speak of them as consituting a refrain, almost her own song, a technique O'Neill used many years later when he wrote *The Iceman Cometh*. The music of her lines picks up the same repeated ideas: when Keeney tries to comfort her, she responds hysterically, saying, "Oh, I can't bear it! I can't bear it any longer!—

> All this horrible brutality, and these brutes of men, and this terrible ship, and this prison cell of a room, and the ice all around, and the silence. (125)

And a few moments later:

> I won't stand it—I can't stand it—pent up by these walls like a prisoner. . . . Take me home, David! I can't think any more. I feel as if the cold and the silence were crushing down on my brain. I'm afraid. Take me home! (126–27)

Still again, when Keeney remarks, horrified, at the deranged look in her eyes, a look he's never seen before, she responds: "[*Laughing hysterically*] It's the ice and the cold and the silence—they'd make any one look strange" (127). She repeats the same images throughout the scenes of struggle between husband and wife, as if by sheer force of language she could impress upon her husband the terror she feels as the walls of ice and silence close around her, emblems of her ever-increasing dementia.

For Mary Tyrone, too, silences are the hallmarks of her imprisonment and her ghostly solitude. In act 2, scene 2, of *Long Day's Journey*, when Mary has begun to slip more completely into her twilight zone of indifference, the lines of dialogue are scored by repeated indications of "silence"—in particular, "dead" silence, as if O'Neill wanted to emphasize the morbid, blank, and hopeless quality of these pauses. Detachment and death are thus fused in our minds. She speaks of their house with the bitter insight that characterizes one of her moods in the play: "It's unreasonable to expect Bridget or Cathleen to act as if this was a home. They know it isn't as well as we know it. It never has been and it never will be." A "*dead silence*" immediately precedes her next speech, and she continues on "*with a return of her detached air.*" "No, no. . . . It was never a home," she says to Tyrone,

> You've always preferred the Club or a barroom. And for me it's always been as lonely as a dirty room in a one-night stand hotel. In a real home one is never lonely. (72)

As the scene goes on, her detachment increases, and there is another "*dead silence*" before the telephone call that interrupts her reveries, the call that informs Tyrone of Edmund's tuberculosis. These blank silences punctuate and inform the dramatic process, because silence is Mary's natural environment. The silence, reminders of her loneliness and imprisonment, and her growing indifference and emotional sterility are analogous to Mrs. Keeney's lament about the ice, the cold, and the silence. Both women are trapped in a void they cannot understand but which, to them, threatens their lives; yet it is silence, more than anything, that is the enemy.

This feature of their entrapment is one hallmark of O'Neill's incipient feminism. As Nancy Rule Goldberger and her colleagues have observed, women tend to ground their sense of themselves and their place in the world in metaphors suggesting listening and speaking rather than visualizing; Goldberger and co-workers suggest that for women a sense of voice and a sense of mind appear to be inseparable.[12] O'Neill anticipates this understanding of women's difference when he presents Mrs. Keeney and Mary lamenting the silences that pervade their lives and when he focuses our attention on the women's inability to find a voice.

O'Neill also reveals what today we might call a "feminist consciousness" in his presentation of Mrs. Keeney's understanding of the idea of home and her articulation of what home means to her. For Mrs. Keeney, the longing to be home has a very special meaning—namely, returning to a place where she can find solace in connection with other women. Mrs. Keeney cries: "[*Intensely*] Oh, I want to be home in the old house once more and see my own kitchen again, and hear a woman's voice talking to me and be able to talk to her," and her next association links her sense of separation from sisterly comfort to her own feeling of ghostliness: "Two years!" she exclaims: "It seems so long ago—as if I'd been dead and could never go back" (128–29). Her real self, fulfilled only in her remembrances and recollections of home, seems to vanish under the pressure of her isolation from other women. "My memory is leaving me—up here in the ice," she says, struggling to envision their house as it must be. Then, as if in a dream,

> It's June now. The lilacs will be all in bloom in the front yard—and the climbing roses on the trellis to the side of the house—they're budding. [*She suddenly covers her face with her hands and commences to sob.*] (130)

From these fragments of a stifled voice, we can reconstruct her misery and the pain she experiences at being cut off from all the natural elements that mean "home" to her. The images of blooming roses and lilacs merge with the idea of "a woman's voice talking to me" (128), warming her, returning her to life and bloom herself. But her husband's implacable will obstructs this longing for life, and the final moments of the play reveal her descent into madness. As the curtain falls, she is left alone on stage, playing the organ *"wildly and discordantly,"* as *"her fingers move faster and faster"* (134) over the keys: the music of her mind is finally deranged.

Mary Tyrone is presented similarly because Mary also speaks of her loneliness again and again. She seems without women friends and resorts to drinking with Cathleen out of sheer desperation for companionship. Although we know the two are not close friends, Mary *"talks to Cathleen with a confiding familiarity, as if the second girl were an old, intimate friend"* (97–98). It is as if Mary is trying to create for herself that companionable good cheer she imagines her husband and sons share when they visit their clubs and barrooms. But O'Neill reveals what we already sense: that Mary is only using Cathleen because she is terrified of being alone: *"In nearly all the following dialogue there is the feeling that she has Cathleen with her merely as an excuse to keep talking"* (98). And talk she does, of her continual dislocation as Tyrone's wife ("I've never felt at home in the theater. . . . I've had little to do with the people in his company, or with anyone on the stage. . . . Their life is not my life" (102). She thus reminds us of the irreparable split between her and Tyrone: they do not share "company," both in the sense that Mary uses the word and the sense of shared purpose and understanding. Like the Keeneys, they are inhabiting the same space without sharing their spirits.

Mary, like Mrs. Keeney, identifies happiness with an imagined group of women friends, and she also longs for this all-important company. "If there was a friend's house where I could drop in and laugh and gossip awhile," she longingly wishes in act 2; and then the bitter recollection: "But, of course, there isn't. There never has been" (85–86). She tells the bitter story of how she came to lose her women friends:

> At the Convent I had so many friends. Girls whose families lived in lovely homes. I used to visit them and they'd visit me in my father's home. But, naturally, after I married an actor—you know how actors were considered in those days—a lot of them gave me the cold

shoulder. And then, right after we were married, there was the scandal of that woman who had been your mistress, suing you. From then on, all my old friends either pitied me or cut me dead. (86)

"Dead" is an appropriate word: unconsciously, Mary is signalling how she came to be what she is—a tormented and lost soul, who, in Tyrone's words, will be nothing but a "mad ghost" by the time the night is through (123). But Mary's sense of the loss of close women friends is only part of her feeling of ghostly dislocation: an even more important symbol of her isolation emerges when she tries to talk to the Virgin Mary but finds she has no voice anymore with which to reach her. That thread of solace—of feminine healing—is one of the last dreams she must surrender during this night of disillusionment. Earlier, Mary imagines a wonderful "some day" when all will be well:

> .... some day when the Blessed Virgin Mary forgives me and gives me back the faith in Her love and pity I used to have in my convent days, and I can pray to Her again—when She sees no one in the world can believe in me even for a moment any more, then She will believe in me, and with Her help it will be so easy. I will hear myself scream with agony, and at the same time I will laugh because I will be so sure of myself. (94)

This is Mary's dream of renewed life, when, through the love and mercy of the Virgin, she will overcome her pain and torment. It is no coincidence that Mary shares her name with the Virgin, for the Virgin Mary is a reflection of the strength, love, and courage Mary herself has lost. The Virgin is Mary's lost soul, the part of herself she has silenced. One of the most shattering moments in the play occurs when Mary tries to pray to the Virgin but cannot, having no voice. "You expect the Blessed Virgin to be fooled by a lying dope fiend reciting words!" she sneers at herself: "You can't hide from her!" (107). Unable to find or restore that precious connection, unable to speak to this ultimate feminine principle, Mary despises herself. She feels so worthless she is not even worthy of speaking to the Virgin. Thus, her last resort, the one "woman friend" she might speak to, is lost to her.

Both Mrs. Keeney and Mary Tyrone represent O'Neill's portraits of ghostly alienation and self-neglect: feeling dead, detached, worthless, and silenced, these women illustrate O'Neill's compassion for women cut off from themselves, their potential, and their power. When Mrs. Keeney sits alone, her fingers madly drumming the keys, and when Mary circles the house like the "mad ghost" of Tyrone's prophecy, they fulfill the pattern O'Neill saw in his own mother's martyrdom. It is not O'Neill's misogyny but his empathy with these women that is striking. Creatures of a crepuscular mood, these two women signify the tremendous waste he perceived in his own mother's fate. He seems particularly aware, as few male dramatists have been, of women's need for each other and of their singular need for shared voices as well as shared lives.

Notes

1. Louis Sheaffer, *O'Neill: Son and Artist* (Boston: Little, Brown, 1973), p. 500.
2. Ibid., p. 501.
3. James A. Robinson, "Ghost Stories: Mary Tyrone and *Iceman's* Absent Women," paper delivered at the Eugene O'Neill Conference ("Eugene O'Neill: The Later Years"), 31 May 1986.
4. Sheaffer, *O'Neill*, p. 500.
5. Henrik Ibsen, *Pillars of Society*, in *The Complete Major Prose Plays*, trans. Rolf Fjelde (New York: Farrar, Straus, Giroux, 1978), p. 117.
6. Arthur and Barbara Gelb, *O'Neill* (New York: Harper and Brothers, 1962), p. 11.
7. Ibid., p. 11.
8. Eugene O'Neill, *Desire Under the Elms*, in *Nine Plays by Eugene O'Neill* (New York: Modern Library, 1954), p. 136. Subsequent references are cited parenthetically by page number in the text.
9. Eugene O'Neill, *Anna Christie*, in *Anna Christie, The Emperor Jones, The Hairy Ape* (New York: Random House, Vintage ed., 1972), pp. 132–33. Subsequent references are cited parenthetically by page number in the text.
10. O'Neill, *Long Day's Journey into Night* (New Haven: Yale University Press, 1955), pp. 153–54. Subsequent references are cited parenthetically by page number in the text.
11. Eugene O'Neill, *Ile*, in *Seven Plays of the Sea* (New York: Random House, Vintage ed., 1972), p. 115. Subsequent references are cited parenthetically by page number in the text.
12. Mary Field Belenky, Blythe McVicker Clinchy, Nancy Rule Goldberger, and Jill Mattuck Tarule, *Women's Ways of Knowing: The Development of Self, Voice and Mind* (New York: Basic Books, 1986).

THEATRICALITY AND OTHERNESS IN *ALL GOD'S CHILLUN GOT WINGS*

Bette Mandl

When Eugene O'Neill's *All God's Chillun Got Wings* was to be staged at the Provincetown Playhouse in 1924, advance notices describing it as a play about miscegenation, in which white actress Mary Blair would kiss the hand of black actor Paul Robeson, provoked a furor. O'Neill, as well as several others in the company, were harrassed by hate mail and threats of legal action. Kenneth Macgowan later commented, "It is no risk at all to say that *All God's Chillun* received more publicity before production than any play in the history of the theatre, possibly of the world."[1]

Response to the play was far more moderate, perhaps anticlimatic, once it opened to less than favorable reviews. *All God's Chillun*, however, remains a controversial piece in the O'Neill canon, inspiring both praise and blame, particularly for its treatment of race. Like *The Dreamy Kid* and *The Emperor Jones*, *All God's Chillun* has a distinctive place in theater history for having been one of the first plays to offer serious roles to black actors. Virginia Floyd, like other critics and biographers of O'Neill, suggests that the playwright's concern with matters of race can be linked, in part, to his family's response to the snobbery they experienced in Yankee New London. Floyd underscores the engagement with O'Neill's subject matter that is suggested in his first notation on *All God's Chillun* in 1922.[2] O'Neill wrote:

> Play of Johnny T.—negro who married white woman—base play on his experience as I have seen it intimately—but no reproduction, see it only as man's.[3]

Margaret Loftus Ranald comments on how the play has fared in the intervening years. She agrees that it "remains the first important and thoroughly serious treatment of white-black relations of this century." Nonetheless, she says, "Prejudiced language, sim-

Theatricality and Otherness

plistic racial sentiments, and inherent stereotypes have dated the play more than might have been initially anticipated."[4] She articulates a general feeling that the work was a substantial contribution but that its shortcomings are sometimes uncomfortably apparent to a contemporary audience.

In this paper, I consider how both the power of the play and its limitations derive from the conceptual forms that the dramatist used to give it shape. O'Neill, an artist who early cultivated a courageous adversarial stance in relation to his society, believed, as he claimed, that *All God's Chillun* would "help toward a more sympathetic understanding between the races, through the sense of mutual tragedy involved."[5] It was easier for him, however, to renounce the explicit racial bias of his culture than it was for him to create an imaginative structure for his drama that did not implicitly reinforce the conditions he challenged. The analysis I propose is an attempt to examine the ways in which aesthetic form imposed its own dictates on the psychological and social elements that converge in the play.

Autobiography was central to the shaping of *All God's Chillun*. As Louis Sheaffer points out, the play "dramatizes some of the playwright son's feelings about the union of Ella Quinlan, gently reared, and James O'Neill, who struggled up from the meanest poverty."[6] The Ella and Jim of the play have some clear resemblances to O'Neill's parents, as they have to the Tyrones of *Long Day's Journey,* whom they anticipate. Such an approach seems encouraged by O'Neill's insistence that "the suggestion that miscegenation would be treated in the theater obscured the real intention of the play."[7] The statement O'Neill wrote before the play opened de-emphasized its racial elements:

> The play itself, as anyone who has read it with intelligence knows, is never a "race problem" play. Its intention is confined to portraying the special lives of individual human beings. It is primarily a study of two principal characters, and their tragic struggle for happiness.[8]

While O'Neill was fending off charges that his play would incite race riots, his remarks have a striking resemblance to those made by Ibsen, when he declined the praise he received for championing women's rights:

> I have been more of a poet and less of a social philosopher than people generally tend to suppose. . . . Of course it is incidentally desirable to solve the problem of women . . . My task has been the portrayal of human beings.[9]

O'Neill's declaration, like Ibsen's, seems important to a long history of controversy regarding the often uneasy relationship of art to politics. In our own moment in time, however, when representations of difference and otherness invite particular scrutiny, it also demands our attention for what it implies about the metaphoric use of race, as well as gender. Peter J. Gillet agrees with T. S. Eliot "that the play points through and beyond questions of race to all those differences which thwart and pervert human affections." However, Gillet warns against critics who regard *All God's Chillun* as "*only* a universal drama of souls, or who can see the play *only* as a drama of marriage."[10]

In her recent book, Leslie Catherine Sanders offers a perspective on Genet's *The Blacks*, which is useful in shaping a response to *All God's Chillun*. Sanders says:

> *The Blacks* is not primarily concerned with black people. Rather, it uses them and their experience both as metaphor of more general aspects of the human predicament and as mask for Genet's personal experience and philosophy.[11]

Sanders considers in her own work the problems that "the use of the black as projection and mask" posed for the development of black theater and a "black stage reality."[12] Her insights suggest the difficulties inherent in the aesthetic effort to appropriate the visibility of otherness to represent what O'Neill called "the special lives of individual human beings."[13]

Crucial to an understanding of *All God's Chillun* is O'Neill's use of polarities to develop the drama. As John Henry Raleigh says, "The impulse toward contrast tends to be more obsessive in the earlier plays and is often schematic."[14] Contemporary theory suggests that the paradoxical responses the play elicits are directly related to this technique. The discussion in a recent article on colonialist literature has some relevance for an understanding of the impact of what Abdul R. JanMohamed calls a "manichean allegory":

> a field of diverse yet interchangeable oppositions between white and black, good and evil, superiority and inferiority, civilization and savagery, intelligence and emotion, rationality and sensuality, self and Other, subject and object. The power relations underlying this model set in motion such strong currents that even a writer who is reluctant to acknowledge it and who may indeed be highly critical of imperialist exploitation is drawn into its vortex.[15]

Theatricality and Otherness

It is possible, then, to assume that the dualistic vision that informs *All God's Chillun* itself embodies assumptions and anxieties that undercut socially progressive aims. These metaphors of contrast have an inextricable connection to social realities and inevitably comment on them. Film theorist Laura Mulvey talks of "the difficulty of envisaging change from within the conceptual framework of a polarized mythology."[16] The problems inherent in a bipolar structure are enhanced in this play by the superimposition of racial difference on a paradigm of gender difference that is highly charged. In his earlier play *Welded*, O'Neill anticipated this conception of a Strindbergian marriage seen in terms of racial contrast. When Eleanor and Cape of *Welded* are reunited after a bitter quarrel and separation, they come together "*like two persons of different races, deeply in love but separated by a barrier of language.*"[17] In *All God's Chillun*, the otherness of Jim as black is complemented by the otherness of Ella as female. Such raw material invited a theatrical interplay of difference that ultimately complicated the presentation of these scenes from a marriage.

Early in the play, contrasts between black and white are made with expressionistic relentlessness. O'Neill says in his stage directions, which in *All God's Chillun* have their own narrative impact:

> *People pass, black and white, the Negroes frankly participants in the spirit of Spring, the whites laughing constrainedly, awkward in natural emotion. Their words are lost. One hears only their laughter. It expresses the difference in race.* (301)

In the separate streets of black and white, contrasting music reinforces the polarization, always with the suggestion that the way of the blacks is more "natural." The world of Jim and Ella as children, where he is called "Jim Crow" and she "Painty face" (302) to denote her rosy complexion, is a relative Eden for them racially. Yet even here, Jim and Ella express affection for each other with a consciousness of difference, he talking of drinking chalk water to become white, she wanting to be black as he is.

From the opening scene, the basic polarities of gender and race are conflated. They are also aligned in significant ways along a vertical axis between the above and below, which Jan Kott identifies in his study of Greek drama as "one of the most universal and most perennial archetypes."[18] The relative positions of Jim and

Ella, he as male and black, she as female and white, are modulated hierarchically throughout the course of the play.

When Jim and Ella are teenagers, Ella, then the girlfriend of Mickey, a white boxer, is no longer interested in Jim. In response to Jim's offer of help, she says, "You're certainly forgetting your place!" (310). At this point in their lives, Jim's effort to rise on the social ladder by graduating from high school on his second try is resented by his friend Joe, who demands that Jim express his solidarity with his own race.

It is not until Ella "falls," having been abandoned by Mickey and having had a child who died of diphtheria, that she starts to see Jim again, calling him the "only white man in the world!" (314). Although she rejects Shorty's offer to set her up as a prostitute, she barely escapes that way of life through her reliance on Jim, who, we are told, "*has grown into a quietly-dressed studious-looking Negro with an intelligent yet queerly baffled face*" (315).

Jim and Ella marry and go to France in hope of a better life. For a while, among people less concerned with their racial difference, they live as brother and sister as a result of Ella's sexual inhibitions, the polarized intensity of the relationship briefly in abeyance. As Ella becomes more unbalanced, however, they return to face what they had tried to flee.

At this point, the Congo mask is introduced into the play.[19] Jim's sister, Hattie, who gave it to him as a wedding gift, describes it as:

> a mask which used to be worn in religious ceremonies by my people in Africa. But, aside from that, it's beautifully made, a work of Art by a real artist—as real in his way as your Michael Angelo. (328)

Its description in the stage directions concurs, in part, with Hattie's idea of it. However, the Congo mask is also referred to as "*a grotesque face, inspiring obscure, dim connotations in one's mind*" (322). Like the photograph of Jim's financially successful father, gotten up in "*outlandish lodge regalia*" (322), the mask has echoes of the primitive world of Brutus Jones. John Cooley's assertion that *The Emperor Jones* "exploits those stereotypes in the white imagination which associate blacks with the savage and a jungle landscape"[20] points toward similar issues in *All God's Chillun*.

In the apartment where Jim and Ella join Hattie and Mrs. Harris, the mask has what O'Neill calls "*a diabolical quality that*

Theatricality and Otherness

contrast imposes upon it" (322). Its demonic impact is evidently intended to be experienced by the audience as well as by Ella, who responds to it alternately with terror and hostility. Through this device, which Travis Bogard feels is "introduced into the play somewhat arbitrarily"[21] and never fully integrated dramatically, O'Neill further defines the conceptual space of the drama. The mask delineates the below, bringing into relief through contrast the heaven of the title, which is the above of the vertical axis, and, as becomes increasingly apparent, the only place where "all god's chillun" can be in harmony. From this point forward, intensity builds through fluctuations in the topographical space of the drama that make it compelling theater but ultimately delimit its possibilities. Jim and Ella remain confined to some intermediate space, between above and below, where frenetic movement is possible, but no exit.

Jim's effort continues to be focused on trying to rise, to pass the bar exam and become a lawyer. Through his sensitive characterization of Jim Harris, O'Neill suggests very effectively the subtle racism he confronts. Of the reaction of his white classmates to his faltering answers to questions, Jim says, "They don't laugh, hardly ever. They're kind. They're good people. . . . They're considerate, damn them! But I feel branded!" (316). At times, Ella urges Jim forward. She says at one point, "I want you to climb and climb" (329). Like Eleanor in *Welded*, however, she is a woman who thwarts a man's aspirations. She is also emblematic of white racist society blocking the way of blacks, a symbolic burden she essentially bears alone in this play. In one of her mad moments, Ella addresses the Congo mask that, for her, embodies Jim's blackness, saying:

> How dare you grin at me? I guess you forget what you are! That's always the way. Be kind to you, treat you decent, and in a second you've got a swelled head, you think you're somebody, you're all over the place putting on airs . . . (338)

Jim remains fully supportive of her in her madness, confident, as he has told Hattie, that Ella's racism is "Deep down in her people—not deep in her" (334).

Ella, in a frenzy of release when she learns that Jim has not passed his exam, stabs the Congo mask. She is euphoric, insisting that "The devil's dead." She confesses,

> I wouldn't let you sleep. I couldn't let you. I kept thinking if he sleeps good then he'll be sure to study good and then he'll pass—and the devil'll win! (341)[22]

Jim ultimately commits himself fully to the care of Ella, regressing willingly with her to the games of their childhood, offering to "play right up to the gates of Heaven" (342).

The portrait of Ella, and that of Jim suffering at her hands, situates *All God's Chillun* in that region that Sandra M. Gilbert and Susan Gubar define in their recent study of modernism as a "no man's land of mad women and unmanned or maddened men."[23] Gilbert and Gubar uncover a pattern in their examination of modernist texts by male writers that reveals a widespread anxiety induced by the shifting gender roles of an era. *All God's Chillun*, like many of its modernist counterparts, suggests a perpetual and universal conflict of male and female, albeit redeemed by interludes of reconciliation. Linking the enduring struggle of Ella and Jim, however, with issues of race implicitly denies the possibility of social change. In seeking to avoid an explicitly political comment by focusing on individual reality, the play unwittingly makes one through its design that is much less progressive than O'Neill would have intended consciously.

It is interesting to consider why the characterization of Jim's sister, Hattie Harris, a militant young woman who is bright and confident, has such little influence on the overall impact of the play. O'Neill describes her as "*a woman of about thirty with a high-strung, defiant face—an intelligent head showing both power and courage. She is dressed severely, mannishly*" (322). As Ranald suggests, Hattie prefigures Beneatha of Lorraine Hansberry's *Raisin in the Sun*.[24] She also has a resemblance to characters in the recent fiction of black women writers, such as Dee/Wangero in "Everyday Use" by Alice Walker and Kiswana Brown in Gloria Naylor's *The Women of Brewster Place*. Hattie is lucid in her appraisal of the social world and of her brother's painful marriage. Her portrait could be seen as distinctively innovative. I suggest, however, that Hattie's significance is bracketed because O'Neill presents her as an androgynous figure in a play that so insistently compels attention through a passionate conflict of opposites. Although her departure from the apartment she and her mother leave to Jim and Ella could signal alternative resolutions, the play mutes all other possibilities and inevitably draws us back to the marriage of Jim and Ella and to a theatrically intense conclusion of religious exaltation.

Earlier, Jim had cried out, "You with your fool talk of the black race and the white race! Where does the human race get a chance to come in?" (336). The response O'Neill attempted in *All God's Chillun Got Wings* is still not yet fully formulated. As Sandra

Theatricality and Otherness 55

Harding says of our own time, "If we find it difficult to imagine the day-to-day details of living in a world no longer structured by racism and classism, most of us do not even know how to start imagining a world in which gender difference . . . no longer constrains the ways we think, feel, and act."[25] Only the plurality of voices now becoming more available could inspire visions and re-visions of difference beyond the considerable achievement of O'Neill.

Notes

1. Quoted in Arthur and Barbara Gelb, *O'Neill* (New York: Harper and Brothers, 1962), p. 551.
2. Virginia Floyd, ed., *Eugene O'Neill at Work: Newly Released Ideas for Plays* (New York: Frederick Ungar, 1981), p. 176.
3. Ibid., p. 53.
4. Margaret Loftus Ranald, *The Eugene O'Neill Companion* (Westport, Conn.: Greenwood Press, 1984), p. 19.
5. Eugene O'Neill, quoted in Gelb, *O'Neill*, pp. 550-51.
6. Louis Sheaffer, *O'Neill: Son and Playwright* (Boston: Little, Brown, 1968), p. 80.
7. Gelb, *O'Neill*, p. 555. See also Travis Bogard, *Contour in Time: The Plays of Eugene O'Neill* (New York: Oxford University Press, 1972), p. 192. John Henry Raleigh, *The Plays of Eugene O'Neill* (Carbondale: Southern Illinois University Press, 1965; Arcturus Books, 1972), points to the Jim of *The Adventures of Huckleberry Finn* by Mark Twain as a model for Jim Harris. Michael Hinden, "The Transitional Nature of *All God's Chillun Got Wings*," *The Eugene O'Neill Newsletter* 4, no. 1-2 (1980): 3-5, considers Jim and Ella as an extension of Yank and Mildred of *The Hairy Ape*. Michael Manheim, *Eugene O'Neill's New Language of Kinship* (Syracuse: Syracuse University Press, 1982), suggests that Jim anticipates Edmund Tyrone of *Long Day's Journey into Night*. For a discussion of miscegenation in drama, see Joyce Flynn, "Melting Plots: Patterns of Racial and Ethnic Amalgamation in American Drama Before Eugene O'Neill," *American Quarterly* 38 (1986): 417-38.
8. Gelb, *O'Neill*, p. 550.
9. Michael Meyer, *Ibsen: A Biography* (Garden City, N.Y.: Doubleday, 1971), pp. 774-75.
10. Peter J. Gillet, "O'Neill and the Racial Myths," *Twentieth Century Literature* 18 (April 1972): 113.
11. Leslie Catherine Sanders, *The Development of Black Theater in America: From Shadows to Selves* (Baton Rouge: Louisiana State University Press, 1988), p. 1.
12. Ibid., pp. 1, 2.
13. Eugene O'Neill, quoted in Gelb, *O'Neill*, p. 550.
14. Raleigh, *The Plays of Eugene O'Neill*, p. 174.
15. Abdul R. JanMohamed, "The Economy of Manichean Allegory: The Function of Racial Difference in Colonialist Literature," in *"Race," Writing, and Difference*, ed. Henry Louis Gates, Jr. (Chicago: University of Chicago Press, 1986), p. 82.

16. Laura Mulvey, "Changes: Thoughts on Myth, Narrative and Historical Experience," *History Workshop* 23 (Spring 1987): 12.

17. Eugene O'Neill, *Welded*, p. 480. Quotations from *Welded* and *All God's Chillun Got Wings* are from *The Plays of Eugene O'Neill*, vol. II (New York: Modern Library, 1982). Subsequent references are cited parenthetically by page number within the text.

18. Jan Kott, *The Eating of the Gods: An Interpretation of Greek Tragedy*, trans. Boleslaw Taborski and Edward J. Czerwinski (New York: Random House, 1970), p. 4.

19. See O'Neill's discussion of his use of masks in "Memoranda on Masks," in *Playwrights on Playwriting: The Meaning and Making of Modern Drama from Ibsen to Ionesco*, ed. Toby Cole (New York: Hill and Wang, 1960), pp. 65–71.

20. John R. Cooley, "The Emperor Jones and the Harlem Renaissance," *Studies in the Literary Imagination* 7 (Fall 1974): 80.

21. Bogard, *Contour*, p. 203.

22. Ella's violent racist impulses invite comparison with those of Lula in Imamu Amiri Baraka's 1965 play, *Dutchman*.

23. Sandra M. Gilbert and Susan Gubar, *No Man's Land: The Place of the Woman Writer in the Twentieth Century, Volume I: The War of the Words* (New Haven: Yale University Press, 1988), p. 40.

24. Ranald, *The Eugene O'Neill Companion*, p. 20.

25. Sandra Harding, *The Science Question in Feminism* (Ithaca: Cornell University Press, 1986), p. 19.

PART 2
ARTHUR MILLER

THE EXCHANGE OF WOMEN AND MALE HOMOSOCIAL DESIRE IN ARTHUR MILLER'S *DEATH OF A SALESMAN* AND LILLIAN HELLMAN'S *ANOTHER PART OF THE FOREST*

Gayle Austin

One of the most influential texts in feminist theory is Gayle Rubin's "The Traffic in Women": Notes on the 'Political Economy' of Sex."[1] In it, Rubin summarizes and comments on the theories of Marx, Lévi-Strauss, and Freud to develop a theory of how women are exchanged among men, mainly through marriage, to maintain the "sex-gender system" of a society. In discussing the anthropological view of the kinship system, Rubin mainly uses Lévi-Strauss's *The Elementary Structures of Kinship*, which further developed the idea first advanced by Marcel Mauss of the giving and receiving of "gifts" as an organizing principle of a society. Lévi-Strauss added the ideas that "marriages are a most basic form of gift exchange, in which it is women who are the most precious of gifts" and that "the incest taboo should best be understood as a mechanism to insure that such exchanges take place between families and between groups."[2] Rubin goes on to state the core of her contribution in this piece:

> If it is women who are being transacted, then it is the men who give and take them who are linked, the woman being a conduit of a relationship rather than a partner to it. . . .
> To enter into a gift exchange as a partner, one must have something to give. If women are for men to dispose of, they are in no position to give themselves away. . . . Women are given in marriage, taken in battle, exchanged for favors, sent as tribute, traded, bought, and sold. Far from being confined to the "primitive" world, these practices seem only to become more pronounced and commercialized in more "civilized" societies.[3]

The difference between Rubin and Lévi-Strauss is that she takes the time to say that the exchange of women is not "natural" or a cultural necessity.

Many feminist critics have used Rubin's ideas in their own fields, such as literary criticism. Eve Kosofsky Sedgwick, in *Between Men: English Literature and Male Homosocial Desire*,[4] has developed some of Rubin's ideas into her own theory of "male homosocial desire," in which women are exchanged among men in order to facilitate the men's relationships with each other. In an earlier article, Sedgwick defines male homosocial desire as "the whole spectrum of bonds between men, including friendship, mentorship, rivalry, institutional subordination, homosexual genitality, and economic exchange,"[5] illustrating how the "traffic in women" takes place in consonance with these bonds in two examples from English literature: Wycherley's play *The Country Wife* and Sterne's novel *A Sentimental Journey*.

Sedgwick makes several points about *The Country Wife* that will be useful later in analyzing *Salesman*:

> "To cuckold" is by definition a sexual act, performed on a man, by another man. Its central position means that the play emphasizes heterosexual love chiefly as a strategy of homosocial desire.
> ... The status of the women in this transaction is determiningly a problem in the play: ... their ambiguous status of being at the same time objects of symbolic exchange and also, at least potentially, users of symbols and subjects in themselves. The play teaches that women are in important senses property, but property of a labile and dangerous sort.[6]

Sedgwick's book deals mainly with eighteenth- and nineteenth-century novels written by men, but her use of Rubin, combined with the idea of "erotic triangles" taken from René Girard, does have application to contemporary American drama. The core of her approach is that "patriarchal heterosexuality can best be discussed in terms of one or another form of the traffic in women: it is the use of women as exchangeable, perhaps symbolic, property for the primary purpose of cementing the bonds of men with men."[7] About erotic triangles, she notes Girard's observation that "the bond that links the two rivals is as intense and potent as the bond that links either of the rivals to the beloved" and that most of the triangles he discusses are "those in which two males are rivals for a female."[8] Today, of course, it is possible to trace many other kinds of triangles as well.

These theories are quite applicable to drama, particularly post-war American drama, informed as it is by capitalist, psychoanalytic social conditions. I apply them to Arthur Miller's *Death of a Salesman* (1949), the "Daddy" of American drama and a frequently utilized paradigm for what American drama *is* or should be. By pointing out how the women in the play are exchanged among the men and how they are represented as objects to be so exchanged, it can be shown how this pattern eliminates women as active subjects in the play. The valorization of this play in the American canon mitigates toward cutting women's experience as subjects out of consideration for "serious" drama. The effect of this play, with its frequent revivals, strong critical approval, and class use on many levels of education, can hardly be overestimated.

The basic family structure of *Death of a Salesman*, that of father, mother, and two dissimilar sons, is a classic one. From the first family in the Bible to Eugene O'Neill's *Long Day's Journey Into Night* (written before but produced after *Salesman*), this family structure has been a popular one for serious writers of all genres. From a feminist perspective, the biggest problem with this family structure is the absence of the daughter. Woman is portrayed only as wife and mother, and, with a few exceptions, her drama is not central to the action of the plays. *Salesman* is not one of the exceptions.

The main action of the play involves the triangle of Willy and his two sons, Biff and Happy. The wife and mother, Linda, is restricted before the play begins by her description in the opening stage directions. She is characterized as loving and admiring of her husband, who overtly demonstrates his longings, *"which she shares but lacks the temperament to utter and follow to their end."*[9] That is the end of the possibility of that woman acting on her own behalf. She was traded long ago and has no "temperament" to change the terms of the deal. Although a triangle occasionally may include Linda, Biff-Willy-Happy is dramatized mostly and has the greatest importance attached to it. Both sons love the father and have competed for his love in different ways since childhood, never receiving enough of the right kind. Biff has a pattern of "stealing" and Happy one of "whoring" to try to compensate for the lack of satisfactory paternal relationship. One has turned to merchandise, the other to women as objects of exchange.

Neither son has married, although at thirty-four and thirty-two they are at an age which, were they women, would lead them to be called "old maids." Both reveal their attitudes toward women and marriage in the scene between them in their old bedroom early in act 1. Biff concedes" "Maybe I oughta get married. Maybe I oughta get stuck into something," while Happy lists among the objects his money can buy "My own apartment, a car, and plenty of women" (23). Women are clearly objects of exchange for Happy. Several times in the play, he "gets" a girl for his brother or offers to do so to gain his brother's favor. Before the play begins, they have been out on a double date, and the restaurant scene in act 2 shows Happy picking up one girl and arranging another for his brother. He does not get satisfaction, however, from his conquests. He admits to Biff that "it gets like bowling or something. I just keep knockin' them over and it doesn't mean anything"(25). He admits that one reason for his conquests is competition with the other men at his office. The girl he was out with before the play begins was engaged to a man "in line for the vice-presidency of the store" where he works, and "maybe I just have an overdeveloped sense of competition or something, but I went and ruined her, and furthermore I can't get rid of her. And he's the third executive I've done that to." He even admits "I don't want the girl, and, still, I take it and—I love it!"(25). What he loves is winning something that the men "better" than he is don't have—yet. He is still competing with his brother and winning on that front, but it is not enough.

Happy competes using women to try to gain some relationship with the other man involved in each instance. In the case of the executives, he even goes to their weddings. He offers Biff "any babe you want" to try to gain his approval. But Happy has always come out second in the race for his father, and he knows it. His whoring may be an unconscious patterning after his father, which he can still do because he was not scarred, as was his brother, by the climactic "primal scene" Biff witnessed in a Boston hotel room at the age of seventeen. That scene has put Biff off women almost entirely, except for the gestures he makes to reciprocate the "gift" of women he receives from his brother. Biff tries to gain his father's approval through setting up a business deal. Happy has already "succeeded" at work; when he feels needy or guilty, he says he will get married. At the end of act 1, after Willy has encouraged Biff in his business endeavor, Happy says, out of nowhere, "I'm gonna get married, Mom. I wanted to tell you" (68). And after Biff and Willy have their last exhausting confrontation, ending with Willy's strong feeling that Biff loves him, Happy adds his contribution: "I'm getting married, Pop, don't forget it. I'm changing everything. I'm gonna run that de-

The Exchange of Women

partment before the year is up"(133–34). He will bring home a woman for his parents in exchange for their approval of him.

The play is structured toward the primal "climax" when Biff found his father in a hotel room with "The Woman" (she has no name, mythic but also anonymous, like the sex Willy enjoys with her). The message of that scene, and of the restaurant scene that precedes it, is that women come between men and their fathers. "The Woman," Miss Forsythe, and Letta are whores, with no power and almost no characterization. They are objects that can be traded, but, because they are not wives, they are not totally under the men's control. They can "tempt" sons to desert their father in a restaurant or, worse, cause a father to alienate his son. Women are indeed property of a dangerous sort.

The play leaves the overpowering impression that, for men, sex with women is empty, mothers and wives are necessary but ineffectual, and the most important thing is to bond successfully with other men. The problem is that this play has become a paradigm for what the "serious American play" should be. Next to some of O'Neill's work, it is the most lauded and most imitated play in the canon. Most playwright "sons" of Miller try to beat the old man at his own game sooner or later. Even Sam Shepard's "family" plays can trace some of their roots to this play. It is the *Oedipus Rex* of American drama for many people, and the continuation of its centrality effectively cuts women's experience out of consideration for "serious" drama.

In contrast to *Salesman* is Lillian Hellman's *Another Part of the Forest* (1946). Written during the same period, Hellman's play represents women in a very different way, as active subjects, making efforts to arrange their own exchange among men. Although it has not entered the canon of "important" American plays nor been positively evaluated by some feminist critics because of its "poor role models," it is important to examine it seriously and contrast it with Miller's play. *Another Part of the Forest* gives an unusual view of the exchange of women: Hellman allows the female "property" to act and speak for themselves as subjects, even as we see them being exchanged by the men on stage as if they were objects.

Produced seven years after *The Little Foxes* (1939), the play shows some of the same characters as its better-known sister, but at a point twenty years earlier in their lives. In *Foxes*, set in 1900, Regina has married Horace Giddens, has a daughter, and schemes to gain some economic control of her life, which has always been circumscribed by her brother, Benjamin. Her other brother, Oscar, is overbearing toward his wife, Birdie. Back in the 1880 setting of *Forest*, Regina is a girl of twenty in love with Birdie's cousin. In the course of the play, the family balance of power shifts from her father, Marcus, to her brother, Ben. The reason for the shift is the revelation to Ben by their mother, Lavinia, of damaging evidence against her father. Because of this shift, Ben gains the upper hand in his siblings' love lives. It is foreshadowed that Regina will be forced to marry Horace, and Oscar, who loses his "working-girl" love, Laurette, will be forced to marry Birdie, whose family is in desperate financial straits.

Like *Salesman*, *Forest* is a family play, with a mother, father, and two dissimilar sons, but in this case the missing daughter is added. Unlike *Salesman*, this is a "history play," set in an earlier period than when it was written, but it deals with some of the same post-world War II issues of American materialism that Miller used three years later. Both are basically passing-along-of-the-phallus plays, but unlike Miller, Hellman keeps the father alive at the end of her play, pushed aside but still a physical reminder of the passage of power. (Perhaps sons, more than daughters, actually need to "kill off" the father to achieve their climax.)

All four of the main women in the play have enough characterization and perform significant enough actions to be seen as active agents, although by the end of the play two have left town and the other two are to be married off at Ben's discretion. They struggle within their circumscribed roles, even though they are overcome in the end. Like Miller, Hellman shows the rise of son over father, but she stresses that it is caused by social and accidental factors, not the inevitable superiority of sons over daughters. Regina is just as worthy a successor to her father as Ben, but, because Ben was around when Lavinia decided to share her secret, Ben received the tool with which to overpower the old man. The women in the play need not be taken as idealized role models for female behavior, any more than Willy, Biff, or Happy are male role models. Putting that demand on a woman playwright in order to consider her play feminist is unrealistic and counterproductive. The women's behavior in this play allows them to be participants in the game, which is more than can be said of Miller's women.

Lavinia embodies several aspects of stereotypical female behavior, but, at the same time, she tells truths and determines the outcome of the play. Hers is the last presence in each of the first two acts, leaving a lasting impression. Her leave-taking is the next to last moment of the play. But she appears to be both passive and crazy. There are many reasons suggested for Lavinia's madness, one of them her husband's brutality. Her passivity, which has been called the "deception of passivity" by one critic,[10] may also be seen as a response to her husband and has a well-suppressed anger under it. In act 3, she tells Ben that she has always been afraid of Marcus and of Ben, too. "I spent a life afraid. And you know that's funny, Benjamin, because way down deep I'm a woman wasn't made to be afraid."[11] For one moment, we see the strong young woman she once must have been and her painful self-awareness. Rubin offers some insight into Lavinia: "the creation of 'femininity' in women in the course of socialization is an act of psychic brutality" and it "leaves in women an immense resentment of the suppression to which they were subjected" but also "few means for realizing and expressing their residual anger."[12]

Regina, Birdie, and Laurette are all twenty years old, a peak age for being exchanged. The irony is that Laurette, who is considered socially inferior to every other white person in the play, is the only woman who is in a position to trade herself, and does so. She goes to the highest bidder, but she controls the transaction. Regina and Birdie have Ben trading them, cementing the social and economic bonds among three families as he does so. Birdie tries to do some trading herself, when she asks for a loan on property which is not hers to transact. In the end, Ben gives her the loan for his own reasons, but it is made clear that the only commodity that will successfully be traded will be Birdie herself, in marriage to Oscar, arranged by Ben.

Regina tries to avoid her mother's fate of a loveless marriage by attempting to arrange for her own marriage to John Bagtry. She uses sex to lure him, but, in the end, she lacks the economic power to carry out her plans and is forced to align with Ben. In this way, we see that Ben will have the power to trade her to the Giddens family in return for their money and prestige, which, along with Birdie's cotton, will make him even more powerful than his father had been. By the end of the play, it is clear that both Ben and Regina will not allow love to block their quest for power. The action of *The Little Foxes*, held in the back of the mind while reading or seeing this play, bears out the lovelessness of their lives. But *Forest* gives an understanding picture of how both got that way and how Regina's options were limited by her gender.

Looking at *Salesman* and *Forest* through Rubin's work provides a new perspective. From the point of view of women, a play may represent woman by a shell of a character, embodied on stage by a female actress. She may seem convincing when played, but, when seen within the text of the play itself, she is usually only an exchangeable object, cementing the relationships of men. One difference between a male and female writer's perspective can be seen by examining a play written by a woman, in which the female characters may have some of the same fates as male-written objects but serve as subjects acting on their own behalf. The difference is striking. Feminist theory can aid in this examination of plays, part of an ongoing effort to write women into the history of drama.

Notes

1. Gayle Rubin, "The Traffic in Women: Notes on the 'Political Economy' of Sex," in *Toward an Anthropology of Women*, ed. Rayna R. Reiter (New York: Monthly Review Press, 1975), pp. 157–210.
2. Ibid., p. 173.
3. Ibid., pp. 174–75.
4. Eve Kosofsky Sedgwick, *Between Men: English Literature and Male Homosocial Desire* (New York: Columbia University Press, 1985).
5. Eve Kosofsky Sedgwick, "Sexualism and the Citizen of the World: Wycherley, Sterne, and Male Homosocial Desire," *Critical Inquiry* 11 (December 1984): 227.
6. Ibid., pp. 228–29.
7. Sedgwick, *Between Men*, pp. 25–26.
8. Ibid., p. 21.
9. Arthur Miller, *Death of a Salesman* (New York: Viking Press, 1949), p. 12. Subsequent references are cited parenthetically by page number within the text.
10. Mary L. Broe, "Bohemia Bumps into Calvin: The Deception of Passivity in Lillian Hellman's Drama," *Southern Quarterly* 19 (Winter 1981): 26–41.
11. Lillian Hellman, *Another Part of the Forest*, in *The Collected Plays* (Boston: Little, Brown, 1972), p. 382.
12. Rubin, "The Traffic in Women," p. 196.

WOMEN AND THE AMERICAN DREAM OF *DEATH OF A SALESMAN*

Kay Stanton

Arthur Miller's stated intention for *Death of a Salesman* was to create a "tragedy of the common man."[1] Although commentators argue over the meaning of "tragedy" in this phrase,[2] the word "man" has been taken as sexually specific rather than as generic in most responses to the play. Undoubtedly, the play is heavily masculine. Willy Loman is the tragic protagonist, and the effects of his tragic flaws are clearly engraved upon his sons. The roots of Willy's tragedy seem to be in his lack of attention from his father and his perceived inadequacy to his brother, Ben. All conflicts seem to be male-male—Willy versus Biff, Willy versus Howard, Willy versus Charley—so it has been easy for productions, audiences, and commentators to overlook, patronize, or devalue the significance of women in the play.[3] The tragedy of Willy Loman, however, is also the tragedy of American society's pursuit of the American Dream, which the play both defines and criticizes. Careful analysis reveals that the American Dream as presented in *Death of a Salesman* is male-oriented, but it requires unacknowledged dependence upon women as well as women's subjugation and exploitation.

The masculine mythos of the American Dream as personified in Willy Loman has three competing dimensions: the Green World, the Business World, and the Home. All three have ascendant male figure heads and submerged female presences. The Green World is the "outdoors" realm of trees, animals, handcrafting, planting, and hunting, and it takes both pastoral and savage forms. The pastoral aspect is associated with ancestral flute music and Willy's yearnings for his father and, in the next generation, with Biff's enjoyment of farm and ranch work, that which provokes Happy to call Biff "a poet," "an idealist."[4] The savage element is seen in Willy's beliefs about Ben.[5] Whereas Father Loman was a creative figure, moving in harmony with nature by making and disseminating music, Ben is an exploiter and despoiler of nature. In both pastoral and savage aspects, the Green World represents freedom and self-reliance and is a place to test and demonstrate one's masculinity. To Willy, "A man who can't handle tools is not a man" (44), and Biff tells Happy that "Men built like we are should be working out in the open" (23). As Ben is said to have walked into the jungle when he was seventeen and walked out when he was twenty-one, rich, the Green World was the means through which he entered manhood. What is submerged in both aspects is the femininity of nature and the dependence of the masculine on it. Biff states, "There's nothing more inspiring or—beautiful than the sight of a mare and a new colt" (22), and the jungle of Ben is a feminine symbol ("One must go in to fetch a diamond out" [134]), but the feminine is the raw material upon which the male asserts himself. Biff tells Happy that they should "Raise cattle, use our muscles" (23), and the jungle must yield its riches to Ben's mastery. Ben's superior masculinity is also proved by his having seven sons, but his wife is only mentioned as the communicant of the news of his death. Yet she is both producer-sustainer and survivor of life. Thus the female is the necessary element in the production of masculinity, but her role must be severely circumscribed.

The Loman family history can be pieced together through Willy's flashback conversation with Ben[6] (partly conflated with his conversation with Charley) and his present conversation with Howard. Apparently, Father Loman was a travelling maker and seller of flutes who went off to seek adventure in Alaska and deserted Mother, leaving her with two boys to raise alone. Then Ben ran off when he was seventeen and Willy was not quite four years old. Thus Willy and Mother were left alone together. The desertion by his father left Willy feeling "kind of temporary" (51) about himself and provoked Ben to imitate and surpass what his father had done. Both sons mythologize the father: to Willy he was "an adventurous man" with "quite a little streak of self-reliance" (81); to Ben he was "a very great and a very wild-hearted man" who with "one gadget" (the flute) supposedly "made more in a week" than a man like Willy "could make in a lifetime" (49). Both trivialize the role of their mother. Ben calls her a "Fine specimen of a lady" and the "old girl" (46) and assumes she would be living with lesser son Willy. But she is the woman who bore and raised Ben, whom he deserted and made no attempt to contact, not even knowing that she had "died a long time ago" (46). Willy's only other stated information about

Mother Loman is his memory of being "in Mamma's lap" listening to "some kind of high music" coming from "a man with a big beard" (48). The mother thus provided the position of comfort from which to attend to the father. Mother is never mentioned again, although hers would be an interesting story. How did she support and raise the four-year-old Willy? Willy seems to have had no further communication from his father, which implies that Father Loman never sent money.[7] Mother must have had "quite a little streak of self-reliance" also.

Willy entreats Ben to tell his boys about their grandfather, so they can learn "the kind of stock they spring from" (48).[8] Mother Loman and her stock and Linda and hers seem to have had no bearing on the production of the boys. An Edenic birth myth is implied, with all Loman men springing directly from their father's side, with no commingling with a female.

In both Ben and Willy, the first desire of manhood is reunion with the father. When Ben ran off, it was "to find father in Alaska." Willy's questions about whether Ben found him and where he is are not answered directly. Ben states that he had had a "very faulty view of geography"; discovering that he was headed due south, he ended up in Africa rather than Alaska. Thus Ben avoids saying whether he knows anything about Father by returning attention to himself. But what he does reveal inadvertently is that, in trying to run toward his father, he actually ran further away in the opposite direction. He discovered his mistake "after a few days" (48), so he could have changed direction but did not. Instead of joining his father, he obviously decided to beat him.

Whereas Ben follows his father's path by running off for adventure, Willy follows it by becoming a travelling salesman. When Willy was "eighteen, nineteen," only slightly older than Ben had been at his departure, he was "already on the road" as a salesman. Yet, unsure "whether selling had a future" for him, Willy at that age "had a yearning to go to Alaska," to "settle in the North with the old man" (80–81) and to be with his older brother. Mother was most likely still alive at this point, and Willy felt that he must break from her to establish his manhood, as he believes his father and brother had done. But, less independent than they were, Willy wishes for a family connection that includes only the three male members, a rebuilding of the family *without* Mother. Willy continually attempts to find or build an all-male realm of patriarchal-fraternal community.[9] This yearning provides the basis for his refrain of the "liked" and "well liked," which are set apart from the "loved." Willy probably had decided that Ben, as first son, had been "well liked" by their father, and he was only "liked," if regarded with affection at all. Willy would have been loved by his mother, but because that love had not been earned or seized but given freely, it did not have the same value as being "well liked" by his father. Linda, as Willy's wife, seems to have picked up where Mother left off, replacing her. Linda sings Willy to sleep with lullabies and "mothers" him in countless ways—and she is made to seem responsible for Willy's rejection of Ben's proposition to go with him to Alaska.[10] But Linda is obviously being made the scapegoat in this episode. Ben's offer is not for the two brothers to work together: Ben merely proposes a job in Alaska, where he had "bought timberland" and needs "a man to look after things" for him because he is heading back to Africa. Even without Ben, Willy finds the offer tempting in terms of pastoral male community: "God, timberland! Me and my boys in those grand outdoors!" (85). Ben interprets it more aggressively: "Screw on your fists and you can fight for a fortune up there."[11] Linda's strongest objection is "why must everybody conquer the world?" (85)—she sees no value in cut-throat competition—but her supporting points are Willy's own statements about his career fed back to him. Willy refuses the offer after Linda makes reference to Dave Singleman.

When the adolescent Willy had "almost decided to go" to find his father in Alaska, he met Dave Singleman, an eighty-four-year-old salesman who had "drummed merchandise in thirty-one states" and who could now simply go into his hotel room, call the buyers, and make his living in his green velvet slippers. Willy saw that and "realized that selling was the greatest career a man could want" (81). Obviously, Willy found in Dave Singleman a substitute father figure. Singleman had explored and imposed his will (through selling) upon a vast territory, as Father Loman had, but Dave Singleman had managed it in a civilized and comfortable way: in a train rather than a wagon, a hotel room rather than around a fire, and with the Green World transformed into the ease of the green velvet slippers, which he wore even in his death in the smoker of a train. The myth of Dave Singleman is equally as strong for Willy as the myth of his father, imaging as it does for him the perfect life and death, as Dave Singleman died the "death of a salesman," with "hundreds of salesmen and buyers" at his funeral and sadness "on a lotta trains for months after that" (81). Singleman's name implies his lack of dependence on women, and he demonstrates to Willy that a life of material comfort without pioneer ruggedness can still be manly. The realm of comfort had probably been associated in Willy's mind with his mother. Through Dave Singleman's model, Willy realizes that it is possible to establish himself as "well liked" in an all-male community outside of and larger than the male immediate family. This community is the Business World, which provides more stability and comfort and more variety of and competition among consumer goods than those handcrafted in the vast outdoors. In the face of both temptations to choose the Green World, Willy chooses the Business World, the realm of his surrogate father, Dave Singleman.

The Business World has the potential to swallow up the achievements of the Green World: Willy tells Ben that "The whole wealth of Alaska passes over the lunch table at the Commodore Hotel, and that's the wonder, the wonder of this country, that a man can end with diamonds here on the basis of being liked!" (86). The myth of the American Business World provides Willy with the fantasy means of beating his father and his brother. But the complexity of the Business World also defeats the simplicity of the Green World. Ben proudly claims to have had many enterprises and never kept books, but such practices are impossible in the Business World. Decision-making and increased competition take the place of handcrafting and manual exploitation of resources. Yet women are the submerged element in this realm, too. As the male realm moves indoors, it brings in the female to attend to the details of daily maintenance considered too trivial for male attention—typing letters, keeping records, collecting evidence, and, perhaps the most important function, screening out lesser men. Instead of testing himself directly on feminine nature, a man in the Business World must test himself by making an important impression on the female secretary-receptionist before meeting with the male decision-maker. Thus the female provides access to the patriarchal male authority. This element is seen clearly in Biff's attempt to make a date with Bill Oliver's secretary to gain access to him, after waiting five hours unsuccessfully, and in The Woman's statement that Willy has "ruined" her because, after their sexual liaison, she now sends him directly to the buyers, without waiting at her desk. Woman as trivialized Earth Mother in the Green World becomes Woman as trivialized Bitch-Goddess Success in the Business World.

Women in the Business World are marked as whores simply because they are there, perhaps because of their function as access givers, although the reconstitution of the submerged shows them to be otherwise. As Willy, deeply and loudly involved in one of his flashbacks, approaches Charley's office to borrow money, Jenny, Charley's secretary, tells Bernard that Willy is arguing with nobody and that she has a lot of typing to do and cannot deal with Willy any more. She is an insightful, kind, put-upon, hard-working woman. When Willy sees her, he says, "How're ya? Workin'? Or still honest?", implying that her income is made through prostitution. To her polite reply, "Fine. How've you been feeling?", Willy again turns to sexual innuendo: "Not much any more, Jenny. Ha, ha!" (90).

Assertion of success for Biff, and especially for Happy, is also bound up with sexual exploitation of women. In their first appearance, they alternate between discussing their father and their own past and current lives, always coming to an association with women. When they recall their "dreams and plans" of the past, an immediate connection is made with "about five hundred women" who "would like to know what was said in this room." They hark back crudely to Happy's "first time," with "big Betsy something," a woman "on Bushwick Avenue," "With the collie dog": "there was a pig."[12] Happy states that he "got less bashful" with women and Biff "got more so"; when he questions what happened to Biff's "old confidence" (20–21), Biff returns the discussion to their father. Biff's self-confidence rests on sexual confidence; its diminishment is tied to his father.[13] For Happy, success is measured using women as markers, as he moves up from the initial "pig" with a dog to "gorgeous creatures" that he can get "any time I want" (24–25)—but to him they are still "creatures," not human beings like himself. Although Biff and Happy agree that they each should marry, find "a girl—steady, Somebody with substance," "somebody . . . with resistance! Like Mom" (25), Happy delights in turning other men's "Lindas" into his private objects of sport. He attributes his "overdeveloped sense of competition" (25) to his habit of "ruining," deflowering, the fiancées of the executives at the store where he works, then attending their weddings to savor his secret triumph publicly. Because he cannot accept his low status in the Business World, he must take what he interprets to be the possessions of his superiors—their women—robbing them of their supposed only value, the gold of their virtue and jewels of their chastity, and delivering the damaged goods for his superiors to pay for over a lifetime of financial support.

Happy uses women as Ben used the jungle and timberlands,

and he carves out this territory for himself as Ben had. Just as Ben sought adventure like his father but found it in another direction, Happy sought the self-confidence of the older brother Biff and found sexual confidence, and it is now where he has superiority over his brother. Although they both hope to have a fraternal life together—male bonding with limited, sex-defined participation of women—they have competing versions. Biff, more attracted to the Green World, wants to buy a ranch that they both can work, and Happy plans for them to go into business together, share an apartment, and for himself to oversee Biff's having "any babe you want" (26). Later, in the restaurant, when Biff tries to tell Happy about his attempted meeting with Bill Oliver, to put forth Happy's own plan for going into business together, Happy turns Biff's attention to the "strudel" he has been attempting to pick up,[14] insisting that Biff demonstrate his "old confidence" (21) before he speaks of the Oliver meeting. Happy wishes to establish a safety net of sexual confidence to protect them against news of failure that he may anticipate and fear, and he perhaps wants unconsciously to show off his "success" to contrast Biff's probable failure. Magnanimous Happy will give this choice female morsel to Biff if he will only say he wants her—assuming in advance that she has no choice but to acquiesce.

During his assault on the "strudel," the "Girl" in the restaurant (later named Miss Forsythe), Happy quickly defines himself as a salesman and asks, "You don't happen to sell, do you?", with a double entendre on prostitution. Her answer is "No, I don't sell"; she is a model whose picture has been on several magazine covers. But Happy continues to insist to Biff that "She's on call" (101–2). At Happy's entreaty, she rounds up a friend, Letta, who is not a prostitute either.[15] Letta is to begin jury duty the next day, so we may assume that she is a responsible citizen without an arrest record, one qualified to hear evidence and evaluate testimony. When she asks whether Biff or Happy has ever been on a jury, Biff answers, "No, but I have been in front of them!" (114). This is supposedly a joke, but it later proves to be true when we learn that Biff had served three months in jail for theft. Woman as nurturer and care-giver was the submerged element in the Green World; Woman as judge and determiner of truth and value is the submerged element in the Business World.

Yet men in the Business World both need and despise the presence and participation of women, who are continually regarded as whores. Stanley, the waiter in the restaurant, calls the two women, whom he had never seen before, "chippies," presumably because they left with Biff and Happy. The double standard in full force, women are allowed no sexual adventurism: one real or supposed sexual experience and they are "ruined" forever by male standards.[16] Happy makes women like Miss Forsythe and Letta the scapegoats for his inability to marry: it is a "shame" that "a beautiful girl like that" (Miss Forsythe) can be "had" by him. He cannot marry because "There's not a good woman in a thousand" (103). This slander covers Happy's submerged fear that if he tries to marry a woman, another man might do as he does and "ruin" her. He cannot invest himself in one woman because he fears competing men who might rob him of his woman's supposed only value, the chastity of virginity and sexual fidelity.

In his initial conversation with Biff in the play, Happy himself makes a connection between his taking of women and taking of money: "Manufacturers offer me a hundred-dollar bill now and then to throw an order their way. You know how honest I am, but it's like this girl, see. I hate myself for it. Because I don't want the girl, and, still, I take it and—I love it!" (25). It is Happy, not any woman in the play, who is a prostitute. He is not only more sexually promiscuous than any of the women, but he also takes money under unsavory circumstances. Thus he projects his own whorishness onto women in the play's clearest character depiction of male-female Business World dealings. As Woman is present in the public world of business, her ultimate function is to absorb the projection of what the men cannot acknowledge in themselves.

Just as the Green World overlaps with and is transformed into the Business World, so the Business World overlaps with and transforms the Home, which also maintains remnants of the Green World. The Home is the only realm where Willy can be the father, the patriarchal authority, so he invests it with sanctity.[17] Much is made of the physical details of the Loman home in the opening stage directions. The home is *"small, fragile seeming,"* against a *"solid vault of apartment houses."* The house is symbolic of Willy, the apartment houses representative of the big-uncaring society that has "boxed in" the little man. An *"air of the dream"* is said to cling to the Loman home, *"a dream arising out of reality."* We are given a few particulars of the reality: *"The kitchen at center seems actual enough,"* with its table, chairs, and the refrigerator, the palpability of which is underlined later through discussion of its repair needs. Other "real" elements are the brass bedstead and straight bedroom chair and *"a silver athletic trophy*" (11). The set reflects Willy's mind, and these elements are most real in life to him. The kitchen and bedroom are the traditional areas of Woman and Linda, and the trophy is the one tangible piece of evidence of Willy's son Biff's "success."

The house evidently also represents the myth of the man's Home being his castle—or here, castle in the air, the *"air of the dream"* (11) clinging to the Home. Willy's failure to get love from his father and brother in the Green World and his failures in the Business World can be obfuscated in the Home, where he is what he defines himself to be. In his interaction with his wife, Linda, Willy habitually patronizes, demeans, and expresses irritation at her; anything he says, no matter how trivial or self-contradictory, is made to seem more important than anything she says. Yet in one of his very few compliments to her, he says, "You're my foundation and my support, Linda" (18). His praise of her is not only placed wholly in the context of himself, but it also partakes of architectural imagery, defining Linda's place in the Home. She is the foundation and support of the Home, the "real" element that Willy can extrapolate from and return to as he constructs his fantasy life.[18]

The Loman men are all less than they hold themselves to be, but Linda is more than she is credited to be.[19] She is indeed the foundation that has allowed the Loman men to build themselves up, if only in dreams, and she is the support that enables them to continue despite their failures. Linda is the one element holding the facade of the family together. Yet even Miller, her creator, seems not to have fully understood her character.[20] Linda is described in the opening stage directions as follows: *"Most often jovial, she has developed an iron repression of her exceptions to Willy's behavior—she more than loves him, she admires him, as though his mercurial nature, his temper, his massive dreams and little cruelties, served her only as sharp reminders of the turbulent longings . . . which she shares but lacks the temperament to utter and follow to their end"* (12). She thus seems inferior to Willy; yet she demonstrates a level of education superior to his in terms of grammatical and mathematical ability, and she is definitely more gifted in diplomatic and psychological acumen. In her management of Willy, she embodies the American Dream ideal of the model post-World War II wife, infinitely supportive of her man. She makes no mistakes, has no flaws in wifely perfection. But the perfect American wife is not enough for American Dreamers like Willy. He has been unfaithful to her, and he rudely interrupts and silences her, even when she is merely expressing support for him. She can be the foundation of the house; he must rebuild the facade.

If the Loman house represents the Loman family, with Linda as the steady foundation and support, the facade is constructed with stolen goods. The enemy apartment buildings that so anger Willy have provided the materials that he and his sons used in such projects as rebuilding the front stoop. Linda knows that they need not have been "boxed in" by the apartment buildings; she says, "We should've bought the land next door" (17). Possibly she had suggested the idea at the appropriate time but was ignored. But Willy prefers to transfer the blame for the diminishment of his Green World: "They should've had a law against apartment houses. Remember those two beautiful elm trees out there? . . . They should've arrested the builder for cutting those down" (17). Of course, there is a law against stealing property, which Willy thought nothing of disobeying when he encouraged the boys to steal from the construction site, calling them "fearless characters" (50). Laws are for lesser men to follow, not the Loman men. In the realm of the Home, Willy and his sons are associated with rebuilding through theft, and Linda is associated with cleaning, mending, and repair.

In Willy's flashback sequences, Linda habitually appears with the laundry, suggesting that it is her responsibility to clean up the males' dirtiness, on all levels. In both past and present, she is shown mending, not only her own stockings but also Willy's jacket. Often when Linda speaks, she discusses repairs, which she oversees; she must mend the male machinery. Willy is "sold" by other salesmen or advertisements on the quality of products and fails to recognize that even the "best" breaks down from daily wear and tear—including Willy himself. Although Linda's functions of cleaning, mending, and overseeing repairs are traditionally "feminine," they are significant because they are the ones maintained when other traditionally "feminine" elements are appropriated by Willy. It is not Linda but Willy who asserts the importance of physical attractiveness, who prefers a fantasy life of glamor to the reality of daily toil, who suffers from the "empty nest syndrome," and who insists on having the most significant role in child-rearing.

Willy works hard at preventing Linda from having any substantive impact on shaping the boys' characters; he tries continually to make them his alone, just as he had implied that they had sprung from his "stock" alone. After thanking God for Adonis-like looks in his sons, Willy confesses to Linda that he himself is "not noticed," "fat," "foolish to look at," and had been called a "walrus" (37).[21] Evidently, the physical attractiveness, strength, and resilience of the boys derive from Linda rather than Willy, but "God," not she, is given credit. Although Linda is the continual presence in the boys' lives at home, as Mother Loman had been for Willy, Willy undermines Linda's authority when he returns from the road. In a flashback sequence, Linda disapproves of various manifestations of Biff's bad behavior and runs from the scene almost in tears after Willy refuses to support her. She represents human dignity and values: cooperative, moral, humane behavior as opposed to lawless assertion of self over all others through assumed superiority. Just as Woman was unacknowledged creator-sustainer of life in the Green World and determiner of value in the Business World, in the Home, Woman, through Linda as submerged element, is the measure of human dignity and the accountant of worth.

Linda is the foundation and support not only of the Loman Home and Willy himself but also of the plea for sympathy for Willy of the play itself. She is used to establish Willy's significance as a human being to the boys and to the audience. In her most famous speech, she asserts that, although not a "great man," not rich or famous, and "not the finest character that ever lived," Willy is "a human being, and a terrible thing is happening to him. So attention must be paid. . . . Attention, attention must finally be paid to such a person" (56). Linda thus articulates his value and notes the real worth beneath the sham presentation. But the boys have been taught too well by Willy to disregard her message. When she reveals that the company had taken Willy's salary away five weeks before, and Biff calls those responsible "ungrateful bastards" (57), she states that they are no worse than his sons. The male world is ungrateful, unappreciative of such contributions as Willy made; only Linda understands and values them. Whenever she attempts to bring Biff and Happy to consideration for their father, they habitually shift blame away from themselves, pretend there is no problem, and/or change the subject and start bickering between themselves on their competing ideas and ideals. Just as Willy leaves the repair of household appliances to Linda, the boys leave the repair of their broken-down father to her.

The Loman men do see Linda as a validator of value, but they objectify virtue in her and assume that, if they have a woman like her, they will possess virtue and not need to develop it on their own. Both Biff and Happy wish to marry a girl just like the girl who married dear old Dad, and they believe such possession will immediately transform their lives and bring them to maturity. They, like their father, want to subtract value from a woman to add to their own; none of the Loman men is able to keep an accurate account of himself. In the Loman Home, only Linda understands what has value, what things cost, and how much must be paid to maintain and repair the Home life. Her other function, therefore, is computing the family finances, doing the family math. She must tactfully bring Willy to face the truth of his commissions from his inflated exaggerations of success to maximize such resources as there are, and Willy resents her for returning him to the foundation of himself as lesser money-earner from his dreams of wealth. As representative and accountant of worth, she must be trivialized and devalued, as must math.

As noted above, besides Linda and her spheres, the only other real element to Willy in the Loman Home is Biff's athletic trophy. Linda's significance in the Home is suppressed largely through the elevation of sports. The Loman men's idolatry of aggressive male-male competition relegates women into being the devalued objects and instruments of sports. Happy states that the "only trouble" with his promiscuity with women is that "it gets like bowling or something. I just keep knockin' them over and it doesn't mean anything" (25). Similarly, The Woman in the Boston hotel room, disabused of the idea that she means anything to Willy, interprets herself as his football. As instruments of sports, women are the means for starting the competitive game, the object they fight over, and the possession that marks the winners and assures them of being "well liked."

The worst mistake that Willy makes with his sons is in his foisting upon them the notion that sports success guarantees financial success. The adult Happy feels superior because he can "outbox, outrun, and outlift anybody in that store," so he cannot bear to "take orders from those common, petty sons-of-bitches" (24). He believes that the strength of his masculinity should overcome all competitors, although selling merchandise has little to do with displays of physical prowess. The adult Biff also finds holding a job difficult because of his self-image of athletic superiority. This is the "spirit" that Willy successfully manages to "imbue them with" (52), the spirit that he associates with Ben. Not only does Ben assert that making a fortune depends on screwing on one's fists, but he also provides a demonstration by challenging Biff, tripping him, and aiming an umbrella's point at his eye in phallic threat, saying "Never fight fair with a stranger, boy. You'll never get out of the jungle that way" (49). Biff and Ben are family members, not "strangers," but Ben's aura is partly maintained by establishing distance between himself and other men: no man is allowed to seem his peer or comrade. This "over-developed sense of competition" that Willy cultivates in his boys, which can only be satisfied by being "number-one man," puts the boys in competition with each other (seen most clearly in their dream of selling sporting goods by heading competing teams) and ultimately in competition with their father.

Sports in the play partakes of Green World elements by providing an arena in which to test and demonstrate masculinity in its most elemental form. When Charley appears in his golf pants in one of Willy's flashbacks of Ben, Willy says, "Great athlete! Between him and his son Bernard they can't hammer a nail!" (51). Charley had been "man enough" to father Bernard, so he can still be a sports participant; similarly, the adult Bernard, father of two boys, is shown with tennis rackets. But golf and tennis are genteel, civilized sports; real men shine in boxing (shown in Willy's gift to the boys of a punching bag) and, especially, football. Because football is played outdoors on a green field and involves seizing territory in pursuit and manipulation of a valued object, it recaptures the savage Green World of Ben in the jungle with the diamonds. Because football is a male team sport that provides opportunity for an individual to "make an impression," "create personal interest," and be "well liked" (33), it epitomizes the Business World. The football star, Biff in high school, brings to the Home a trophy as validation of value, and feminine support comes in having "a crowd of girls behind him" (32) and in having "the girls pay for you" (28). For Willy, therefore, football becomes the ideal means of synthesizing the realms of Green World, Business World, and Home into his desired male community. As such a synthesis, football assumes mythic proportions; on the day of the Ebbets Field game, Biff appears "Like a young god. Hercules—something like that. . . . A star like that, magnificent, can never really fade away" (68).

This fantasy synthesis, however, does not pass the test of reality. The values of sports fail to overcome the combined challenge of the feminine and math. Just as the Loman house is partly constructed with stolen materials, so Biff's success in high school is partly established through theft of knowledge, especially of math, from Bernard. Like Linda and the suppressed feminine elements of the Green World and Business World, Bernard in the sports synthesis is a demeaned and exploited presence. Because he "loves" Biff, without feeling a need to compete with him, Bernard is "anemic" (32), emasculated, made feminine by the hypermasculine standards of sports.

Through their belief in the justified predominance of male-male competition over feminine measurement of value, the Loman men can rationalize, even sanctify, theft. Willy steals from Linda the respect of parenting and steals through The Woman a higher place in the Business World than he deserves. Happy steals the women of his superiors to avoid competition in the prescribed arena and to inflate his sense of self-worth. Thus both younger sons, Willy and Happy, compete primarily through Woman as object, but older son Biff, like older son Ben, competes more directly with the male, making defeated men like women through emasculation.

Biff's theft of answers from Bernard, who loves him, is of a piece with his theft of a football from the locker room (indirectly from the coach) and the carton of basketballs and gold fountain pen from Bill Oliver. All involve theft of masculinity from a trusting and approving male authority figure. The confused Loman male sense of mathematics is such that one can only be something if everyone else is nothing. One must add to himself by seizing from others and never subtract from himself through giving to others; giving is what women and lesser men must do. Therefore, one becomes the most valuable by taking that which signifies value from all others, male and female. Female value in this system is relegated to support and sexual functions, and male value resides in the phallus. But one cannot have all and be number-one man unless one ultimately castrates the father. Each of Biff's thefts is a preparation for and rehearsal of the theft of his father's phallus.[22]

Sports, then, only seems to be the perfect synthesis of the three realms and thus of the patriarchal-fraternal community that Willy seeks continually. Pushed to its inevitable conclusion, the sports mythos demonstrates that a paternal-fraternal community cannot exist in its forum. Willy wants to celebrate an ideal of brotherhood for lesser men (who are actually like himself) to follow, while he would be the patriarchal authority, idolized by all, especially Biff. Yet when Willy is rational, he believes that although Biff has the potential to be number-one man he himself does not. Biff cannot be both more than Willy and less than Willy: there is a glaring contradiction in logic—it does not add up. In fulfilling his expected potential, Biff would have to grow up, to surpass Willy, to recognize that his father is less than himself. For the "young god" to become an adult god, he would have to dethrone, "castrate," the "fake" god, Willy.

Even before the Boston incident, Willy was dangerously close to being "found out" as less than his stolen, self-constructed image in the boys' eyes.[23] He had promised to take the boys on a business trip; if he had done so, they would have seen that he was a "fake," that the waves did not part for him. If he had not taken them, he would have been a "liar." If Biff had not learned of The Woman, Willy would have had to confront the math teacher and probably fail to get the extra points for Biff. But these crises of faith in the father are forestalled because Biff witnesses him with The Woman.

When Willy and Biff meet in Boston, both have failed: Biff has failed math, and Willy has failed marital fidelity. These failures are accompanied by masculine dream-value system failures: Willy has failed to uphold the family as the sacred cornerstone of success, and Biff has failed to be universally well liked by lesser men. In present time, each blames the other for his failure, but The Woman is made the foundation of the failed relationship between father and son.[24] Although the Loman men contrast Linda as "somebody with resistance" with the women of the Business World, who can be "had,"[25] The Woman epitomizes those women, and she overlaps with and parallels Linda.

Willy continually links Linda and The Woman unconsciously. Linda's attempted ego-inflating praise of Willy in a flashback as the "handsomest man in the world" (37) to her (after he had confessed feeling foolish to look at) brings on a flashback within a flashback in the laughter and then the first appearance of The Woman. Although in context the laughter signifies The Woman's enjoyment of Willy's company, the dramatic effect is that she is laughing at him rather than with him. As he comes out of the flashback within flashback to the flashback, Linda's laughter blends with that of The Woman. The Woman's laugh returns when evidence of Biff's bad behavior, provided by Linda and Bernard, haunts Willy's flashback, testifying that Willy raised Biff by the wrong standards—his rather than Linda's.

The Woman is not even dignified by a name in the list of characters and speech headings, although her name may be Miss Francis. By being simply The Woman, she figures as a temptress, a femme fatale, and this impression is reinforced by her laughter, the music accompanying her appearances, and her appearance in a black slip. Yet her description in the stage directions is at odds with this impression. She is "*quite proper-looking, Willy's age*" (38). Furthermore, she is far from being a prostitute—she is a business contact of Willy's, someone (probably a secretary-receptionist) with the power to choose whom the buyers will see—and she lives with her sisters. Her payment for sex with Willy is silk stockings. She needs silk stockings to wear to work and can probably ill afford them on her salary. Yet the stockings also become an important symbol. When she mentions the promised stockings, Biff understands his father's relationship with her, and when Linda mends her own stockings, it reminds Willy of his guilt. Thus Linda and The Woman are bound together by the stockings, which reinforce their other connections: they are good-humored women of about the same age who both genuinely like Willy.[26] The essential difference between them is that one has chosen to marry and work inside the Home, and the other has chosen not to marry and to work in the Business World. Linda herself is like a mended stocking, torn and tattered by Willy but still serviceable through the strengthening of her own moral fiber. The Woman is a "new" silk stocking, new territory on which Willy can test himself. Both are made to be objects, but both also witness the failures of masculine values.

Contrary to surface appearance, then, there are not two kinds of women in the play, good and bad. All of the women are conflated in the idea of Woman: all share more similarities than differences, particularly in their knowing, and having the potential to reveal, masculine inadequacy, although generally they have been socialized not to insult a man by revealing their knowledge to his face. The Loman men all agree that the truth of masculine inadequacy or failure must be kept from women, because if women do not know, men can maintain their pretenses among other men and to themselves. What most upsets Biff about his father's flashback ravings is that "Mom's hearing that!" (27), and Happy habitually lies about himself and other men to women. When Willy borrows money from Charley, it is to pretend to Linda that it is his salary—but Linda know about the loans. Willy tries to force Biff into a fabricated version of the meeting with Bill Oliver, supposedly so he can have good news to bring to Linda—but it is he, not Linda, who craves good news from Biff. Linda also knows and tells her sons that Willy has been trying to commit suicide. Like Letta, she is associated with collection and evaluation of evidence. Not only does Linda find the rubber gas hose (during her repairs), but she knows of other suicide attempts that Willy has made with the car. As she begins to tell the story of the witness, she says, "It seems there's a woman," and Biff quickly responds, "What woman?" (58–59), obviously assuming that Linda means The Woman in Boston. Linda not only overlaps the function of Mother Loman, but she and the insurance company's woman witness are alike in knowing about Willy's suicide attempts; the woman witness is linked to The Woman in Biff's mind; Willy treats Jenny as he probably had treated The Woman; and, in the restaurant, Miss Forsythe and Letta provoke Willy's memory of The Woman, as had Linda. The synthesis that Willy seeks among the Green World, Business World, and Home is achieved not by male community but collectively through the women, who independently rise from their positions as submerged elements to join in a circle of femininity and summation of value that closes in, without acknowledgment, on the truth of the Loman men.

The emergence of suppressed Woman occurs in the midst of an intended paternal-fraternal celebration of triumph in the restaurant.[27] Linda was not invited; the savoring of success was for the men only. Willy was to have wrested a New York job for himself from his symbolic "son" Howard, and Biff was to have convinced his symbolic "father" Bill Oliver to invest in Happy's idea of the Loman Brothers sporting goods teams. But the dreams of success for the day failed to become realized. Howard, delighting in being a "father" himself (evidenced by his pride over his son's performance on the wire recorder)[28] is not impressed by Willy's assertion of fatherhood (his supposed fraternal relationship with Howard's father and his exaggerated claims to have "named" Howard) and in fact fires Willy for failing to "pull his own weight" (80). Biff fails also, not even making an impression on the secretary, let alone Bill Oliver, who sees him only momentarily and does not remember him. Enraged at being treated like a lesser man, Biff re-enters Oliver's office and steals his gold fountain pen, completing the castration of the symbolic father from whom he had stolen basketballs years before. Thus, once again, as in Boston, Willy has failed as father and Biff has failed as son. The restaurant scene recapitulates as well as calls forth the Boston scene as the double failures unfold, but now a transfer of phallic power takes place. Willy seems unable to face his failure to his family until he sees his sons grow into the same action. As Willy "betrayed" the family with The Woman, so Biff and Happy "betray" him by deserting him in the restaurant and leaving with Miss Forsythe and Letta.

In an early line in Willy's culminating flashback—"Willy, Willy, are you going to get up, get up, get up, get up?" (114)—The

Woman's iteration of "get up" implies not only getting up to answer the knocking at the door but also getting up the ladder of success and, perhaps, erection. Sexual performance is one realm where a man cannot be a fake—the woman knows if he fails. Woman is the means not only of phallic inflation but also of phallic deflation, both by satisfying his need of her and by her potential for intimidation to impotence. Yet The Woman, like Linda and the women in the restaurant, complies by providing the man with what he desires, the necessary boost in self-confidence. Although her baby-talk manner of speech is meant to make her seem otherwise, The woman has a sense of responsibility about her job and the intelligence to sense masculine feelings of inadequacy and say the "proper" things to dispel them, even if her own humiliation results. But she also grants herself the freedom of taking sexual initiative: "You didn't make me, Willy. I picked you" (38). And she unabashedly enjoys sex: "Come on inside, drummer boy. It's silly to be dressing in the middle of the night" (116). This implies that she has not yet been satisfied by Willy, and perhaps the laughter so often associated with her also represents his fear that she will laugh at his inadequacy/impotence, which he must overcome by diminishing her.

The Woman insists that Willy acknowledge the knocking, which literally is Biff knocking at the door and symbolically is Willy's own conscience knocking, which he tries to deny. Before Willy opens the hotel room door, he hides The Woman in the bathroom, associating her with "plumbing" and bodily functions. But The Woman becomes the means of destroying the masculine mythos by coming out of the bathroom.

When Willy lets Biff into the room, Biff confesses his math failure. Willy is shocked and tries to displace blame onto Bernard. But Bernard has not failed in loving submission to Biff—although he "stole" from Bernard, Biff only "got a sixty-one" (118). The numbers, so denigrated before, are extremely important now, and Biff needs Willy to get him the extra four points. If they had left then, Willy's failure would have remained secret, but his authority would have to be tested against that of another patriarchal figure. Biff, however, goes on to rationalize his failure. This unimportant math class comes right before all-important sports, so he "didn't go enough" (118), avoiding submission to its alternative value system. Then, too, he is not "well liked" by the teacher; Mr. Birnbaum "hates" Biff for doing a comical imitation of him in front of the class. Biff steals the teacher's self-esteem by imitating him and showing him as a lesser man. Thus, although

Biff failed, he succeeds in displacing another male authority figure. Biff increases his own esteem of his classmates by decreasing their esteem for the teacher, and he repeats his imitation for his father's approval. Willy pauses to savor Biff's triumph over male authority and to share male communion by laughing at a supposed lesser man who holds Biff's fate in his hands. But just as Mr. Birnbaum had walked into the midst of Biff's ridicule, so does The Woman intrude into its repetition by joining in their laughter and coming out of the bathroom.

Undoubtedly, most readers and audience members feel tension as Biff and Willy talk, knowing that The Woman is hidden in the bathroom, and they are upset when she makes her presence known. The scene is set up in such a way as to protect the males and to put the blame entirely on her. If only she had kept her mouth shut! If only she had stayed in the bathroom where she belonged! But she does not; she insists on being part of the fun, of sharing in the male-defined game. When she enters, she not only laughs, but she also lisps her lines, imitating Biff's imitation of Mr. Birnbaum—but a woman must not be allowed to share in male camaraderie or to ridicule a lesser man.

To dispel Biff's shock at her presence, Willy begins his "striving for the ordinary." He names her, probably giving her real name, but promoting her: "This is Miss Francis, Biff, she's a buyer" (119). Her promotion is in a sense true—she *has* been a buyer of what Willy is selling—himself as a likeable commodity.[29] She had also bought into the idea that she was a human being to him. But when she sees herself treated as an embarrassment, merchandise no longer desired, she insists at least on the material terms of agreement. Willy tries to force her out into the hall without her clothes, but she demands her promised stockings. Willy tries to deny, but she is armed with numbers: "You had two boxes of size nine sheers for me, and I want them!" (119). And Willy finally produces them for her.

What seems to make "Miss Francis" a "bad" woman is that she refuses to be walked on the way Linda is, that she dares to insist on being recognized and dealt with according to the terms of the contract, and that she understands and resents being humiliated. After she identifies herself as the football that has been kicked around in the male game, she takes her clothes and leaves. The Woman literally has been undressed and Willy literally has been dressed, but Biff has symbolically witnessed Willy defrocked of the patriarchal mantle and has encountered the deflated phallic reality of his father. Through the stockings, Biff has seen the sanctity of family life reduced to an exchangeable commodity: "You—you gave her Mama's stockings!" (121), he says, as he bursts into tears and gives up on his life in terms of Business World success. For once he seems to identify with Linda; if she as wife-mother can be reduced to an object of exchange by his father, so can he as son. Biff accuses his father of being a "liar" and a "fake" (121) and departs.

The projection of the undressed state onto The Woman, however, has left the resolution of the phallic conflict betwen father and son unresolved until the double masculine failures repeat themselves. In real time, Biff is now armed with two stolen phalluses: Bill Oliver's gold pen, representing the symbolic paternal power of the Business World, and the rubber gas hose, Willy's self-destructive phallus in the Home. Without either of them consciously recognizing it, Willy is "emasculated," put into the position of The Woman, as Biff deserts Willy, leaving his father "babbling in a toilet."[30]

Just as The Woman was the scapegoat for Willy's desertion and failure of the family, so Miss Forsythe and Letta are the scapegoats for his sons' desertion and failure of him. But as masculine failure had been the means of bringing The Woman out of the bathroom of the Business World, so it brings Linda out of her limited position of foundation and support in the Home. Significantly, Linda is at her most assertive and ominous after the incident with The Woman. She flings down the boys' proffered bribe of flowers, presented by Happy as he displaced blame onto women for his and Biff's desertion of their father. But in her wrath, Linda is a superior match for both boys. They cannot cover up or smooth over the truth in her presence, although they sheepishly continue to try. Linda can be threatening not in her own right, but for Willy. Her reaction in this scene is perhaps what could be expected from a woman whose husband had been unfaithful. Yet her devotion to Willy is such that we believe she would not have come at *him* that way. Although Linda has bought into the system enough to condemn the women as "lousy rotten whores" (124), she blames her sons more for going to them. She attempts to throw the boys out of the house and stops herself from picking up the scattered flowers, ordering them, for once: "Pick up this stuff, I'm not your maid any more." Linda finally declares her independence from her role, recognizing that she is better than they are.[31] For both Linda and The Woman, male failures have provoked female sense of injustice and realization of victimization. Happy turns his back on Linda's order, refusing to acquiesce to feminine dominance, but Biff gets on his knees and picks up the flowers, as he understands that he is a failure as a man. Willy has been put into the position of the humiliated and abandoned one, like The Woman, the football kicked around in the competition. Linda achieves this position through empathy with him but rises above it into female control, short-lived as it is: women can take charge when the men are defeated by one another. When Linda accuses Biff, "You! You didn't even go in to see if he was all right!" (124), she is condemning him partly for shunning all of her influence, the nurturing and tending, the human compassion. But Biff insists on seeing Willy now, over Linda's objections. Because he has become as bad as Willy in betraying Linda, he and Willy can understand each other.

Recognition of his own and Biff's failures in both the Business World and Home makes Willy revert to the Green World as he attempts to reclaim his lost masculinity after the disaster in the restaurant. "The woods are burning!" (107), as he has previously noted, so he must buy some seeds, because "Nothing's planted. I don't have a thing in the ground" (122). His action will be futile in his yard, the remnant of the Green World remaining in the Home realm, because, as Linda knows, "not enough sun gets back there. Nothing'll grow any more" (72). The Green World has become a sunless/sonless void through male depletion of it, but Willy must continue to assert his masculinity on it, imposing the hoe, as Green World phallic symbol, on Mother Earth. In planting his seed, he attempts to renew Biff's conception—his own of Biff and Biff's of him, to start over as new father and new son on a pastoral basis.

The three realms of Green World, Business World, and Home, however, cannot be separated in Willy's mind, and, as he plants, he considers with a hallucinated Ben his suicide plan—he is actually digging his own grave. His previous suicide plans recapitulate his past and have submerged feminine elements. In the first attempt, femininely witnessed, he was driving down the road, went off track into a little bridge, and was saved only by "the shallowness of the water" (59). The road is symbolically connected with being "on the road" of the Business World, the bridge is perhaps sex as a connection out of his loneliness that he got off track into, and the shallowness of water the prescribed shallow but supportive function of Woman that "saved him." The second plan, associated with the Home, involves the phallic rubber hose, but the success of that attempt rests on the "new little nipple" (59), a feminine symbol, on the gas pipe. The third plan is formulated in "pastoral" aspect and approved of in "savage" aspect in the Green World, and it uses elements of the Business World and Home realms as well, thus becoming a replacement for the failed synthesis of the three realms in the sports forum. The suicide will be feminine in being a return to the womb, the pre-competitive sanctum. But as such, it will be another scapegoat for masculine failure.

The suicide plan provides Willy with the fantasy means of reestablishing a fraternal relationship with Ben. Although he had "missed the boat" of Ben's success, Willy can catch the "boat" of death to join the recently dead Ben and, through him, their dead father. In this proposed paternal-fraternal community, Woman is again made the foundation. Willy asserts to the hallucination of Ben that the proposition is "terrific" because "the woman has suffered" (126). But what his understanding of Linda's (and through his ambiguous phrasing, The Woman's) suffering is not revealed. Apparently she has suffered because he has failed to live up to his own standard, not that he has ever seriously considered hers: "A man can't go out the way he came in, Ben, a man has got to add up to something" (125). Thus, the suicide synthesis, like the sports synthesis, involves a confused fantasy appropriation of math. Rather than continuing to live while "ringing up a zero" (126), Willy wants to turn himself into money through death as he perceives Ben had. His plan is a "twenty-thousand-dollar proposition" that is "Guaranteed, gilt-edged" (126). The money, which he will try to steal from the insurance company by making his death seem accidental, will be Willy's gold. Gold had been the value symbol associated with Business World success through Bill Oliver's gold fountain pen and with sports success as Biff in the legendary Ebbets Field game had appeared "in gold." But the death is also imaged as a "diamond, shining in the dark, hard and rough, that I can pick up and touch with my hand" (126). While he puts his seed into the earth, he wants to get something out, the diamonds that his brother found but that he had missed, the value to be appropriated from the Green World as he simultaneously adds and subtracts. A diamond is "Not like—like an appointment!" (126) that is soft in contrast to the manly hardness of the diamond. The death would be tangible in the money, but Willy quickly jumps to another appointment: the funeral, which he envisions will be "massive," attended by "all the old-timers" from four states, because, as Biff never realized in thinking him "nothing," "I am known!" (126). The suicide plan thus becomes the perfect merging of Green

World, Business World, and Home, as he, like Ben, will go into the dark jungle of the unknown and come out rich; will, like Dave Singleman, have the death of a salesman in a grand funeral and secure the hero-worship of Biff in the legacy of controlling Biff's future. In forming this synthesis, Woman is exploited once more. Although the plan had begun in relation to Linda, because "the woman has suffered," she has been left out of the grand male scheme again because the money will go to Biff, not her, so that Willy can "amount to something" by masculine standards by regaining the phallus and looking "big" in Biff's eyes.

Although the gold of the gilt-edged insurance policy and the diamond of suicide are presented in masculine terms, they too have submerged feminine significance, because gold and diamond are the elements of a wedding ring. Rather than interpreting gold and diamond as objects to be stolen, Willy could recognize that he already has them in Linda, could understand that value can be achieved rather than objectified and seized, if he submits himself to Linda's system of worth. In her system, big or little, inflated or deflated, are irrelevant to having compassion and dignity and sharing love. But Ben is the primary rival to that vision; he and the suicide plan ultimately represent infidelity to a true marriage with Linda.

Willy is preparing himself to enter the dark, yet he really wants to "get back to all the great times" that "Used to be so full of light and comradeship" (127). One of his main problems is that he yearns for the boys' adolescence that provided him with his own, out of which he and the boys have never quite grown. But the joy of their fraternal adolescence died in their struggle for phallic patriarchal power, and now Biff enters to take the hoe, the last remaining phallic symbol, away from Willy and to assert paternal authority by demanding that Willy return to the Home to "tell Mom" of their failures as father and son. As Willy has been trying to re-establish roots in a pastoral Green World, Biff has determined to uproot himself by leaving permanently for his pastoral Green World.

The confrontation scene between Willy and Biff begins in the Green World remnant, the yard, but it must be played out in the Home, in front of Happy as lesser man, and especially Linda. When they enter, Linda withdraws into her support function for both of them, gently asking Willy, "Did you plant, dear?" (128), and allowing Biff the "public" credit for her idea, in fact demand, that Biff leave the Home forever. But Biff cannot leave without wanting Willy to shake his hand, thereby acknowledging his defeat and Biff as the winner. Neither Biff nor Willy is ready for it to be over until one has asserted authority over the other, so they begin a contest of competing reasons for Biff's failure: blaming it on Willy or attributing it to Biff's spite. Willy repeatedly turns to Linda to ratify his version, spite. Yet what Willy wants here is for Biff to maintain the masculine system of conspiracy, which involves protecting Woman (and themselves) from the truth of male failure. If he can make Biff submit to this version, Willy will both triumph over Biff and be safe in Linda's eyes. Although Biff repeatedly denies attributing blame to his father, Willy is too agitated to hear Biff's response. Instead, he accuses Biff of "trying to put a knife in me" (130)—using phallic weaponry against him. Then Biff rises to the challenge, not with a knife but with the rubber hose.

Just before he shows the hose, Biff says, "All right, phony! Then let's lay it on the line." The implication, especially through the word "phony," is that Biff will reveal Willy's infidelity in front of Linda and Happy, conflating infidelity with the suicide attempts. But both Linda and Happy already know about the hose and try to prevent Biff from disclosing that they know. It is like presenting the naked phallus in public: indecent exposure. Willy pretends not to recognize the hose, but it is the revelation of Willy's rising ("What is this supposed to do, make a hero out of you?") and falling ("This supposed to make me sorry for you?") phallus. But even this is not enough; Biff perseveres that Willy is "going to hear the truth—what you are and what I am!" When Happy interrupts, Biff begins with him: "You big blow, are you the assistant buyer?", asserting that Happy is "full of it! We all are! And I'm through with it" (130–31). This affirmation, along with Biff's statement a few lines earlier that "We never told the truth for ten minutes in this house!" (131), implies that Linda is included, but not if we remember that she has never been given the status of being one of them. She alone has told the truth of what Willy is, what the boys are, and of Willy's suicide plans (albeit to the boys but not Willy). Again she is discounted, but with her value appropriated yet unacknowledged.

Now that Willy's phallic flaws have been made public, Biff must confess his own: "I stole myself out of every good job since high school!"—and he had spent time in jail for theft. Although Biff had earlier absolved Willy from blame, he places it now: Biff "never got anywhere" because Willy "blew me so full of hot air I could never stand taking orders from anybody! That's whose fault it is!" The tumescent image here connects with his calling Happy a "big blow" (131), and both reveal Biff's recognition of the artificially inflated phalluses of all the Loman men; he tries to make himself and them face their own deflated condition.[32] Willy's response is "Then hang yourself! For spite, hang yourself!" Thus Biff's confession of failure leads Willy unconsciously to the same conclusion as his own of suicide. But Biff answers that "Nobody's hanging himself" (131–32). He has finally learned that acknowledging limitations does not lead necessarily to self-annihilation but to choosing alternate paths—for him, acceptance of the pastoral Green World and rejection of the Business World.

Biff's castration of the Business World in his theft of the gold pen has resulted in his recognizing the pointlessness of stealing other men's phallic power to "become what I don't want to be" (132)[33] and his accepting the Green World as the appropriate realm for his truest inclinations. But because the Green World also involves asserting manhood, Biff still cannot be free to enter that realm until he completes his "castration" of Willy by imposing his new-found truth. He now turns, significantly, to the "real math" of value computation to do so, asserting to Willy that "I'm a dime a dozen, and so are you!", that Willy is only a "hard-working drummer" and Biff himself, on any turf, is "one dollar an hour." Furthermore, Biff is "not bringing home any prizes any more" (132), and Willy is not to expect them. Once he has defined himself as "nothing," Biff can and does cry. We have only seen him cry once before, in the hotel room, and these tears connect these two incidents. They culminate in the conclusion of the conflict, which had been delayed by sustaining the masculine myth between them. But this resolution has taken place on the grounds of relating represented by Linda: the emotional, compassionate way of interaction. Willy turns to Linda for an explanation of Biff's tears, recognizing that she can understand better. Biff has finally learned to love himself and Willy for what they are, pretensions stripped away—what Linda has been advocating and has demonstrated throughout, without recognition.

Biff asks to be let go, for Willy to "take that phony dream and burn it before something happens" (133). But he cannot carry through and re-establish a relationship on compassionate terms; he can only escape: "I'll go in the morning." And once again, Linda is made to do the difficult part: "Put him—put him to bed" (133).

At first it seems strange that Willy, who has gotten what he wanted—the return of Biff's love—still intends to commit suicide. He is enraptured because Biff has become a boy again; they have gone back to the day when Biff confronted him in the hotel room, and it has been "made right," with Biff acknowledging Willy as the one in control and with the power to "take and burn that phony dream." But neither Biff nor Willy follows through. Neither can handle a relationship that is based on "feminine" compassion and mutual self-recognition. Yet Willy is pleased because he now believes that Biff will accept the money; perhaps he has an idea that his suicide will burn away the phoniness from the dream but leave the dream intact.

Linda alone feels the danger and asks Willy to come to bed. But Willy must seize and make the most of this moment of glory, take the ball and run with it, listening to Ben again. Willy makes the same mistake that he has always made: not appreciating real moments of value as they happen because they have always got to be topped with bigger dreams for the future. That prevented his full enjoyment of the boys' youth, and that prevents him from living on. He can only think to top this moment by leaving Biff twenty thousand dollars. If Biff has done a great thing in crying to Willy, sacrificing his self-image to his father, Willy must sacrifice his life for Biff, still competing with him. Happy appropriately asks for recognition now, behaving as if he had been the source of the trouble, maintaining that he is going to be the perfect son, replacing Biff, staying and living out the dream. But Willy cannot even acknowledge his younger son as he pays increasing attention to his older brother. Therefore, Linda must give Happy the comfort he needs.

As Biff and Happy go to bed, only Linda remains as a living interactive presence for Willy. In his last moments on stage, he alternates between attending to the real voice of Linda and the fantasized voice of Ben. Linda continually entreats him to follow her, and she is put into direct competition with his desire to follow Ben. Willy cannot acknowledge the superiority of the feminine value system to his own, so he must choose Ben. Ben's way is presented erotically—"One must go in to fetch a diamond out" (134)—one must enter sexually, impose the phallus, to get a diamond—son—out. Linda's "I want you upstairs" (134) is both a command and, perhaps, a sexual invitation, to counter the sexuality of Ben's offer. But Willy cannot satisfy Linda on her terms. When Linda says, "I think this is the only way, Willy," meaning that Biff should leave, Willy conflates it with the suicide plan: "Sure, it's the best thing." And Ben agrees: "Best thing!" (134). Here is the only point where all three agree, but two are agreeing

Women and the American Dream

to a plan between them, to a dream in which Woman is left out, not to the basis of the real experience just past.

Willy is finally left alone with Ben, as he wishes. The male-male connection can now be savored only by males, with no female commentary. He shares with Ben his wonder that Biff loves him and always has. But instead of being content with love, Willy must inflate it to worship which he seeks to provoke in Biff by his suicide that Ben now urges him toward, promising, "It's dark there, but full of diamonds." When Linda calls, his reply, "Coming!" (135), answers Ben more than her.

Before following Ben, Willy *"elegiacally"* relives the preparation for the Ebbets Field game, the day of Biff's stardom, when Willy was the authority figure. After much advice, he says, "There's all kinds of important people in the stands" (135) and suddenly recognizes his aloneness in the male-defined game. Willy starts asking for Ben, but instead Linda calls again. She has repeatedly offered acceptance on the terms of love for being what he is, average, and Biff has just offered the same, but Willy must make one more grandstand play. Yet it is obvious that accepting love, the feminine way, frightens him. Responding to Linda's call, he tries to quiet her, but his "sh!" unleashes *"sounds, faces, voices"* (136) that swarm in upon him, and he tries to "sh" them too. They are probably the voices of truth represented by Woman, the contradictions and failures in his world view. In the midst of his "sh"-ing, the ancestral flute music of his father stops him, rising in intensity *"to an unbearable scream"* (136). The music of male harmonic blending is now the only thing he hears, although Linda, and even Biff following her lead, calls out again. But the music draws Willy to the car, another symbol of masculine unity in the play, and Willy, the car, and the music all crash, *"in a frenzy of sound, which becomes the soft pulsation of a single cello string,"* which further develops into *"a dead march"* (136). Willy has crashed the car and killed himself, driven to the beat of the male song.

The scene dissolves into a dumb show of preparation for the funeral, with the *"leaves of day"* appearing *"over everything"*(136), suggesting Willy's final rest in the pastoral dream that was just as much death for him as were the other dreams. But as the Requiem begins, Charley notes that "It's getting dark, Linda" (137). Willy is finally put to rest in the darkness that he had sought, the void that the competing realms made of Woman, and he exists now only in the competing summations of his value presented by Linda, Charley, Biff, and Happy.

Critics have often been puzzled at Linda's speech of incomprehension at the grave, because she knew Willy was trying to kill himself.[34] But what she cannot understand is why. The reason is partly that Willy could not accept no longer being a boy or having a hope of boyhood in his sons—that the dreams could not be realized. Linda is always patronized for not understanding Willy's "massive dreams," but she comprehended the dreams well enough. Willy Loman's "massive dreams" were little more than adolescent male dreams of *being massive*. What Linda cannot understand is why those dreams of inflated masculinity are more important than family love, compassion, and respect—why real virtues are seen to have no honor and the "little man" cannot accept his dignity.

As the male characters present their competing versions of who Willy was and what he represents, it becomes evident that they understand him less than Linda does. Each identifies himself with Willy, making a male synthesis to contrast and outdo Linda. Biff relates to the camaraderie and construction, the "nice days" such as "Sundays, making the stoop." Forgetting that the stoop was constructed from stolen materials, Biff muses fondly, "there's more of him in that front stoop than in all the sales he ever made." Linda's reply may be meant as a punning sexual tribute: "He was so wonderful with his hands."[35] But then Biff says his famous lines, "He had the wrong dreams. All, all, wrong." Happy responds angrily, but Biff continues, "He never knew who he was," speaking as much about himself as Willy. Charley begins his "Nobody dast blame this man" speech partly to break up a pending fight between the boys. Oddly, in saying what a salesman is, Charley has to specify what he is not, including "He don't put a bolt to a nut"—which Willy actually did, albeit not as a salesman. Charley also is talking partly about himself: he has been the one unaccustomed to using the tools of reconstruction. Furthermore, it is Charley, the unsentimental, non-dreaming realist, who now says, "A salesman is got to dream, boy. It comes with the territory," thus combining his reality with acceptance of Willy's dream. This speech does little to reconcile Biff and Happy, who ignore it and continue their rivalry. Once again, Biff suggests his fraternal dream—that Happy go with him—but Happy says, "I'm not licked that easily" and refers once more to his fraternal dream, "The Loman Brothers!" Happy reaffirms the part of Willy that he identifies with: "the only dream you can have—to come out number-one man" (138–39). He plans to show Biff and everybody else that Willy Loman did not die in vain.

What Willy did die for if not in vain is not clear in any of the characters' minds, particularly not in Happy's, because not much earlier he had denied that Willy had any "right" to kill himself. Happy's speech is meant to be received by the audience as pathetic, and it is. For one, it defines the only dream possible as coming out "number-one man," women excluded, other men trampled beneath. Biff has now rejected it and turns to his mother. But Linda sends the men on their way, so that she, the only one who truly loved Willy, can be alone with him, and the flute music plays through her speech.

Alone at his grave, Linda asks Willy to forgive her for not being able to cry. Her loyalty and dedication to Willy are such that she wishes to do the expected, appropriate, female supportive behavior even when Willy is no longer there to require it. The two notes sounded alternatively throughout the speech are that she cannot cry and she cannot understand it. Thus part of what she cannot understand is why she cannot cry. On the one hand, Willy's death seems like just another of his absences, when she carries on, managing the bills, etc., as always. She has made the last payment on the house today, and "there'll be nobody home," considering herself, as Willy had, to be nobody. But suddenly a sob rises as she says, "We're free and clear." The idea of freedom releases her to sob more fully: "We're free . . . We're free" (139). What she cannot yet sort out, perhaps, is that she could not cry for Willy because of her unconscious sense of his oppression of her and her sons. She will no longer have to bend under the burden of the masculine ego. Biff is free of the patriarch now, and so is she: free and crying in the emotional intensity that her freedom releases.

Although mystified to seem otherwise, the male American Dream of *Death of a Salesman* is, as the play shows, unbalanced, immature, illogical, lying, thieving, self-contradictory, and self-destructive. Only Willy literally kills himself, but the Dream's celebration of the masculine mythos is inherently self-destructive in its need to obliterate other men or be obliterated, to castrate or be castrated.[36] It prefers to destroy itself rather than to acknowledge the female as equal or to submit to a realistic and balanced feminine value system. This tragedy of the common *man* also wreaks the suffering of the common *woman*, who has trustingly helped the man to maintain and repair the Dream and has helplessly watched him destroy it and render her sacrifices meaningless. One could argue that Linda as common woman possesses more tragic nobility than Willy.[37] Her only flaw was in harnessing all of her talents and energies to support the self-destructive American masculine mythos that requires Woman's subjugation and exploitation. Yet, at the end of the play, Linda lives—and even, for once, gets the last word. Biff, under her unacknowledged influence, now even shows her some tenderness as they leave the stage. But Happy exits last, alone, with the male music of the flute remaining, reminding us of the perpetuation of the Dream.

Thus the audience and readers are left with a choice between Happy and Linda, as Willy had had a choice between Ben and Linda. We can continue to side with the immature masculine mythos in degrading and ignoring Woman while making her the scapegoat for failures in American male-dominated society, or we can free Woman to rise from her oppression by choosing with her the appreciation of love and compassion, the recognition of the values of human dignity, and the worthwhile contributions of men *and* women.

Notes

1. See Arthur Miller, "Tragedy and the Common Man" [1949], in *The Theater Essays of Arthur Miller*, ed. Robert A. Martin (New York: Viking Press, 1978), pp. 3–7, and "Introduction" to Arthur Miller, *Collected Plays* (New York: Viking Press, 1957), pp. 3–55, especially pp. 31–36.

2. Much of the criticism on the play involves the question of whether it can properly be called a tragedy. For a summary of the various positions, as well as for a distillation of analysis of the work as social drama and for discussion of its place in theater history, see Helene Wickham Koon, "Introduction" to *Twentieth Century Interpretations of* Death of a Salesman, ed. Helene Wickham Koon (Englewood Cliffs, N.J.: Prentice-Hall, 1983), pp. 1–14.

3. Note the example of "Private Conversations" (produced, directed, and photographed by Christian Blackwood), the 1985 PBS documentary in the *American Masters* series that was a commentary on the filming of the televised version of the 1984 Broadway production of *Death of a Salesman*, starring Dustin Hoffman. In it, the male lead actors, director, Miller, and even male guests made pronouncements on the play, but no comments from Kate Reid, who played Linda, were included, although Dustin Hoffman's flirting with a female stagehand and his remark about the physical endowments of Kathy Rossetter as The Woman were.

4. Arthur Miller, *Death of a Salesman* (New York: Viking Press, 1949), p. 23. Subsequent references are cited parenthetically by page number within the text.

5. Although some mention that Ben has achieved mythic stature in Willy's mind, I seem to be alone among critics in believing, and finding Linda capable of believing, that Ben was just as much of a "fake" as Willy; lying and exaggera-

tions of success do seem to be typical traits in Loman men. Ben keeps his two visits short and gives supposedly profound but actually vague explanations of his wealth. Although he offers Willy a job, he surely knows that there is no danger of Willy's accepting it. His gift of a diamond watch fob to Willy hardly constitutes proof of his success in diamond mines, because he could have simply bought or stolen one to dazzle Willy. If Ben were as rich as he claims to be, he could have made some provision for his only brother in his will (if only to impress him further), even if he did have seven sons. But what Ben really was matters less to Willy than what he believed Ben to be.

6. I use the word "flashback" for convenience; Miller, in "Introduction" to *Collected Plays*, maintains that "There are no flashbacks in this play but only a mobile concurrency of past and present" (p. 26).

7. My interpretation here is directly opposite to that of Lois Gordon, "Death of a Salesman: An Appreciation," in *The Forties: Fiction, Poetry, Drama*, ed. Warren French (Deland, Fla.: Everett/Edwards, 1969), who states that "The first generation (Willy's father) has been forced, in order to make a living, to break up the family" (p. 278).

8. Barclay W. Bates, "The Lost Past in *Death of a Salesman*," *Modern Drama* 11 (Fall 1968): 164–72, suggests that Willy tries to function as the "dutiful patriarchal male intent upon transmitting complex legacies from his forbears to his progeny" (p. 164).

9. Willy's dream of a male patriarchal-fraternal community corresponds to the American Dream of the United States as male-dominated capitalist (patriarchal)/democratic (fraternal) nation.

10. Many critics blame this incident on Linda. For example, Barry Edward Gross, "Peddler and Pioneer in *Death of a Salesman*," *Modern Drama* 7 (February 1965); 405–10, says, "Linda discourages him from accepting the one opportunity which would allow him to fulfill his pioneer yearnings . . . [she] frustrates the pioneer in Willy because she fears it. . . . What Linda does not understand is that Willy was brought up in a tradition in which one had worlds to conquer and that the attempt to conquer them was the mark of a man" (pp. 407–8).

11. Paul Blumberg, "Sociology and Social Literature: Work Alienation in the Plays of Arthur Miller," *American Quarterly* 21 (1969): 291–310, determines that, in sociological terms, Ben represents the nineteenth-century robber baron, "hard, unscrupulous, firm, self-reliant, full of . . . self-confident energy," whereas Willy represents "the new, salaried, pathetically other-directed middle class" (p. 300).

12. Note the Green World implications in the animal images, and in the nature association and sexual pun of the "Bushwick" location, of this woman.

13. Both Richard J. Foster, "Confusion and Tragedy: The Failure of Miller's Salesman," in *Two Modern American Tragedies: Reviews and Criticism of Death of a Salesman and A Streetcar Named Desire*, ed. John D. Hurrell (New York: Charles Scribner's, 1961), pp. 82–88, and Joseph A. Hynes, "Attention Must Be Paid. . . ." *College English* 23 (April 1962): 574–78, reprinted in *Arthur Miller, Death of a Salesman: Text and Criticism*, ed. Gerald Weales (New York: Viking Press, 1967), pp. 280–89, note inconsistencies in the play, particularly in the character of Biff, but neither, nor any other critic I have read, detects what is to me a troubling contradiction. When were Biff and Happy together conducting those seductions of "About five hundred women"—before or after the incident in Boston? If Biff, brimming with sexual confidence, had

already had several successful experiences and had supervised Happy's initiation *before* he had gone to Boston, he surely would not have been so shocked and devastated at learning of his father's affair. He conceivably could have begun and brought Happy into a rampage of promiscuous sex as a reaction to Willy's adultery, but that interpretation seems to be at odds with Happy's mention here of Biff's mysterious change in character toward bashfulness and loss of "confidence."

14. By calling this woman a "strudel," Happy continues in his habit of self-centered definition of women by projection: when he went to his first woman to satisfy *his* "natural" but "animal" urges, *she* was framed in natural, animal images; here, as he is in a restaurant, Miss Forsythe is an item on *his* menu—a delicacy to be ordered, "bought," devoured, and digested to provide him with sustenance.

15. Thomas E. Porter, *Myth and Modern American Drama* (Detroit: Wayne State University Press, 1969), like many critics, calls these women "prostitutes" (p. 143). Eric Bentley, *In Search of Theater* (New York: Knopf, 1953), asks, "Has [Miller] given us a suitable language for his tarts (in the whoring sequence)?" (p. 87), without thinking to question whether the language of the women might be right and the unreliable Happy's assumptions about them wrong.

16. Note that male and female interpretations of female "ruin" do not correspond: The Woman sees her "ruin" not in being "used goods" but in allowing her job performance to be affected by a sexual relationship.

17. In Arthur Miller, "The Family in Modern Drama" [1956], in *Theater Essays*, ed. Martin, pp. 69–85, Miller postulates that all plays considered "great" or even "serious" examine this problem: "How may a man make of the outside world a home? How and in what ways must he struggle, what must he strive to change and overcome within himself and outside himself if he is to find the safety, the surroundings of love, the ease of soul, the sense of identity and honor which, evidently, all men have connected in their memories with the idea of family?" (p. 73).

18. Whereas I see Linda as the foundation of what is good in Willy as opposed to his "massive dreams," in which he separates himself from association with her, many critics make Linda the foundation for Willy's problems. For example, Guerin Bliquez, "Linda's Role in *Death of a Salesman*," *Modern Drama* 10 (February 1968): 383–86, states that "Linda's facility for prodding Willy to his doom is what gives the play its direction and its impetus" and projects onto Linda the play's thematic "cash-payment fixation" (p. 383). Karl Harshbarger, *The Burning Jungle: An Analysis of Arthur Miller's* Death of a Salesman (Boston: University Press of America, 1980), misappropriates "feminism" to advance his theory that Linda, beneath her "show of the 'perfect' wife" is "attempting to destroy her husband" (p. 7). He twists her statements of support of Willy into attacks (pp. 8–21) and even accuses her of an incestuous desire for Biff (p. 28).

19. Critics often give Linda even less credit than does her family. Henry Popkin, "Arthur Miller: The Strange Encounter," *Sewanee Review* 67 (1960): 34–60, calls Linda "not in the least sexually interesting" (p. 56), forgetting Willy's statement to her that "on the road I want to grab you sometimes and just kiss the life outa you." As Linda is so thoroughly compliant with Willy's other desires, there is no reason to assume her to be otherwise in connection with sex. Similarly, Brian Parker, "Point of View in Arthur Miller's *Death of a Salesman*," *University of Toronto Quarterly* 35 (1966): 144–57, reprinted in *Twentieth*

Century Interpretations of Death of a Salesman, ed. Helene Wickham Koon (Englewood Cliffs, N.J.: Prentice-Hall, 1983), pp. 41–55, discounts Linda's "traditional values and her downtrodden, loving loyalty" because they "blind audiences to the essential stupidity of Linda's behavior. Surely it is both stupid and immoral to encourage the man you love in self-deceit and lies" (Koon, p. 54). Yet, as is noted by Irving Jacobson, "Family Dreams in *Death of a Salesman*," *American Literature* 47 (1975): 247–58, "given Loman's inability to accept disagreement from his sons or Charley, it is hard to suppose that he would tolerate a less acquiescent wife" (p. 257). Besides, rather than "encouraging" Willy's "lies," Linda instead balances delicately and skillfully between helping to maintain Willy's self-esteem and trying to keep him grounded in reality.

20. In Arthur Miller, "The American Theater" [1955], in *Theater Essays*, ed. Martin, pp. 31–50, Miller tells the story of Mildred Dunnock's efforts to secure the role of Linda in the original 1949 production: "We needed a woman who looked as though she had lived in a house dress all her life, even somewhat coarse and certainly less than brilliant. Mildred Dunnock insisted she was that woman, but she was frail, delicate, not long ago a teacher in a girls' college, and a cultivated citizen who probably would not be out of place in a cabinet post. We told her this, in effect, and she understood, and left." She returned the next day, "had padded herself from neck to hem line to looks a bit bigger, and for a moment none of us recognized her, and she read again. As soon as she spoke we started to laugh at her ruse; but we saw, too, that she *was* a little more worn now, and seemed less well-maintained, and while she was not quite ordinary, she reminded you of women who were. But we all agreed, when she was finished reading, that she was not right, and she left." But on every following day, "she was there again in another getup," and "each day she agreed with us that she was wrong; and to make a long story short when it came time to make the final selection it had to be Milly, and she turned out to be magnificent" (pp. 46–47). Thus it seems that Dunnock, better than Miller, understood Linda Loman to be a bright woman "disguising" herself to seem inferior to meet male expectations.

21. Miller had originally written "shrimp," changed it to "walrus" to fit Lee J. Cobb in the original 1949 production, then changed it back to "shrimp" for Dustin Hoffman in the 1984 production.

22. In "Introduction" to *Collected Plays*, Miller mentions having received "innumerable letters asking if I was aware that the fountain pen which Biff steals is a phallic symbol" (p. 28), and some critics continue to interpret the pen thusly, although none to my knowledge have discovered the other phallic symbols that I discuss, nor have they examined the castration theme further than do Schneider and Field, whom I cite below.

23. According to Miller in "Introduction" to *Collected Plays*, one of the "simple images" out of which the play grew was that of "the son's hard, public eye upon you, no longer swept by your myth, no longer rousable from his separateness, no longer knowing you have lived for him and have wept for him" (p. 29).

24. In Olga Carlisle and Rose Styron, "Arthur Miller: An Interview" [1966], in *Theater Essays*, ed. Martin, pp. 264–93, Miller calls the father-son relationship "a very primitive thing in my plays. That is, the father was really a figure who incorporated both power and some kind of a moral law which he had either broken himself or had fallen prey to. He figures as an immense shadow. . . . it had a mythical quality to me" (pp. 267–68).

25. Benjamin Nelson, *Arthur Miller: Portrait of a Playwright* (New York: David McKay, 1970), unfairly burdens Linda with responsibility for the Loman men's dichotomizing of women into Madonna/whore categories, in order to blame her for their sexual misconduct: "In her well-meaning prudery and naïveté, and in her unswerving loyalty to Willy, she has unconsciously fostered adolescent sexual attitudes in all three of her men by creating an image of herself as the maternal counterpart of the infallible father. The more she is a paragon of virtue to them the less are they able to relate to her as adult males to a wife and mother. That view of her is pantingly adolescent and distorts all their relationships with women." Thus Happy's "image of Mom as goddess is partially responsible for his shoddy encounters with girls who are never fit to bring home to her, as well as for his father's cheap and pathetic adultery and Biff's traumatic reaction to it" (p. 113).

26. Beverly Hume, "Linda Loman as 'the Woman' in Miller's *Death of a Salesman*," *Notes on Modern American Literature* 9 (1985): item 14, also sees connection between the two characters, but her interpretation finds in Linda an "intense materialism" that places her "in league with 'the Woman,'" who "is manipulating Willy only for money (or stockings)."

27. Psychoanalyst Daniel E. Schneider, *The Psychoanalyst and the Artist* (New York: Farrar, Straus, 1950), pp. 246–55, suggests that the dinner was to be a "totem feast in which the sons recognize the father's authority and sexual rights" (p. 250).

28. Eric Bentley, *What Is Theatre?* (New York: Atheneum, 1968), states that "one never knows what a Miller play is about: politics or sex. If *Death of a Salesman* is political, the key scene is the one with the tape recorder; if it is sexual, the key scene is the one in the Boston hotel" (p. 261). To me, the play is not about politics or sex but politics *of* sex, so even the scene with the tape recorder (actually a "wire recorder") is sexually political. Howard's presentation of the three females in his private life—daughter, wife, and maid—recapitulates in miniature the treatment of women elsewhere in the play. Although Howard had bought the recorder for dictation, he tries it out on his family—testing Business World techniques in the Home. His daughter, the first guinea pig, whistles "Roll out the Barrel," then Howard whistles the same song, perhaps to demonstrate superiority over her. She is seven years old, and her chief value is in being "crazy for" her father. Howard's son, however, is the important one—five years old and reciting the state capitals, in alphabetical order. Father and son are the best performers, with the females only to express devotion, provide entertainment, or demonstrate supposed inadequacy to the male standard. The maid "kicked the plug out," but later Howard will depend on her to support the machine by recording radio programs for his convenience. Howard's wife is bullied into speaking into the machine, but she proves such an embarrassment that he interrupts her dissension by shutting off her voice. Willy's function throughout this episode is to admire but to be interrupted and silenced when the son displays his talents. Willy is thus put into the position of Woman, into the same role that he expects Linda to play. Furthermore, Willy even replays the actions of the wire-recorded women: like the daughter, Willy calls forth the admired father (Howard's father); like the wife, he has no interest in the recorder but is forced to interact with it; and like the maid who accidentally unplugs the machine, Willy (a "servant" of Howard's firm) accidentally turns it on, thereby becoming an embarrassment to be "shut off," again like the wife. Howard the "son" then begins the symbolic castration (completed by Biff)

of Willy the "father" by asking him to turn in his samples, his two salesman's cases, representing his testicles.

29. In "Introduction" to *Collected Plays*, Miller relates that "when asked what Willy was selling, what was in his bags, I could only reply, 'Himself'" (p. 28).

30. Schneider, *The Psychoanalyst and the Artist*, labels as "castration-panic" Willy's flight to the bathroom after hearing of Biff's theft of Oliver's pen (p. 250).

31. Cf. the hideous portrayal of Linda's self-assertion by Schneider, *The Psychoanalyst and the Artist*: "Her rage at being old and dried-up is implicit as she fights like a she-tiger against the sons who have cast off the father for their own sexual philandering" (p. 251).

32. B. S. Field, Jr., "Death of a Salesman," *Twentieth Century Literature* 18 (1972): 19–24, reprinted in *Twentieth Century Interpretations of* Death of a Salesman, ed. Helene Wickham Koon (Englewood Cliffs, N.J.: Prentice-Hall, 1983), pp. 79–84, interprets Willy's *hamartia* to be his success in making his sons in his own image: "One may . . . say of Willy that 'he's got no balls.' And neither have his sons . . . They are morally and socially castrated. . . . he has made moral eunuchs of his own sons" (Koon, p. 84).

33. As is noted by Chester E. Eisinger, "Focus on Arthur Miller's *Death of a Salesman*: The Wrong Dreams," in *American Dreams, American Nightmares*, ed. David Madden (Carbondale: Southern Illinois University Press; London and Amsterdam: Feffer & Simons, 1970), pp. 165–74, Biff "cannot and need not rely on a mere symbol of manhood. This conviction transcends the phallic value of the pen and sustains Biff in his honest self-knowledge at the end of the play" (p. 172).

34. Note Parker's explanation in "Point of View": "After thirty-five years of marriage, Linda is apparently completely unable to comprehend her husband: her speech at the graveside . . . is not only pathetic, it is also an explanation of the loneliness of Willy Loman which threw him into other women's arms" (Koon, p. 54).

35. Miller, in "Introduction" to *Collected Plays*, remembers that he "laughed when the line came, laughed with the artist-devil's laugh, for it had all come together in this line, she having been made by him though he did not know it or believe in it or receive it into himself" (p. 30).

36. In Phillip Gelb, "Morality and Modern Drama" [interview, 1958], in *Theater Essays*, ed. Martin, pp. 195–214, Miller states that because he kills himself, Willy cannot be an "average American man," yet he "embodies in himself some of the most terrible conflicts running through the streets of America today. A Gallup Poll might indicate that they are not the majority conflicts; I think they are" (pp. 199–200).

37. In "Introduction" to *Collected Plays*, Miller, recalling some of the widely varying evaluations of the play, says that "The letters from women made it clear that the central character of the play was Linda" (p. 28). But those women were not alone. Several critics have made a case for Biff as the play's tragic protagonist, and one (Schneider) has even done so for Happy. Recent criticism sometimes cites these readings, but it is much less often remembered that some early reviewers sketched in a similar possibility for Linda. Robert Garland, "Audience Spellbound by Prize Play of 1949," *The New York Journal-American*, 11 February 1949, p. 24, reprinted in *Arthur Miller*, ed. Gerald Weales (New York: Viking Press, 1967), pp. 199–201, saw Linda as the "the play's most

poignant figure" whose "all-too-human single-mindedness holds *Death of a Salesman* together," and he found the "most tragic tragedy" to be her powerlessness to prevent Willy from being his "own worst tragedy" (Weales, p. 200). Similarly, William Beyer, "The State of the Theatre: The Season Opens," *School and Society* 70 (3 December 1949): 363–64, reprinted in Arthur Miller, ed. Weales, pp. 228–30, interpreted the play to be "essentially the mother's tragedy, not Willy Loman's. Willy's plight is sad, true, but he is unimportant and too petty, commonplace, and immature to arouse more than pity, and the sons are of a piece with their father. . . . We can only sympathize since they reflect human frailties all too common among men. Within her circumscribed sphere of living, however, the mother makes of her love a star which her idealism places on high, and when it is destroyed her heavens are wiped out. What the mother stands for is important, and when she goes down the descent is tragic" (Weales, p. 230).

PAPER DOLLS[1]
Melodrama and Sexual Politics in Arthur Miller's Early Plays

Jeffrey D. Mason

In his first four major full-length plays—*All My Sons* (1947), *Death of a Salesman* (1949), *The Crucible* (1953), and *A View from the Bridge* (1956)—Arthur Miller drives the action to a climactic moment of decision and then separates the protagonist from his family, pushing the women aside and requiring the man to choose in isolation. In contriving these penultimate scenes, Miller borrows the methods and espouses the sexual politics of melodrama.

In the classic American melodrama of the mid-nineteenth-century, gender was a key factor in determining the degree of interpersonal power—that is, the freedom to influence one's destiny, measured in terms of options and restrictions—allowed to each of the principal characters. Man was either villain, the agent of the action, or hero, the often wayward champion of the sentimental social order. Woman was heroine, the embodiment of virtue, and the passive victim of both the villain's schemes and the hero's weaknesses. The effect was to deny Woman her right to act or choose and to confer both the privilege and the burden of initiative on Man.

Miller adopts the melodramatic vision of individuals as either wholly good or wholly evil and so divides the women into wives and whores, the first loyal, acquiescent and virtuous, and the second tempting, sexual, and dangerous. He divorces the women from the crucial decisions, instead using them to help create the situations with which the men must cope. Although melodrama affirmed middle-class family values, Miller's plays demonstrate the collapse of the family as intimacy leads to the estrangement of men and women and then to the agony of the final scenes.

Miller's families are what used to be called "typical," whose interactions are based on "typical" assumptions. Man and

Woman co-exist in an atmosphere of wary playfulness, each conceding the other's role but constantly testing the limits. Man measures Woman in terms of sexual attractiveness and its implications in terms of marriage, childbearing, and romantic status, and Woman measures Man in terms of ability to provide as husband and father. In *All My Sons*, Sue Bayliss complains when Jim's female patients telephone him, and he says of Ann Deever that the "block can use a pretty girl. In the whole neighborhood there's not a damned thing to look at"(62). He advises Ann never to count "your husband's" money, and Sue later recommends Chris Keller for his affluence—he has promised to "make a fortune" for Ann—asserting that "as soon as a woman supports a man he owes her something. You can never owe somebody without resenting them"(92).[2] Joe Keller equates his wife with the maid in that they do the same work; the difference is that Kate's wifely obligation represents Joe's early success and the maid's contract his later prosperity. In *A View from the Bridge*, Marco comes to America to fulfill his male duty, although it means leaving his family. When Beatrice wants to buy a new tablecoth, Eddie reaches into his pocket to give her the money, to do her a favor. Life is what Eddie brings home—coffee, bananas, spiders, or money.

In these conventional families, men make the decisions while women can only hope to influence them. When a plumbing company offers Catherine a job, she, Beatrice, and Eddie all take it for granted that she will accept it only if Eddie approves. George Deever travels seven hundred miles to prevent Ann's engagement and order her to accompany him, but his neighbors consider such behavior only a slight variation from the norm. It is indicative of Miller's attitude that the seminal story for *All My Sons* involved a daughter who had exposed her father and that Miller, even before putting pen to paper, transformed her into a son, although one who lacked her moral daring.[3]

These people assume that men and women cannot truly know each other. Eddie disputes the fact that Beatrice could understand the world as he does, saying "You lived in a house all your life, what do you know about it? You never worked in your life"(387). Linda Loman never fully comprehends her husband's aspirations, even when standing over his grave, and Willy warns Biff that making promises to girls can lead to misunderstanding. Chris confesses that he has not seen Ann for five years, but, because he was brought up next door to her, he cannot imagine anyone else as his wife, and they marry for lack of options, acting on the memory of their childhood familiarity. If they love, they love at a hazy distance.

All My Sons

In *All My Sons*, the men must discover the truths that the women already understand, and Miller manipulates the situation by allowing the women to divulge their information only in fragments and at intervals. Kate Keller most clearly perceives the imbalance in the moral equation—Joe has failed and lied, sending twenty-one pilots to their deaths, his partner to prison, and his elder son to a sacrificial suicide. There is a moral debt still to be paid, and Kate knows the price, but she postpones the reckoning for three and a half years, freezing time by insisting that Larry is coming back and forcing Joe and Chris to humor her as she inhibits action and makes an ultimately futile effort to deny Joe's deceit and guilt. This false equilibrium is revealed as such when Chris invites Ann to the house and George follows to force a confrontation. Kate can no longer control the situation, so she smashes Joe in the face to keep him quiet, then turns on Chris.

> Your brother's alive, darling, because if he's dead, your father killed him. Do you understand me now? As long as you live, that boy is alive. God does not let a son be killed by his father.(114)

Kate articulates the moral imperative of the play, yet she cannot confront its consequences; as soon as she permits herself to imply the truth to Chris—a moment that Miller justifies only in terms of Kate's emotions, not her reason—she literally deserts the stage, leaving the men to work out the implications of what she has said.

Chris faces Joe in complete isolation. Kate has fled and Ann has gone to pursue her brother; there is no one to help the son judge his father, and he weeps, repeating, "What must I do? . . . what must I do?"(116). He must act, but he cannot; he is paralyzed. When he returns from a lonely drive in the car, both women are waiting to hear his decision, but he has chosen only to flee his own guilt and impotence. Ann understands that action is required but believes that Chris is the one who must choose, that she cannot assume that prerogative. She knows how Larry died, but she, whose lover fell from the sky and whose father fades in prison, has been content to let her brother and her new lover act on her behalf. She tells Chris to "do what you have to do!"(123) and begs Kate to command him. When he remains helpless, even when Joe asks whether Chris wants him in jail, Ann overrules Kate's final attempt to forestall confrontation and gives him Larry's letter. As he reads, the women watch and wait, knowing all the strands of the story, unable or unwilling to act on their knowledge, wondering whether Chris will rise from his lethargy. Ultimately, it is Joe who takes the moment, realizing that Larry's letter has made him a stranger in his own home. He seems to intend to turn himself in, but Kate, having begged Chris to keep the letter a secret, now denies Joe's impulse to expiate himself. Comfortless, he walks upstairs to sit alone in his room, lift the gun, and fire the pointless bullet in his head—the final cowardice. Both men must endure the learning and the moment of choice—Chris failing to act and Joe acting with disastrous results—without help from the women who love them.

Death of a Salesman

Death of a Salesman resembles *All My Sons* in that the son chooses to explore the family and reveal the truth within it, and the father must choose a way to cope with the discovery. Biff suffers to learn what he is, then he struggles to tell his father, failing twice and meeting only resistance from both Happy and Linda. When he finally says what he must, Willy refuses to accept his revelation.

Linda Loman dominates the situation that engulfs Willy. She is a wife in the Keller tradition, that is, a housekeeper—no less than three times does she enter into Willy's memory carrying the family wash. She is the patient little woman for whom Willy sells and dreams and lies, and she reincarnates the melodramatic wife as victim, waiting at home with the rubber hose while Willy leaves to drive off the edge of a bridge. According to John von Szeliski,

> Linda seems another vestige of the sentimental tragedy. She is like the long-suffering and incredibly patient women of the lachrymose eighteenth-century dramas who brought tears to the audience's eyes with their ability to forgive in the face of their husbands' infidelity.[4]

It is that infidelity—not the lifetime of lying—that destroys Biff's faith in his father and finally leads to the salesman's self-destruction. The wife and mother is the virtuous woman who is synonymous with the family, and man defines himself partly in terms of how keenly he feels imprisoned in this female preserve. Biff perceives Willy's infidelity as a crime against Linda and a betrayal of the family, so he withdraws his respect. Willy could have withstood his own guilt, but he cannot brook Biff's rejection, killing himself so his son—not, oddly, his wife—can collect on his insurance policy.

Linda is for Willy, as a flag for a nation, the emblem of the ideals that inspire action. Yet an emblem cannot participate, so Linda offers neither help nor support. She makes excuses for Willy even when he is ready to confront his problems, avoiding the truth of his many failures. Guerin Bliquez explains how she makes conflicting demands on him:

> Objectively Linda is the proof of her husband's ability as provider and subjectively the negation of it..... Like the house and garden, she must be constantly secured, maintained, planted, and cultivated. She is the goal of the salesman's futile activity as a man, a goal that can never be achieved.[5]

Linda and Willy are not totally estranged from each other; if they were, their alienation would be less moving. At the beginning of act 2—perhaps the most optimistic scene in the play, because Biff has gone to meet Bill Oliver and make his fortune—the husband and wife talk easily and intimately together. Yet Linda's presence both obligates Willy and inhibits him. Ben is Willy's dream but her nightmare; the diamonds would satisfy both of them, but Willy cannot risk the stability of his home to pursue the quest. She has, without malice, trapped Willy in a double bind, imposing expectations that he cannot satisfy. Lois Gordon has suggested that

> Linda, as the eternal wife and mother, . . . is also Willy's . . . destroyer. . . . Linda has accepted Willy's greatness and his dream, but while in her admiration for Willy her love is powerful and moving, in her admiration for his dreams, it is lethal. She encourages Willy's dream, yet she will not let him leave her for the New Continent, the only realm where the dream can be fulfilled.[6]

Linda's good intentions ruin Willy. Like Kate, Linda would shield her husband from the truth while her son would confront him with it, and, like Joe, Willy is alone when he makes his final decision. Linda has gone upstairs to bed, and even the vision of Ben has walked off impatiently; Willy is left by himself, trying to quiet the silent voices that surround him.

Biff's elegy for his father is "He never knew who he was" (221). Willy Loman is a man lost in the gulf between his role and his abilities. He is a husband, so he must provide. He is a father, so he must set an example for his sons. He cannot grasp the power that should be his, so he lies in order to maintain appearances, borrowing from Charley and pretending to Linda, who knows the truth but will not speak it, that the money is his pay. Willy is sadly miscast, a little man assigned the wrong dreams, who in turn dramatizes those around him: Ben is a demi-god, Biff and Happy embody Willy's hopes and fears, and, as the product of Willy's uncontrollable imagination, Linda is a confusingly contradictory role, shifting attitudes capriciously between lines. Willy's paragon is Dave Singleman, the single man, the old salesman who, unmarried, spent his life in smoking cars and hotel rooms, not even seeing his buyers, speaking to voices over the telephone with only his green velvet slippers for company. Willy would assume a similar role but with a family, not realizing that success, as Ben and Singleman define it, requires that he stand alone. Miller has trapped him in a metatheatrical net of his own misconceptions.

A View from the Bridge

Sexuality lurks beneath the action in both *All My Sons* and *Death of a Salesman*. Chris loves Ann but seems unable to express himself in sexual terms, leading her to complain that he kisses her "like Larry's brother" (84). Kate defines sex as the final, irrevocable betrayal of Larry's memory, telling Ann that "the night [Chris] gets into your bed, his heart will dry up" (121–22). Biff and Happy have spent much of their lives chasing after women, treating them as quarry, prizes to be won as in an athletic contest. Happy insists that he'd like to find a girl just like his mother, "somebody with character, with resistance!"(140), but the girls he chooses seem to have no resistance at all. In *Death of a Salesman*, Miller casts the women in roles that he apparently considers to be polar opposites: Linda is a wife/mother, and the other three, to use the simplistic label of melodrama, are whores—one of them simply and significantly known as "The Woman." They please men and entrap them, satisfying their sensuality but seducing them away from their respectable roles.

Eddie Carbone is a man whose passion renders his role untenable as the conventional husband and father, and the morality of melodrama combines with his Italian immigrant's sense of honor to blind him to the sexuality that consumes him. He evaluates Catherine's job offer in terms of the kinds of men that will see her as she walks to and from her office, and when Beatrice alludes to the recent waning of their sex life, he retreats from the question and denies the problem, insisting vaguely that he hasn't been feeling well. He cannot believe that Rodolpho's interest in Catherine is unselfish, insisting that he only pretends to love her to win his citizenship. Catherine's sexuality gives him "the willies"—he believed that she would remain a child, innocent, asexual, and happily subject to his authority. When Rodolpho reveals her sexual maturity, Eddie kisses her full on the mouth, tasting what was not his but which he feels someone has stolen from him. Then he pins Rodolpho's arms and kisses him, too, an act that so shocks Beatrice that she can only allude to it.[7] He has raised Catherine to be a wife just like Beatrice—acquiescent, obedient, and supportive—but he cannot reconcile his idealization of her with the response she evokes in him. He sees her as both madonna and whore, a contradiction that tears him apart.

Eddie must decide whether or not to betray the "submarines" to the authorities and so remove Rodolpho from Catherine's life. His agony over his niece alienates him from his wife, so he turns instead to Alfieri, finding no comfort and then choosing to ignore the offered advice. Miller implies that Rodolpho seduces Catherine just before Eddie throws him out; as in *Death of a Salesman,* sexual intimacy is the catalytic act. Eddie is alone when he calls the Immigration Bureau and alone when he pulls the knife that kills him. He suffers because he wants respect from Beatrice, Catherine, and his neighbors and friends, yet he has sacrificed it to his passion. In the last moments of the play, Beatrice forces Eddie to face the real issue—that he wants Catherine for his own. He had found a lie to help him live with the shame of denouncing Marco, but he cannot find a way to endure this knowledge of himself—that he cannot master his sexual attraction for the girl. Bereft of wife, niece, community, and self, he goes to his death.

The Crucible

Miller offers the clearest expression of his sexual politics in *The Crucible.* The men and women are separated from each other by religious hysteria and social roles; sexuality is a dangerous, alienating trap; and the male protagonist, John Proctor, makes his desperate decision with no guidance, trapped between a wife and a whore—Elizabeth maintaining a magisterial distance from her husband's guilt, and Abigail leading the girls into the woods and then the court to fan the spark of suspicion into a raging fire of accusation.

The courtroom drama is carefully cast along gender lines, for the men of Salem have evolved a patriarchy that reposes all social, political, and religious power in male hands, disempowering the women to the status of children. The men act as both judges and defenders, dividing the women into the accused—those who are older and malicious—and the accusers—those who are innocent children.[8] When Hale assures Tituba that clergymen are impervious to the Devil's seductions, he implies that a minister is the ultimate male and that women are weaker and more susceptible to evil. The men expect obedience from these children/women; Proctor overrides Mary's defiance and compels her to accompany him to court, and although she fears to expose Abigail by testifying to the poppet and the needle, she gives in to him out of habit. There is little substance to her earlier protest that she is a grown woman and not to be commanded.

Miller fuels his witch-hunt not only with the adult fear of children gone wild but also with the male fear of women who have proclaimed their sexuality. Proctor's greatest shame is his copulation with Abigail, not only because he has betrayed his marriage vows and outraged his own sense of morality but also because he has put himself in Abigail's power. Their intimacy restrains him from denouncing the trials, and the most drastic future he can imagine is that he will brand her a whore and himself a lecher, thus discrediting them both beyond redemption. The report of Abigail's dancing impresses Danforth far more than Mary's deposition or the concern of Salem's farmers, and when Proctor denounces her as an adult, sexual person, the judge falters.[9] Sexuality is power, and all the more so in a society that represses it and creates a scarcity of supply. Although the men perceive the women as a menace, the most sexual woman, Abigail, looks to Proctor as her only available outlet, thus relocating the ultimate power back in male hands. Only her religious ecstasy can emasculate him and avenge her humiliation.

What really happened in Proctor's barn? Who initiated the sexual encounter, and how willingly did each embrace the opportunity?[10] Miller's skill is remarkable in that the audience is more likely to sympathize with Proctor than with Abigail. She says that he "took me from my sleep and put knowledge in my heart!" (241), but Miller makes him seem the helpless victim of her charms, implicitly asking us to allow him an indulgence out of keeping with the strength of his character. If Proctor seduced Abigail and then rejected her, we can scarcely respect him; if he raped her, than we must condemn him, and the play falls to pieces. In any case, the episode seems to have paralyzed Proctor, for he condones his wife's decision to turn the girl out and thus suggest her guilt to the community while he evades public censure.[11] Abigail appears as the evil one who has led the upright man astray.[12]

Both Elizabeth and John Proctor face momentous decisions, but Miller denies her the information and options that he grants him. She helps John face his first dilemma—whether or not to expose Abigail before the court—yet it is his decision, not hers, for all she might urge it. When it is time for her to make her most important choice—whether or not to tell Danforth the truth regarding John and Abigail—she is kept unaware of the relevant developments, so she falls into the judge's trap and gives him what he needs to impeach and condemn her husband. Like Kate Keeler, who re-awakens George's suspicion by remarking on her husband's good health, Elizabeth complicates the situation unintentionally; she lies to Danforth to protect her husband, not to provoke catastrophe.

In the crucial scene, Miller brings husband and wife together in complete privacy, with the hangman's scaffold waiting outside to spur their conversation. John asks Elizabeth for advice, and she refuses it not once but five times:

> *Proctor.* I have been thinking I would confess to them, Elizabeth. What say you? If I give them that?
> *Elizabeth.* I cannot judge you, John.
> *Proctor.* What would you have me do?
> *Elizabeth.* As you will, I would have it.
>   . . . .
> *Proctor.* I would have your forgiveness, Elizabeth.
> *Elizabeth.* It is not for me to give. . . .
>   . . . .
> *Proctor.* It is evil, is it not? It is evil.
> *Elizabeth.* I cannot judge you, John, I cannot!
>   . . . .
> *Proctor.* Would you give them such a lie? Say it. Would you ever give them this? *She cannot answer.* (322–24)

Proctor had once feared her judgment and forbade it; now that he needs her counsel, she cannot bring herself to give it. She will neither advise nor forgive, turning his questions back to him and declining to take an active part in this most drastic moment in their marriage. In his other plays, Miller sends the wife from the stage so the husband can grapple alone; here he re-stages the climax so that the wife's presence makes the husband's desolation appear more agonizing. Elizabeth speaks not a word from the moment the judges enter to question her husband, through the signing and the tearing of his statement, until the drums beat for his execution. Hale beseeches her to plead for his confession and save his life, but her only answer is, finally, "He have his goodness now. God forbid I take it from him!" (329).

Melodrama and Gender

Joe Keller insists that there is nothing bigger than the family, yet, when Chris seeks something more, what he rejects is hardly the sanctuary that Miller once described in terms of

> the safety, the surroundings of love, the ease of soul, the sense of identity and honor which, evidently, all men have connected in their memories with the idea of family.[13]

In his plays, the family is a trap, imposing expectations that its members cannot satisfy. He presses them closer and closer together until the attractions repel and create a disastrous fission.

Miller's male point of view defines Woman as Other, either a paper doll devoid of depth and warmth or a source of confusion and the locus of evil. Joe, Willy, and Eddie all assert that they have made sacrifices for "their" women, and Proctor tells Elizabeth that he has thought of nothing else but her pleasure since his episode with Abigail. Yet even while these husbands proclaim their loyalty, they impose a debt on their wives, casting them as adversaries whose presence creates obligations but who do not participate in finding solutions. Miller pays his fathers and sons the tribute of testing their mettle, but he tends to allow the women more leniency. Kate Keller knew of Joe's crimes and remained silent, yet no one holds her accountable, and Harold Clurman has pointed out that Miller scarcely challenges the potentially destructive influence of the mothers in his plays.[14] Each play ends with the wife controlling the stage, standing forth as judge and survivor, one who has observed the dissolution and kept a careful distance from the husband's self-immolation. The wife obligates her husband, and the whore leads him astray, but neither participates with the man in reconciling the contradictions in his life. Miller simplifies Woman and obviates the need for revelatory interaction with Man; the husband does not consult his wife because she is designed to make such an encounter pointless.

Miller has denied Woman the sexuality, freedom, and potential individuality that he offers Man, giving her motherhood without eroticism and making her femininity a form of paralysis. Although Man may be the captive of the woman-centered family, Woman is more so, for she can no more leave the family than she can escape from herself. Miller condemns infidelity, but he unsexes the wives and leaves the husbands little option for their own sexual expression, thus frustrating both partners. Robert W. Corrigan has pointed out that sexuality causes calamity in all four plays; even in *All My Sons*, Ann's visit to Chris is the catalyst.[15] Abigail is more a witch than any she accuses; she is a succubus who can feel Proctor's heat at a distance. Catherine's sexuality leads Eddie to disaster, just as The Woman betrays Willy. When one of Miller's women makes the statement of self that is sexuality, she brings temptation and torture to a man and chaos to society.

The nature of melodrama is polarity, and, in his treatment of men and women, Miller enforces a devastating separation, distributing situations, options, and agony along gender lines, creating women who endure and survive, and men who fail and fall. If Miller writes tragedy, as he has claimed, he makes it a male preserve; the suffering may canonize the protagonist, although it teach him little, but the women are left to deal with a holocaust of ambiguous value.[16] Miller imposes melodrama's conventional vision of gender on his characters, but he denies them its naïve belief that providence will guide the individual toward virtue, and he concludes the plays with calamity instead of reconciliation. The playwright peers into the moral order but turns aside to contemplate the male burden, defining responsibility less than the alienation of gender.

Notes

1. Song by Johnny Black. Used in act 1 of *A View from the Bridge*, p. 396. Quotations from all Miller's plays are from Arthur Miller, *Collected Plays* (New York: Viking Press, 1957).

2. Whether Sue resents Jim for supporting her remains a question for the actor and the director to interpret.

3. Arthur Miller, "Introduction" to *Collected Plays*, p. 17.

4. John von Szeliski, *Tragedy and Fear: Why Modern Tragic Drama Fails* (Chapel Hill: University of North Carolina Press, 1962, 1971), pp. 107–8.

5. Guerin Bliquez, "Linda's Role in *Death of a Salesman*," *Modern Drama* 10 (February 1968): 383.

6. Lois Gordon, "*Death of a Salesman*: An Appreciation," in *The Forties: Fiction, Poetry, Drama*, ed. Warren French (Deland, Fla.: Everett/Edwards, 1969), p. 280.

7. Myles R. Hurd, "Angels and Anxieties in Miller's *A View from the Bridge*," *Notes on Contemporary Literature* 13 (1983): 4–7, has suggested that Eddie is a repressed homosexual whose Italian code of masculinity destroys him.

8. Of the scores mentioned as witches in the play, only four are men—Proctor, Giles Corey, and the unseen George Jacobs and Isaac Ward.

9. Miller clarified his tendency to polarize good and evil in "Introduction" to *Collected Plays*, expressing his wish that he had "perfected" Danforth's evil and going on to say that "there are people dedicated to evil in the world; that without their perverse example we should not know the good" (43).

10. William J. McGill, Jr., "The Crucible of History: Arthur Miller's John Proctor," *New England Quarterly* 54 (1981): 260, points out that the actual Abigail was only 11 and Proctor was 60 and argues that those ages would have made the affair "a patent, and dramatically unattractive, fiction." Be that as it may, Miller clearly adjusted the ages to make the relationship more conventionally plausible.

11. Elizabeth insists that "it needs a cold wife to prompt lechery" (323), thus offering her husband the old justification for philandering and even rape—that the husband was sexually deprived.

12. In June 1953, Miller added a scene (now II-2 in the Dramatists Play Service acting edition) that makes Abigail seem not only driven but actually insane. She and Proctor meet alone in the woods, late at night, and both dialogue and stage directions indicate that Abigail sees herself as victim, messenger of God, and Proctor's savior, acting with full belief that witches torment her and hypocrites surround her. She tells Proctor:

> Why, you taught me goodness, therefore you are good. It were a fire you walked me through, and . . . you burned my ignorance away. As bare as some December tree I saw them all—walking like saints to church, running to feed the sick, and hypocrites in their hearts! And God gave me strength to call them liars, and God made men to listen to me, and by God I will scrub the world clean for the love of Him! Oh, John, I will make you such a wife when the world is white again! *She kisses his hand.* You will be amazed to see me every day, a light of heaven in your house . . .

This is a child whose transition into womanhood, with its awakening into passion and carnality, has hurled her into ecstatic madness.

13. Arthur Miller, "The Family in Modern Drama" [1956], in *The Theater Essays of Arthur Miller*, ed. Robert A. Martin (New York: Viking Press, 1978), p. 73.

14. Harold Clurman, "Arthur Miller's Later Plays," in *Arthur Miller: A Collection of Critical Essays*, ed. Robert W. Corrigan (Englewood Cliffs, N.J.: Prentice-Hall, 1969), p. 145.

15. Robert W. Corrigan, "Introduction" to *Arthur Miller: A Collection of*

Critical Essays, ed. Robert W. Corrigan (Englewood Cliffs, N.J.: Prentice-Hall, 1969), p. 6.

16. Robert Bechtold Heilman, *Tragedy and Melodrama: Versions of Experience* (Seattle: University of Washington Press, 1968), has pointed out that Willy Loman and Eddie Carbone go to their deaths without truly understanding themselves or their dilemmas (pp. 102–3).

BETRAYAL AND BLESSEDNESS
Explorations of Feminine Power in The Crucible, A View from the Bridge, *and* After the Fall

Iska Alter

It hardly needs to be argued that Arthur Miller is preeminently a playwright concerned with exploring the dimensions of male authority and defining the constituents of male identity within patriarchal systems of culture: Joe Keller, Willy Loman, John Proctor, Eddie Carbone, Quentin, and the Franz brothers are proof enough. However, the extent to which Miller also possesses a complex vision of female power, albeit one inevitably determined by masculine necessity, has been scarcely recognized. Critics have simplified the position women occupy in Miller's plays at the very least; some ignore the feminine presence entirely because women, as a rule, do not act in that public arena which seems so frequently to regulate Miller's theatrical geography.[1] Of this evasion, the author himself is aware:

> Critics generally see them as far more passive than they are. . . . The women characters in my plays are very complex. They've been played somewhat sentimentally, but that isn't the way they were intended. There is a more sinister side to the women characters . . . they both receive the benefits of the male's mistakes and protect his mistakes in crazy ways: They are forced to do that. So the females are victims as well.[2]

Miller would have us acknowledge that his women are complicitous in sustaining patriarchy; that they are capable of manipulating its ideology to achieve the power they have; and that they can offer a limited, treacherously ambiguous escape from its most oppressive constraints. They are not only the source of betrayal, guilt, and self-destructive fragmentation but are also the genesis of blessedness, sensual liberation, and generativity. Throughout his work, Miller evolves an elaborate palimpsest of feminine authority, derived from presumptive archetypes representing modes of generalized human behavior, social forms enclosing individual action, and psychoanalytic explanations of personal response.

Central to this intricate design of nurture and treason, shaping Miller's view of the female imperium, is the role of the mother, primary author of the fall into consciousness, into knowledge of praise and subversion, of loyalty and rebellion, of desire and guilt: "It was of course the mother . . . actually the concept of her in a most primordial sense that perhaps only the boy-child, half-lover and half-rebel against her domain, really knows in his mythifying blood."[3] The ineluctable doubleness of the maternal poisons the wellspring of male sexuality just as it explodes the family, transforming the ideal of edenic safety into the battleground of conflicting impulses: "The family is, after all, the nursery of all our neuroses, and it is the nursery of our hopes, our capacity to endure suffering."[4]

Carrying into maturity a self divided by these unresolved Oedipal paradoxes, the male, according to Miller, first attempts to heal such divisions through the traditional machinery of duty and responsibility, the invariable agents of a repressive community. But duty and responsibility are finally insufficient to control the demanding contradictory energies released by psychic breakdown. Instead, the instrumentality by which the shattered masculine self can be integrated and made whole is the redemptive, even sanctifying, possibility of female sexuality. Seeking to live authentically, independent of custom and social orthodoxy, the male invests the women of his childhood with extraordinary power rooted in sensual openness and instinctive spontaneity. Yet this liberating desire cannot by its definition be contained within a stable, enduring monogamy; nor can its anarchic immediacy be tempted, postponed, or curbed by normative institutional arrangements. Rather, active feminine sensuality undermines hypocrisy, nullifies convention, and directly challenges the standard definitions of mutuality. Miller describes the frightening revolutionary potential of such expressive eroticism:

> . . . perhaps it was simply that when the sight of her [Marilyn Monroe] made men disloyal and women angry with envy, the ordinary compromises of living seemed to trumpet their fraudulence and her very body was a white beam of truth. She knew she could roll into a party like a grenade and wreck complacent couples with a smile, and she enjoyed this power, but it also brought back the old sinister news that nothing whatsoever could last.[5]

The mystery of ecstatic unity apparently proclaimed by woman's blessedness dissolves once again into the familiar if dissonant pattern of nurture and treason to be denied or disguised by the claims of ordinary existence.

The increasingly tangled conception of female authority is further complicated by the playwright's insistent identification of the oppositional tensions inherent in the feminine impulse with the origins of his own imaginative and artistic generativity ("The muse has always been a sanctifying woman, God help her"[6]):

> I wanted to stop turning away from the power my work had won for me, and to engorge experience forbidden in a life of disciplined ambition. . . . Cautiously at first, . . . I let the mystery and blessing of womankind break like waves over my head. . . . Fluidity and chance soon poured in to swamp all law, that of the psyche as well as the courts. . . .
>
> the chaos within remained; a youth was rising from a long sleep to claim the feminine blessing that was the spring of his creativity. . . .[7]

But the turbulent contraries of sexual desire—the life force itself, if you will—that Miller finally names as the ultimate source of feminine blessedness and female endowment must be subjugated to the orderliness and predictability of the everyday. The roles of mother, wife, and daughter that patriarchy uses to control woman's rulebreaking threat instead produce the inevitable betrayals and ongoing treacheries that for Miller describe the nature of experience.[8]

From *The Crucible* through *A View from the Bridge* to *After the Fall*, Miller's characters are forced to behave according to the terms dictated by this ambiguous contradictory model of feminine authority, increasingly seen by the dramatist as the inherited condition of human existence. Initially, Miller creates separate characters who seem to embody the self's interior antagonisms: those who betray and those who nurture, while Miller attempts to dispose of the traitors through dramatic action. But the protagonists seem eventually to learn that, to eliminate these externalized combatants, emblems of the unavoidable rifts and cracks of selfhood, is to retreat into murderous innocence. As each play enacts its particular dilemma, the various figures come to recognize to a greater or lesser degree that the divided consciousness—a feminine legacy, as Miller would have it—is the quintessential defining paradox of the individual and as such must be acknowledged and accepted; that blessedness and betrayal emerge from the same psychic matrix; and that betrayal

Betrayal and Blessedness 119

necessarily signifies blessedness because it removes the destructive expectations of deceiving innocence.

1

There is no need to rehearse again the many discussions of the political significance of *The Crucible*. Nor do I wish to deny either its historical importance as a theatrical document bearing witness to the destructive terrors of the nineteen fifties, America's plague years, or its value as a continuing and vital protest against any nation's scoundrel time. I would, however, like to remind the critics that what originally provokes the events of *The Crucible* is not a matter of principle or conscience but rather the experience of sexual desire translated by a repressive patriarchal establishment first into criminal behavior and then into acts of public rebellion. Although an earlier version of the play suggests additional socioeconomic reasons for the communal hostilities driving the prosecutions, and the residue of these explanations remains in its present form, Miller himself attests to the centrality of the sexual, frequently identified with modes of female sensuality, that Puritanism would have equated with demonic agency.[9] Miller reads into Salem's texts presumptive adultery and construes the testimony as an illustration of

> the sexual theme, either open or barely concealed; the Devil himself . . . was almost always a black man in a white community, and of course the initial inflammatory instance that convinced so many that the town was under Luciferian siege was the forced confession of the black slave Tituba. . . . almost all the bewitched women were tempted by a warlock, a male witch. Night was the usual time to be subverted from dutiful Christian behavior, and dozens were in their beds when through window or door, as real as life, a spectral visitor floated in and lay upon them or provoked them to some filthy act like kissing. . . . The relief that came to those who testified was orgasmic; they were actually encouraged in open court to talk about sharing a bed with someone they weren't married to. . . .
> Here was guilt, the guilt of illicit sexuality.[10]

To enhance further this interpretation, Miller alerts historical circumstances: for example, he raises the age of Abigail Williams from eleven to seventeen while lowering that of Mary Warren from twenty to seventeen in order to represent emergent desire and to justify susceptibility; he pushes the Putnams into early middle age to place the couple beyond the possibility of reproduction; he omits any mention of Tituba's husband in order to underscore her isolation and to emphasize her sensual particularity.

The design of The Crucible attempts to make visible two discrete, self-contained and antagonistic expressions of female power to test their legitimacy as authentic definitions of sexual desire. The externalized contest between the impulse that betrays, embodied in the group of accusers led by Abigail Williams, and the force that nurtures, personified by the figures of Rebecca Nurse and Elizabeth Proctor, shapes the choices made by John Proctor on his road to martyrdom. This schematic moral division is clearly drawn. The young women compelled by the anarchic strength of the erotic destroy the righteous and the dutiful for whom instinct is disciplined or submerged in service to family and community. But as the play unfolds, its melodramatic absolutism collapses under the pressure of Puritan authority suspicious of both views, because any knowledge of desire is potentially a transgression; and the too easily assumed virtue that seemed to inform John Proctor's decisions grows darker, more complex and more difficult.

There is no question that the girls—Betty Parris, Ruth Putnam, Mercy Lewis, Mary Warren, and, most especially, Abigail Williams—are suspect and possibly dangerous. Their sexually charged presence in the forest, the Puritan landscape of nightmare, is an explicit violation of publicly affirmed communal norms as well as private standards of right conduct insisted upon by a male-authorized social order sustained by a patriarchal, woman-fearing theology:

> Parris. Now look you, child, your punishment will come in its time. But if you have trafficked with spirits in the forest I must know it now. . . .
> Abigail. But we never conjured spirits. . . .
> Parris. . . . my own household is discovered to be the very center of some obscene practice. Abominations are done in the forest—
> Abigail. It were sport, uncle!
> Parris. [Pointing at Betty.]. You call this sport? . . . I saw Tituba waving her arms over the fire when I came upon you. Why was she doing that? And I heard a screeching and gibberish coming from her mouth. She was swaying like a dumb beast over that fire!
> Abigail. She always sings her Barbados song, and we dance.
> Parris. I cannot blink what I saw, Abigail. . . . I saw a dress lying on the grass.
> Abigail. [Innocently.]. A dress?

Betrayal and Blessedness

> Parris. *[It is very hard to say.]*. Aye, a dress. And I thought I saw—someone naked running through the trees!
> Abigail. *[In terror.]*. No one was naked! You mistake yourself, uncle!
> Parris. *[With anger.]*. I saw it![11]

Having named desire as unnatural, this repressive culture has condemned an inherent, normal biological process as aberrant, criminal, or, worse yet, as profoundly evil, the essential principle of demonic command. The journey into the woods, undertaken as an attempt to deal with and manage the consequences of inchoate sexuality, renders these young women outlaws. Within the dramatic action of the play, the sexually fallen Abigail particularly represents the release of this insurgent, destabilizing horrific energy:[12]

> Betty. You drank blood, Abby! You didn't tell him that! . . . You drank a charm to kill John Proctor's wife! You drank a charm to kill Goody Proctor!
> Abigail, *smashes her across the face.* Shut it! Now shut it! . . . Now look you. All of you. We danced. And Tituba conjured Ruth Putnam's dead sisters. And that is all. And mark this. Let either of you breathe a word, or the edge of a word, about the other things, and I will come to you in the black of some terrible night and I will bring a pointy reckoning that will shudder you. And you know I can do it; I saw Indians smash my dear parents' heads on the pillow next to mine, and I have seen reddish work done at night, and I can make you wish you had never seen the sun go down! (238)

As distrusted adolescents, motherless or poorly mothered, servants, and female, their status is rendered even more equivocal; so they accuse to maintain a measure of control over their societal identities, their passional selves, and the structures of Puritan male dominance that determined their place.

To redeem their problematic illegitimacy, the girls first denounce communal pariahs enacting transgressions that cannot be protected, contained, or disguised by the institutional machinery governing Salem society: the black slave Tituba, whose concupiscent Devil "be pleasure man in Barbados" (313); Goody Osburn, sleeping "in ditches, and so very old and poor. . . . beggin' bread and a cup of cider" (267); "*a bundle of rags*"—Sarah Good (312); and Bridget Bishop "that lived three year with Bishop before she married him" (316).

The effects of denunciation are, ironically, empowering for the accusers, as they forge an alternative if troubling center of matriarchal authority. Abigail's sexuality becomes publicly useful and needs no longer to be hidden:

> Abigail. . . . She comes to me while I sleep; she's always making me dream corruptions! . . . Sometimes I wake and find myself standing in the open doorway and not a stitch on my body! I always hear her laughing in my sleep. I hear her singing her Barbados songs and tempting me with— (256–57)

while Mary Warren's is curiously revolutionary:

> Mary Warren, *hysterically, pointing at Proctor, fearful of him.* My name, he want my name. "I'll murder you," he says, "if my wife hangs! We must go and overthrow the court," he says! . . . He wake me every night, his eyes were like coals and his fingers claw my neck, and I sign, I sign . . . (310)

Even the condemned are oddly liberated by their indictments, because it allows them to utter possibilities that ordinarily would have been restrained by judgment and discretion:

> Tituba, *suddenly bursting out.* Oh, how many times he bid me kill you, Mr. Parris!
> Parris. Kill me!
> Tituba, *in a fury.* He say Mr. Parris must be kill! Mr. Parris no goodly man, Mr. Parris mean man and no gentle man, and he bid me rise out of my bed and cut your throat! *They gasp.* But I tell him "No! I don't hate that man. I don't want kill that man." . . . then he come one stormy night to me, and he say, "Look! I have *white* people belong to me." (258–59)

Awakened by her illicit relationship with John Proctor to the instinctive, rule-dissolving vitality of desire, Abigail recognizes that the function of piety, responsibility, and duty—the conventions of the respectable—is to deny the amoral authority of nature; that behind all legitimate acts of copulation sanctioned by patriarchy to ensure its continued existence is the same driving, rebellious, potentially threatening sexuality:

> Abigail, *in tears.* I look for John Proctor that took me from my sleep and put knowledge in my heart! I never knew what pretense Salem was, I never knew the lying lessons I was taught by all these Christian women and their covenanted men! And now you bid me tear the light out of my eyes? I will not, I cannot! (241)

Puritanism has transformed this risky sexuality into witchcraft, thereby conceding the danger at the heart of feminine power, and has made putative witches out of the entire community, creating the revolution it had thought to contain.

> *Danforth.* . . . You have heard rebellion spoken in the town?
> *Hale.* Excellency, there are orphans wandering from house to house; abandoned cattle bellow on the highroads, the stink of rotting crops hangs everywhere, and no man knows when the harlots' cry will end his life—and you wonder yet if rebellion's spoke? Better you should marvel how they do not burn your province! (318–19)

By challenging the apparently decent men and women of Salem, the young women, led by the knowing Abigail, act to scourge hypocrisy, punish its practitioners, and exact revenge for their socially determined impotence. Rebecca Nurse, for example, is attacked because she seems able to control and direct nature's fecundity ("You think it God's work you should never lose a child, nor grandchild either" [245]); and Elizabeth Proctor because her righteousness seems an instrument for the denial of her fundamental sensuality. For both women, the condemnation demands a necessary reevaluation of the assumptions that conditioned their lives. Rebecca, who has never known suffering, accepts her pain, therefore granting that she cannot master the ambiguous force of natural energy and welcoming her martyrdom. Elizabeth Proctor confesses her complicity in her husband's downfall. ("I have read my heart this three month, John. . . . I have sins of my own to count. It needs a cold wife to prompt lechery" [323]). She finds blessing in acknowledging her participation in a series of complex betrayals provoked by erotic uncertainty, and, with curious irony, Elizabeth is permitted to survive her adulterous if heroic husband because of a pregnancy that in the most obvious fashion reaffirms the sexuality she initially has chosen to repudiate.

In a world shattered by the radical effects of the systemic rejection of women's power signified by the repudiation of nature and the resultant criminalizing of desire, John Proctor, the uncertain, divided protagonist, equivocal in his allegiance to Puritan patriarchal rule, has to discover what constitutes right moral action, then choose to act appropriately.[13] To do so, he must not only accept the insurrectionary strength of the sexual impulse, but he also must publicly indicate his responsibility for the disruptive social consequences of delegitimized private behavior (albeit in the same condemnatory rhetoric used by the dominant and dominating culture—the only language he has been given):

> *Proctor.* How do you call Heaven! Whore! Whore! . . .
> *Danforth.* You will prove this! This will not pass!
> *Proctor, trembling, his life collapsing about him.* I have known her, sir. I have known her.
> *Danforth.* You—you are a lecher! . . . In—in what time! In what place?
> *Proctor, his voice about to break, and his shame great.* In the proper place—where my beasts are bedded. On the last night of my joy, some eight months past. She used to serve me in my house, sir. . . . She thinks to dance with me on my wife's grave! And well she might, for I thought of her softly. God help me, I lusted, and there *is* a promise in such sweat. (304–5)

The respectable citizen has become a malefactor, as proof of personal and communal conscience is seen to reside in the acknowledged inevitability of desire.

Because his wife's confession of instinct denied makes her a culpable third partner in the adultery, he recognizes that goodness is neither absolute, nor unitary, nor prohibited by guilt derived from the violation of culturally determined normative conduct:

> *Elizabeth.* You take my sins upon you, John—
> *Proctor, in agony.* No. I take my own, my own!
> *Elizabeth.* John, I counted myself so plain, so poorly made, no honest love could come to me! Suspicion kissed you when I did; I never knew how I should say my love. It were a cold house I kept! . . . But let none be your judge. There is no higher judge under Heaven than Proctor is! Forgive me, forgive me, John—I never knew such goodness in the world! (323)

Finally, and not without considerable irony, Proctor learns that the price of survival might well betray its worth. He will confess to his own disorderly sins of sexuality, "for sending your spirit out upon Mary Warren" (326); but he refuses to indict the female principle—Goody Nurse, Mary Easty, Martha Corey—at least in its maternal incarnation; nor will he allow his confession to be exploited to justify the validity of their presumptive crimes, "You will not use me! . . . I blacken all of them when this is nailed to the church the very day they hang for silence!" (327). His masculinity, his identity, his name is preserved by his willingness to sustain some vision of female authority.

Betrayal and Blessedness

As John Proctor goes to his martyrdom, the melodramatic structure of *The Crucible* seems to reassert itself although the subtextual content of the play tempers our pleasure at the victory of principle with a curious indeterminacy. After all, notwithstanding the heroic manner of his death, the transgressing adulterous male is punished most severely. The sexually active women remain triumphantly alive: Abigail Williams and Mary Lewis, ironic terrorists of instinct and desire, escape; and honest Elizabeth Proctor, whose one lie, apparently uttered to preserve both her husband's and her own reputations, condemns him, is saved by her pregnancy, surely the most visible sign of the source of female power.

2

If Miller's exploration of the contradictory, male-determined ideology of feminine power in *The Crucible* is dictated by the claims of historical specificity, then *A View from the Bridge*, in both its one-act and two-act versions, attempts to dramatize the tyrannical authority of the primitive formulae of blood and desire identified with the archetypal female imperium hidden in the local and the particular, drawing the Italian community of Red Hook, Brooklyn, back into its tribal past. As Miller describes the genesis of the play:

> You see that story . . . is age-old. I didn't know it when I heard it the first time, but just telling it around a few times to people who lived on the waterfront where I used to live, it was quite obvious that—in its details it was a little different but basically the orphan girl or the niece who is not quite a blood relation living in the house is a stick of dynamite which always ends badly and the betrayal by an individual in a passion—his betrayal of some group is part of it, generally. It had a myth-like resonance for me. I didn't feel I was making anything up, but rather recording something old and marvellous. . . . Raf Vallone has toured Italy three times with it and especially in the small southern towns the people, he tells me, react to it almost as a rite.[14]

Unlike the articulate self-consciousness of the earlier drama, in which the Puritan "not only felt, but constantly referred his feelings to concepts, to codes and ideas of social and ethical importance,"[15] *A View from the Bridge* recovers the inexplicable. Alfieri, the lawyer-narrator who must negotiate among the conflicting demands of the law of matriarchal nature, the rules of the tribe, and the legalisms of civilization, comments on the anarchic force of ancient definitions of the sexual impulse:

—and yet . . . every few years there is still a case, and as the parties tell me what the trouble is, the flat air in my office suddenly washes in with the green scent of the sea, the dust in this air is blown away and the thought comes that in some Caesar's year, in Calabria perhaps or on the cliff at Syracuse, another lawyer, quite differently dressed, heard the same complaint and sat there as powerless as I, and watched it run its bloody course. (379)

Indeed, it seems as if only the very structure of the work—the balance "between the play's formal, cool classicism and the turmoil of incestuous desire and betrayal within it"[16]—guarded by the interpretive rhetoric of Alfieri can contain the unloosened flood of instinct and passion masquerading as destiny.

The first version of A View from the Bridge presents Eddie Carbone's sexual obsession with his niece Catherine as the mythic "awesomeness of a passion which, despite its contradicting the self-interest of the individual it inhabits, despite every kind of warning, despite even its destruction of the moral beliefs of the individual, proceeds to magnify its power over him until it destroys him."[17] The playwright gives his audience as well as his protagonist "an unbreakable series of actions that went to create a closed circle impervious to all interpretation" (47–48). There is no effort to explain Eddie's psychology, nor to offer a contextual justification for his mutinous, life-denying sexuality, nor to provide theatrically for "a conventional investigation in width which would necessarily relax that clear, clean line of his catastrophe."[18] The characters exist "purely in terms of their action . . . because they are a kind of people who, when inactive, have no new significant definition as people."[19]

Notwithstanding the fact that female seductiveness and maternity are essential to enacting Eddie's story, the women are curiously adjunctive participants in the events. Catherine seems almost an arbitrary trigger of desire. The fact that she is Eddie's niece is surely structurally necessary for the tragedy, but Miller concedes only that static necessity. One weakness of this initial version is that Catherine appears too knowing and too aggressive to accept so passive a role as unconscious provocateur. Beatrice, on the other hand, remains unconvincingly naïve as the impotent wife, vaguely disturbed but not allowed by the exigencies of authorial insistence on dramatic inevitability to account for the single-minded trajectory of Eddie's ruin or to intervene in its progress toward devastation. For Miller, the story is Eddie's alone and "to cleave to his story was to cleave to the man."[20]

Betrayal and Blessedness

The two-act revision, or the play as we presently know it, arises from the playwright's recognition that excluding the communal ethos into which Eddie Carbone is bound deprives its protagonist of humanity even as it seems to elevate his presumptive mythic authority:

> The mind of Eddie Carbone is not comprehensible apart from its relation to his neighborhood, his fellow workers, his social situation. His self-esteem depends upon their estimate of him, and his value is created largely by his fidelity to the code of his culture....
>
> In other words, once Eddie had been placed squarely in his social context, among his people, the mythlike feeling of the story emerged of itself, and he could be made more human and less a figure, a force.[21]

Once he re-creates Eddie as less a phenomenon than an individual determined by complex sociocultural ideologies rooted perhaps in the powerful archetypal tensions of an earlier tribal sense of society, Miller also can refashion the presence of the feminine as a significant instrumentality driving the action of the play. He introduces "the autonomous viewpoints of his wife and niece," which are no longer "muted counterpoints to the march of Eddie's career" but have become "involved forces pressing him forward or holding him back and eventually forming, in part, the nature of disaster" (51). More important, however, Miller has reconceived the ways sexuality operates through the characters and events of the play, dramatizing its dangerous unpredictable authority by locating it once again within the oppositional possibilities of the feminine principle. By embodying the insurgent energies of the archetypal matriarchy in Catherine's destructive innocence and B.'s knowing maternity, he has restored the disruptive centrality of female power to the mythic design elaborated in *A View from the Bridge*.

Granted innocence, Catherine's erotic vitality becomes an unconscious element of character. In this play, however, such innocence is costly. Because Miller defines this sensuality as inherent, an innate component of female selfhood, and therefore beyond awareness, Catherine is freed not only from responsibility for its consequences but also from its guilts. That such a formula can be neither satisfactory nor persuasive is clear enough if we are meant to accept B.'s later attempt to impose collective accountability:

> Catherine.... In the garbage he belongs!...
> Beatrice.... *To Catherine.* Then we all belong in the garbage. You,

and me too. . . . Whatever happened we all done it, and don't you ever forget it, Catherine. (436)

Although she is seventeen (the same age of sexual maturity as those troublesome young women of Salem), she remains "Baby," "Katie baby," or "kid" to both Beatrice and Eddie—notwithstanding B.'s increasing discomfort with and Eddie's urgent, compulsive insistence on such a characterization. This process of infantilization, surely a method for defusing and inhibiting Catherine's emergent sexuality, is strengthened by Eddie's frequent recourse to the word *madonna* to describe her conditional naiveté ("With your hair that way you look like a madonna, you know that? You're the madonna type. . . . You wanna go to work, heh, Madonna?" [386]), which finally controls her eroticism by recasting it in suppressive religious terms.

Because her childlikeness has been encouraged, particularly by Eddie's fearful needs, she seems unable to recognize the seductive subtext of her gestural affection that confuses the actions of daughter, wife, and lover, although Eddie certainly can define its absence when those gestures are transferred to Rodolpho:

Catherine. You like sugar?
Rodolpho. Sugar? Yes! I like sugar very much!
  Eddie is downstage, watching as she pours a spoonful of sugar into his cup, his face puffed with trouble. . . . (397)

Ironically named "the blessed one," given the treacherous wisdom she imparts to her niece, only Beatrice, whose awareness has been sharpened by sexual experience and sexual deprivation, can begin the necessary explanations to Catherine of the explosive archetypal power she contains:

Beatrice. . . . you gotta be your own self more. You still think you're a little girl, honey. . . .
Catherine. Yeah, but how am I going to do that? He thinks I'm a baby.
Beatrice. Because *you* think you're a baby. I told you fifty times already, you can't act the way you act. You still walk around in front of him in your slip—
Catherine. Well I forgot.
Beatrice. Well you can't do it. Or like you sit on the edge of the bathtub talkin' to him when he's shavin' in his underwear. . . . if you act like a baby and he be treatin' you like a baby. Like when he comes home sometimes you throw yourself at him like when you was twelve years old.

Betrayal and Blessedness

> *Catherine.* Well I like to see him and I'm happy so I—
> *Beatrice.* Look, I'm not tellin' you what to do honey, but—
> *Catherine.* No, you could tell me, B.! Gee, I'm all mixed up. See, I— He looks so sad now and it hurts me.
> *Beatrice.* Well look Katie, if it's goin' to hurt you so much you're gonna end up an old maid here. . . . I'm tellin' you, I'm not makin' a joke. I tried to tell you a couple of times in the last year or so. That's why I was so happy you were going to go out and get work, you wouldn't be here so much, you'd be a little more independent. I mean it. It's wonderful for a whole family to love each other, but you're a grown woman and you're in the same house with a grown man. So you'll act different now, heh? . . . Because it ain't only up to him, Katie, you understand? (405)[22]

Catherine's awakening to the treasonous demands of desire continues when her own passions become conscious and explicit, aroused by a presumptively acceptable male and sanctioned by those conventions that exist to domesticate the unruly impulses of sexuality. This instinctual release allows her to voice the troublesome ambiguities embedded in her relationship with Eddie, using language that emphasizes the equivocal by blurring once again the distinctions among mother, wife, and lover:

> *Catherine.* . . . I've been here all my life. . . . Every day I saw him when he left in the morning and when he came home at night. You think it's so easy to turn around and say to a man he's nothin' to you no more? . . . I'm not a baby, I know a lot more than people think I know. . . . I can tell a block away when he's blue in his mind and just wants to talk to somebody quiet and nice. . . . I can tell when he's hungry or wants a beer before he even says anything. I know when his feet hurt him, I mean I *know* him and now I'm supposed to turn around and make a stranger out of him? I don't know why I have to do that, I mean.
> *Rodolpho.* Catherine. If I take in my hands a little bird. And she grows and wishes to fly. But I will not let her out of my hands because I love her so much, is that right for me to do? I don't say you must hate him; but anyway you must go, mustn't you? (420–21)

However, as the rhetoric of Catherine's speeches of discovery indicate, she does not resolve these tensions until her uncle's incestuous betrayal and homoerotic fixation collapse the normative categories of gender behavior and familial order. Yet her resolution does little to change the determined course of action. Because as a woman she simply *is* a figuration of the erotic, her influence operates independently of personal choice, so that she can neither alter nor regulate Eddie's obsessional responses; and the arc of his fate impelled by the frightening ineluctable power of female sexuality drives Eddie Carbone to his death.

If the adolescent Catherine embodies the innocence that unwittingly kills, then the mature Beatrice is a version of the archetypal mother, the Great Goddess who knows, and perhaps is, the darkness as well as the redemptive light, the source of Miller's belief in the inevitability of both betrayal and blessedness.

Because her knowledge encompasses the disorderly contradictions that fuel sexual desire, and she understands their threatening power, Beatrice attempts to manage these rebellious forces as they emerge and enclose the knotted relationships among niece, husband, and immigrant cousins. That she fails is not from want of recognizing that she cannot succeed: not only is she aware of the autonomous warrant of the erotic, but she also realizes that as a woman she is an inevitable circumstantial source of the oppositional energies that generate the tragic action.

Beatrice's maternity dictates that she warn Catherine of the dangerous consequences of her childishness, although she knows that her criticism might be stained by sexual jealousy, the result of the niece's unconscious erotic empowerment:

> Beatrice . . . *She reaches over to Catherine's hand; with a strained smile.* You think I'm jealous of you, honey?
> Catherine. No! It's the first I thought of it.
> Beatrice, *with a quiet sad laugh.* Well, you should have thought of it before . . . but I'm not. (406)

She seeks to alleviate the problem of Eddie's physical withdrawal by confronting it:

> Beatrice. When am I gonna be a wife again, Eddie?
> Eddie. I ain't been feelin' good. They bother me since they came.
> Beatrice. It's almost three months you don't feel good; they're only here a couple of weeks. It's three months, Eddie.
> Eddie. I don't know, B. I don't want to talk about it.
> Beatrice. What's the matter, Eddie, you don't like me, heh?
> Eddie. What do you mean, I don't like you? I said I don't feel good, that's all.
> Beatrice. Well, tell me, am I doing something wrong? Talk to me.
> Eddie—*Pause. He can't speak, then.* I can't. I can't think about it.
> Beatrice. Well tell me what—
> Eddie. I got nothin' to say about it! (399)[23]

Betrayal and Blessedness

Yet her barely suppressed anger at the loss of sexual recognition undercuts her genuine concern and makes the confrontation ironic just as it intensifies Eddie's inner divisions, forces him into silence, and further dissolves his public and private allegiances.

Beatrice seems to accept the structure of traditional marriage that denies the sexual source of female power, but to Eddie her acceptance becomes frighteningly provisional as each independently asserted opinion or speech of dissatisfaction is interpreted as a direct challenge to the increasingly unstable determinants of patriarchal authority and male identity:

> Eddie. You used to be different, Beatrice. You had a whole different way.
> Beatrice. I'm no different.
> Eddie. You didn't used to jump me all the time about everything. The last year or two I come in the house I don't know what's gonna hit me. It's a shootin' gallery in here and I'm the pigeon.
> Beatrice. Okay, okay.
> Eddie. Don't tell me okay, okay, I'm tellin' you the truth. A wife is supposed to believe the husband. (426–27)

As John Proctor's case indicated, and as *A View from the Bridge* verifies in representing the trajectory of Eddie Carbone's destruction, it is the male and the male principle that is defeated by this inexplicable, revolutionary surge of desire generated by female presence. Eddie, "as good a man as he had to be in a life that was hard and even" (390), has lived within the unequivocal categories, the clear definitions, and the precisely conceived roles imposed by patriarchy. He knows what it means to be a wife, an uncle/father, and a man. But when "passion . . . moved into his body, like a stranger" (406), the carefully contrived design that controlled his knowledge and ruled his experience unravels. The more powerful and destabilizing his desire becomes, however, the more urgently Eddie needs to maintain the governing distinctions of his life; and the more he is driven to maintain those distinctions, the less he is able to do so.

The wifely B. is re-created as the shrewish Beatrice, whose fearful truths must be denied at all cost:

> Beatrice. . . . What's gonna mean somethin'? Eddie, listen to me. Who could give you your name? . . . if Marco'll kiss your hand outside, if he goes on his knees, what is he got to give you? That's not what you want.

> Eddie. Don't bother me!
> Beatrice. You want somethin' else, Eddie, and you can never have her! . . .
> Eddie, *shocked, horrified, his fists clenching.* Beatrice! . . .
> Beatrice, *crying out weeping.* The truth is not as bad as blood, Eddie! I'm tellin' you the truth—tell her good-by forever!
> Eddie, *crying out in agony.* That's what you think of me—that I would have such a thoughts? *His fists clench his head as though it will burst.* (437–38)

Any recognition of Catherine's adulthood must be dismissed, just as any admission of her active sexuality, symbolized by her wedding, must be repudiated. Rodolpho's masculinity—his blond hair (ironically ascribed to the sexual consequences of the Danish invasion of Sicily), tenor voice, ability to cook and sew, inadequacy as a boxer—must be established as signifiers of homosexuality ("If I tell you that guy ain't right don't tell me he is right" [427]) to reduce his desirability. But such a metamorphosis is dangerous, because it not only sustains Eddie's sense of maleness but also undermines it: if Rodolpho is feminized and still arouses Catherine, then Eddie's potency is rendered problematic. Having subverted personal relationships and disrupted familial order, this incomprehensible, rule-breaking desire finally compels Eddie to a last, self-destructive act of communal betrayal.

Although the concluding moments of the play offer an image of reconciliation or blessedness,

> Eddie. Then why—Oh, B.!
> Beatrice. Yes, yes!
> Eddie. My B.!
> *He dies in her arms, and Beatrice covers him with her body.* (439),

it cannot annul or replace the betrayals that are the consequence of the insurrectionary struggle inherent in the feminine archetype that has doomed Eddie Carbone.

A View from the Bridge, like *The Crucible,* ends with a single-minded absoluteness that disguises a certain discomfort with the subtext of the play's resolution. But if *The Crucible* depends on the consciousness of its characters and culture for its impact, then *A View from the Bridge* dramatizes a story that is contingent on lack of awareness and helplessness. Indeed, Miller insists, through the language and structure of the play, that Eddie is overtaken by a force he neither understands nor controls; that Catherine cannot be held responsible for an erotic power that is

Betrayal and Blessedness

inherent in her identity and is, undoubtedly, a defining condition of femaleness itself; and that Beatrice sees and understands but is unable to intervene in halting the course of events. Yet Beatrice asserts that all are culpable for creating the situation of Eddie's betrayal. That collective guilt is an inappropriate response when there is no consciousness or responsibility, and no control may account for the residual ambiguities that remain embedded in the mythic conventions of *A View from the Bridge*. It is also the crucial issue that greatly disturbs the action of *After the Fall*.

3

Unlike the necessary historicism of *The Crucible* and the tribal ethnicity of *A View from the Bridge* as those forces shape the ambiguous dramatic representations of matriarchal power and female desire, *After the Fall* relies on the causative particularity of the autobiographical. In this play, Quentin's problematic litany attempts to understand and perhaps to control the agents of destructive innocence, inevitable betrayal, and the tentative possibilities of reconciliatory blessedness issuing from the various modalities of feminine authority. Although Miller seems more conscious of the governing archetypes that embody the rule-annihilating impulses of the female imperium and uses these mythic patterns as the structural determinants of the protagonist's confessional fable, *After the Fall* remains a troubled and troublesome depiction of woman's equivocal dominion despite the playwright's increased awareness and qualified optimism.

Throughout *After the Fall*, Quentin's voice, often synonymous with patriarchal convention, establishes the linguistic terms and the behavioral signs describing feminine power and defining its limits as he denounces the genre-fixed categories he has created for the cultural disruption and personal disintegration that fuel such action as the play contrives. Miller's knowing use of the self-exposing monologue organizes Quentin's responses to the demanding complexity of feminine force as enacted by the three women (and their acolytes) who have made, shattered, and recorded his existence: Mother, defined by primary function rather than by individuating name;[24] Maggie, the erotic signifier and the sexually signified; and Holga, balanced and integrated, the completed female self. These women are not only distinct, potentially oppositional figurations of patriarchy's need for and belief in a concept of unitary femaleness that embraces, contains, and disciplines the insurrectionary energies of contradiction. They also are enabling representatives of the quintessential dualism of matriarchal nurture and subversion that support the instruments of communal repression and equate acts of private culpability and shame with forms of public treason, transforming murderous thoughts into an ideology of collected guilt, that final ironic evasion of responsibility.

Echoing the male-generated vocabulary of psychoanalysis, laden with blame and desire, *After the Fall* offers a clear paradigm of emasculating maternal sovereignty in addition to presenting the most obvious statement of the disruptive Oedipal tensions that had been a covert source of the confrontational theatrical strength in the earlier plays:

> Quentin. . . . Why is the world so treacherous? Shall we lay it all to mothers? You understand? The sickness is much larger than my skull; aren't there mothers who keep dissatisfaction hidden to the grave, and do not split the faith of sons until they go in guilt for what they did not do?[25]

Quentin's mother is the primary maternal actor in the mythic Oedipal drama that, in part, determines the action of *After the Fall*. In his reconstructive memory, "so many of my thoughts of her degenerate into some crime" (212), usually murder, including an imagined matricide that erupts into Quentin's violent attempt to kill Maggie's imprisoning hold over him. Mother almost always appears in conjunction with the re-emergence from darkness of the concentration camp tower, the play's most emphatic symbol of human complicity and historic evil. However, because we know within moments that she has died months before her son's testimony, we are necessarily conscious that her residual influence will be enclosed and diminished. Indeed, just as we learn early in the play of Mother's death, in the same way we also discover Maggie's end and Quentin's decision regarding Holga. There is no question that possessing such information reduces significantly the anguished seriousness of Quentin's complaint and minimizes the conflicts that explode *The Crucible* and *A View from the Bridge*. This method of decreasing the play's emotional intensity functions as the technical means of superintending the insurgent claims of the feminine will that would annul social order and dissolve individual repression.

Within the limits constituted by the dramatic machinery, the

Betrayal and Blessedness

playwright restricts further the matriarchal warrant by contriving a representative of matriarchal tyranny that we must condemn. She is conceded to be a figure of betrayal even before she actively enters Quentin's edgy recollections when her death is perceived as the abandonment of a hospitalized and needy husband infantilized over the years by a wife who has maintained her embittering ascendancy by re-establishing and exploiting modes of childhood dependence:

> Dan. . . . How can we walk in and say, "Your wife is dead?" It's like sawing off his arm. . . . Kid, the woman was his right hand. Without her he was never very much, you know. He'll fall apart. (133)

The initial paternal response to the news—"*Father's hand grips his abdomen as though he were stabbed*" (135)—is a reactive gesture to deliberately inflicted pain repeating the physical sign—"*as though stabbed*" (146)—that marked his reply to the first act of traumatic maternal disloyalty that Quentin witnesses. But although we observe the lingering authority of the matriarchal agent, it is presented again in circumscribed fashion. Quentin's father not only survives the presumed devastation of his wife's death, he is allowed the limited triumph of delayed adulthood as he participates for the first time in the traditionally public world of masculine power.

> Quentin. . . . Still, a couple of months later he bothered to register and vote. . . . Well, I mean . . . it didn't kill him either, with all his tears. (136)

Quentin is also granted a qualified victory during this early episode because he, not his brother Dan, becomes the advocate (albeit an ambivalent one) for the certainty, even the inevitability of paternal strength. Only after we have seen the scope of maternal jurisdiction contained are we finally permitted to view the extent of her manipulations and to know the weight of her control.

Although Mother surely has been victimized by male-derived systems of culture,

> Mother. . . . God, I'll never forget it, valedictorian of the class with a scholarship to Hunter in my hand—*A blackness flows into her soul*—and I come home, and Grandpa says, "You're getting married!" It had never come into my mind! I was like .. like with

> small wings, just getting ready to fly; I slept all year with the catalogue under my pillow. To learn, to learn everything! (144–45),

such knowledge offers no reason for sympathy because she ultimately achieves her problematic empowerment through the psychic mutilation of others. She becomes adept at using the patriarchal gender system and the roles assigned within it to subvert their legitimacy. She humiliates the father, undermines the family, and makes Quentin a guilty, resentful accomplice in the process of destabilization.

Mother first appears in a complex re-enactment in which sexual awareness, the failure of capitalism, and the privileging of literacy are knotted together as the contradictory Oedipal sources of wisdom, danger, and complicity. As Quentin remembers, we watch as he is transformed into a reluctant maternal partisan and an unwilling paternal competitor through a manipulative account of his mother's life that both elevates and diminishes his father's potency. Although he is sexually desirable and financially successful—a paradigmatic figure to imitate and envy—he is also illiterate, an emasculating legacy of another mother's betrayal, unlike his son who is learning the empowering force of language at his mother's insistence:

> Mother. . . . Why don't you practice your penmanship . . . ? You write like a monkey, darling.
>
> * * * *
>
> Mother. . . . *With a strange and deep fear:* Please, darling, I want you to *draw* the letters, that scribbling is ugly, dear. . . . (143, 144)

Throughout this play, the ownership of the words, identified with matriarchal supremacy, renders Quentin an accessory, a guilty and shamed parricide:

> Mother. . . . And two weeks after the wedding, Papa hands me the menu. To *read!*
> Quentin. Huh! Yes! And to a little boy . . . who knows how to read; a powerful reader, that little boy!
> Mother. I want your handwriting beautiful, darling; I want you to be . . .
> Quentin. . . . an accomplice! (157)

The remaining action of the episode, noted by Quentin through *"a sharp shaft of light"* suggesting a slightly open door, reinforces his divided and warring allegiances as his father is stripped of his wealth by the Depression and his sexual presence ("*Father is gradually losing his stance, his grandeur. . . . He sits, closing his eyes, his neck bent*" [146–47]) by his wife's harsh words. All that is left is the defeated illiterate, vanquished by an embittered woman for whom the patriarchal contract has collapsed:

> Mother. . . . *Breaks off; open horror on her face and now a growing contempt.* You mean you saw everything going down and you throw good money after bad? Are you some kind of moron? . . . I should have run the day I met you! . . . I should have done what my sisters did, tell my parents to go to hell and thought of myself for once! I should have run for my life! . . . I ought to get a divorce! . . . But your last dollar? *Bending over, into his face:* You are an idiot! (146–47)

It is this term *idiot* that resonates during *After the Fall* as an incantatory summons invoking the mutinous anger of feminine rebellion until Holga's visionary balance reconstructs its meaning to signify an acceptance of the human condition.

Each additional appearance of Mother emerging from the overdetermined associations that drive Quentin's memory is not only a recapitulation of maternal seduction, betrayal, or abandonment but also an uncomfortable reminder of the ongoing authority of the female imperium. Such moments of matriarchal assertion further widen the cracks and fissures within his oppositional consciousness. He becomes increasingly unable to control the murderous impulses embedded in his unresolved Oedipal dilemma until he is forced to enact them and recognize their residual strength before he can acknowledge that all we possess is after the Fall.

Even the other votaries of matriarchy such as Elsie and Louise in their collateral roles as wives practice the treacheries of female seduction and disloyalty, reproducing the first mother's betrayal. Elsie, for example, has compelled Lou (Quentin's professional mentor/father and, therefore, the embodiment of the precarious value of the Law) into his initial act of dishonesty that has made conditional his sense of adult masculinity.

> Mickey. . . . and I remember who made you throw your first version into my fireplace! . . . I saw you burn a true book and write another that told lies! Because she demanded it, because she terrified you, because she has taken your soul! (163–64)

She then denies him the opportunity to recover his identity through the restorative action of self-denying work:

> Lou. . . . but Elsie feels . . . I'd just be drawing down the lightning again to publish now. She even feels it's some unconscious wish for self-destruction on my part. And yet, if I put the book away, it's like a kind of suicide to me. . . . with this book of mine, I want to be true to myself. . . .
> Elsie appears, approaching, hearing.
> Elsie. Lou, I'm quite surprised. I thought we'd settled this. . . . You certainly don't think he ought to publish.
> Quentin. But the alternative seems—
> Elsie, with a volcanic, suppressed alarm. Paul dear, that's the situation! Lou's not like you. . . . He's incapable of going out and . . .
> Lou. . . . Well, dear, I'm not all that delicate, I—
> Elsie—a sudden flash of contempt; to Lou. This is hardly the time for illusions! (151–52)

Only when he seems a despairing failure (largely because of Elsie's intervention) does she nurture and comfort:

> Quentin. . . . *He turns to Elsie, who is lifting Lou to his feet and kisses him.*
> How tenderly she lifts him up—now that he is ruined. (165)

It should be no surprise, given the design of the play's gender relationships, that as surrogate mother/lover she also would attempt to seduce Quentin, re-enacting yet again the traditional Oedipal triad.

Although Quentin, with a narcissist's unpersuasive attempt at honesty, often concedes the validity of Louise's analyses of their personal and marital difficulties, he consigns her to the ranks of "These goddamned women" who "have injured me" (131). But her treason, if it is such, is more apparent than real, as Miller imposes a characterization on Louise that is not borne out by her dramatic experience or ours to justify Quentin's over-determined emotionalism.

Quentin demands from Louise a presumed sensitivity that his own Oedipally conditioned gender behavior cannot return ("Never forget it, dear, you're a man, and a man has all the choices" [143]). Although he expects her to understand the causes and tolerate the excuses for his sexual adventurism, he would prefer normative feminine exclusivity, notwithstanding his smug, unconvincing qualification:

> Louise. . . . Supposing I came home and told you I'd met a man—a man on the street I wanted to go to bed with . . .
> *He hangs his head, defeated.*

Betrayal and Blessedness

because he made the city seem full of lovers. What would you feel? Overjoyed for my discovery?

Quentin—*pause; struck.* I understand. I'm sorry. I guess it would anger me too. *Slight pause.* But if you came to me with such a thing, I think I would see that you were struggling. And I would ask myself—maybe I'd even be brave enough to ask you—how *I* had failed. (182)

He resents her contained, disciplined sexuality, perceiving the only reasons for her withdrawal to be punishment, a mode of repressive familial control, and a function of that dangerous surety that defines innocence as unacceptable. He also insists that Louise acknowledge responsibility for the flawed marriage in encounters that echo the pattern of the initial episode of primal treachery, although the evidence of the dramatic action substantiates the greater extent of Quentin's liability:

Louise. Quentin, you are full of resentment; you think I'm blind?
Quentin. What I resent is being forever on trial, Louise. Are you an innocent bystander here? I keep waiting for some contribution you might have made to what I did, and I resent not hearing it. . . . How much shame do you want me to feel? I hate what I did. But I think I've explained it—I felt like nothing; I shouldn't have, but I did, and I took the only means I knew to—
Louise. This is exactly what I mean, Quentin—you are still defending it. Right now.
He is stopped by this truth.
And I know it, Quentin.
Quentin. And you're . . . not at all to blame, heh?
Louise. But how?
Quentin. Well, for example . . . you never turn your back on me in bed?
Louise. I never turned my—
Quentin. You have turned your back on me in bed, Louise. I am not insane!
Louise. Well what do you expect? Silent, cold, you lay your hand on me?
Quentin, *fallen.* Well, I . . . I'm not very demonstrative, I guess. (167)

It becomes increasingly clear, however, that certitude, absolution, and the recovery of an unfallen world are the problematic concerns of Quentin's investigative recall, the consequences of which are associated with his reaction to all gestures of separation that mark the play but especially with his fear-laden attitude toward his wife's efforts to establish an independent feminine self. Louise's desire for an identity apart from the culturally designated roles that bind her to Quentin forces him to realize grudgingly that every separation, each feminine betrayal, is a mimic Fall, replicating the primary maternal treachery—withdrawal of the nourishing breast—dissolving the unity of nurturing mother and feeding child and losing Eden forever. Whatever its symbolic significance (this world is a broken image of what has been forfeit), its psychological results (the persistence of guilt, rage, and frustration), or its socioideological outcome (the disempowerment of women as cause of the forfeit, guilt, rage, and frustration), the process is biologically inevitable—the necessary, painful severance that transforms child into adult, betrayal into blessedness.

Like the knowing Abigail and the innocent Catherine, Maggie also is the emblem of the insurrectionary power of sexuality—the quintessential element of femaleness, a basic constituent of matriarchal authority, another face of the Great Goddess, as reconstructed by the necessities of the patriarchal imagination. Like them, Maggie becomes an instrument of social and personal destruction once the anarchic eroticism that she embodies has been thwarted by the ideological requirements of patriarchy, as it is initially exploited, contained, and finally suffocated.[26]

Maggie is an obvious representation of life's complex cyclical energies; throughout the play, her symbolic and actual presence is signified by the sounds of her breathing; when those energies fail, her respiration becomes labored; and she dies of barbiturate poisoning that kills "by suffocation. And the signal is a kind of sighing—the diaphragm is paralyzed" (240). From the first, Quentin describes her as "a truth; symmetrical, lovely skin, undeniable" (170). She is defined as a physically encoded being, a figuration of the female sexual principle:

> Quentin. . . . I met a girl tonight. . . . but one thing struck me, she wasn't defending anything, upholding anything, or accusing—she was just *there*, like a tree or a cat. And I felt strangely abstract beside her. (181)

Given the insurgent force of Maggie's authority, this linguistic objectification has the curious effect of confining rather than merely identifying her power. The hermeneutic enclosure of her erotic generativity transforms Maggie into a singular icon to be controlled and used, lest her rule-denying sexuality subverts the conservative structures of patriarchy. Quentin, consciously using the illusionary language of limitless love—"a love not even of

Betrayal and Blessedness

persons but blind, blind to insult, blind to the spear in the flesh, like justice blind" (225)—Quentin acquires Maggie as an archetypical gender transaction, believing that possessing her is synonymous with restoring the primal unity irrecoverably lost by maternal betrayal:

> Quentin. . . . You ever felt you once saw yourself—absolutely true? I may have dreamed it, but I swear I feel that somewhere along the line—with Maggie I think—for one split second I saw my life; what I had done, what had been done to me, and even what I ought to do. (190)

But possession is the exercise of tyranny, not an act of love, and yet another betrayal, although it takes a second expression of near-murderous guilt for Quentin to realize the extent of his treachery and Maggie's complicity:

> Quentin. . . . and God's power is love without limit. But when a man dares reach for that. . . . he is only reaching for the power. Whoever goes to save another person with the lie of limitless love throws a shadow on the face of God. (233)

That Maggie is complicitous in her own fate, if not a willing victim then one who needs victimization for the creation of selfhood, is a liberating recognition for Quentin.[27] As Miller writes of the genesis of Maggie's character from an earlier theatrical probe:

> For she appeared so trusting in her candor, and as strong and nonjudgmental as a fine animal, while within she felt painfully illicit, a kind of freak whose very candor brought her little but disguised contempt in the serious opinion of the world. And so, bewildered and overwhelmed, she secretly came to side against herself, taking the world's part as its cynicism toward her ground down her brittle self-regard, until denial finally began its work, leaving her all but totally innocent of insight into her own collaboration as well as her blind blows of retaliation.[28]

But the consequences of such a position, whether it be Quentin's or Miller's, are disturbing and dramatically irresponsible, eventually discrediting the play's qualified optimism. If Maggie is emblematic sexuality, the physical incarnation of the claims of eros as defined by the man who "loved" her, the patriarchal culture that exploited her, and the playwright who fashioned her, then her identity will always be contingent and tentative, depending for completion on the male other, the very agency that has determined her existence and fixed her meaning. Maggie can never be a whole separate person—her creators have seen to that. Under such circumstances and with considerable unwitting irony, suicide becomes both the final gesture of despair and the first act of the self's independence.

If, as Arthur Ganz has observed, "*After the Fall* . . . show[s] a genuine alteration of temper and attitude,"[29] then the reasons for such a change seem to be embedded in the aptly named character Holga. Although Miller may have "turned from the celebration of innocence to a search for the roots of guilt,"[30] Holga's presence in this essentially grim theatrical enterprise oddly infuses the play with a comic sensibility, if by comedy we mean that generic form that promises renewal and subscribes to recovery in limited proportions.

Although she is not a convincing figure—she is balanced too schematically between the extremes of Mother and Maggie which diminishes her dramatic power to support Quentin's symbolic function—she does offer this pathologically troubled character a methodology of hope. As an archeologist, she puts together shards of the past to explain the rise and fall of civilizations. Because she has both studied and experienced the indeterminacy of history, she neither requires consistency nor values certainty:

> Quentin. . . . I swear I don't know if I have lived in good faith. And the doubt ties my tongue when I think of promising anything again.
> Holga. . . . But how can one ever be sure of one's good faith?
> Quentin, surprised. God, it's wonderful to hear you say that. All my women have been so goddamned sure!
> Holga. But how can one ever be? (140)

She can take Quentin to a concentration camp, then offer him *The Magic Flute*, knowing and accepting the apparent contradiction; as a survivor, she reminds her lover that "no one they didn't kill can be innocent again" (148). Holga teaches him the necessary lesson that guilt, loss, and betrayal are not punishments to be avoided but inevitable signs of the human condition:

> Holga. . . . And for a long time after I had the same dream each night—that I had a child; and even in the dream I saw that the child was my life; and it was an idiot. And I wept, and a hundred times I ran away, but each time I came back it had the same dreadful face.

Betrayal and Blessedness

> Until I thought, if I could kiss it, whatever in it was my own, perhaps I could rest. And I bent to its broken face, and it was horrible . . . but I kissed it.
>
> Quentin. Does it still come back?
>
> Holga. At times. But it somehow has the virtue now . . . of being mine. I think one must finally take one's life in one's arms, Quentin. (148)

This reconciliatory embrace becomes, finally, the process of the play and the content of Quentin's education. By using the rhetoric of nurturing matriarchy, Holga reconstitutes the significance of the term *idiot*, incorporating even the negative resonances, and permits Quentin to redeem both the paternal legacy and the maternal embrace:

> Quentin. . . . To know, and even happily that we meet unblessed; not in some garden of wax fruit and painted trees, that lie of Eden, but after, after the Fall, after many, many deaths. Is the knowing all? And the wish to kill is never killed, but with some gift of courage one may look into its face when it appears, and with a stroke of love—as to an idiot in the house—forgive it; again and again . . . forever? (241)

While *The Crucible* operates within the circumscribed events of a verifiable past and *A View from the Bridge* occurs with the primitive designs of transcultural archetypes, *After the Fall*, interiorizing both historical awareness and mythic perception, remains firmly placed within the interpretive flow of an individual memory. The social concerns—the Depression, the Holocaust, the treacherous fifties—and the archetypal energies emerge from the overdetermined activity of a single unconscious, reflecting psychoanalytic narcissism.

Although the play appears committed to developing a flexible methodology of affirmation based on a balanced unitary vision of feminine wisdom, unlike the earlier works, with their enclosed movement, *After the Fall* also seems to possess an uncomfortable subtext. Perhaps the containment inherent in the play's central structural device can create only problematic optimism and suspect hope. Certainly neither the imagined matricide nor Mother's actual death can resolve the persistent Oedipal tensions issuing from Quentin's obsessive sense of maternal betrayal. His apparent adoption of "the idiot in the house," however sentimentally pleasing the rhetorical gesture, is not entirely convincing. Quentin's response to Maggie's suicide, the ultimate denial of her erotic power and insurrectionary sexuality, seems less conditioned by his liberated, if smug, sensitivity than by the fear of its residual seductiveness.

Yet reconciliation continues to be a possibility even within the limits imposed by Quentin's restrictive consciousness. Holga's truths are no less truths because they are confined by dramatic circumstances; and self-righteousness does not negate the discovery that to ensure our humanity, we must all live as if after the Fall.

Notes

1. It is only in recent years, as current interviews with Miller indicate, that critics and the playwright himself are beginning to move away from the vision of the feminine as simply passive and adjunctive to male authority.
2. Matthew C. Roudané, "An Interview with Arthur Miller" [1985], in *Conversations with Arthur Miller*, ed. Matthew C. Roudané (Jackson: University Press of Mississippi, 1987), p. 370.
3. Arthur Miller, *Timebends: A Life* (New York: Grove Press, 1987), p. 327.
4. Robert A. Martin and Richard D. Meyer, "Arthur Miller on Plays and Playwriting" [1976], in *Conversations with Arthur Miller*, ed. Matthew C. Roudané (Jackson: University Press of Mississippi, 1987), p. 271.
5. Miller, *Timebends*, pp. 370–71.
6. Ibid., p. 328.
7. Ibid., p. 312.
8. Miller's naming of, response to, and elaboration of the ironic doubleness of female power within a patriarchal culture are clearly presented in his autobiography, *Timebends*.
9. This earlier version, a more sprawling play with dramatic energies dispersed throughout a more complex view of Puritan society, can be found in the Billy Rose Collection, New York Public Library, Lincoln Center.
10. Miller, *Timebends*, pp. 340–41.
11. Arthur Miller, *The Crucible*, pp. 231–32. Quotations from *The Crucible* and *A View from the Bridge* are from Arthur Miller, *Collected Plays* (New York: Viking Press, 1957). Subsequent references are cited parenthetically by page number within the text.
12. In the unpublished early version, sexuality is presented as a driving force within Puritan culture in a far more explicit fashion. Not only are Abigail's sexual motivation and behavior made more obvious (she has been engaged in conjuring John Proctor's desire over a long period of time), so too is Mercy Lewis's sexual complaisance. Even the Reverend Parris is touched by the power of the erotic:

> Parris. . . . I did not seek you children by accident last night. I could not sleep, and yet I had no inkling that you were gone from the house. I felt oppressed, as though a cold and sour wind had clamped my bed; and I was silently aroused, do you hear? I was touched and stirred and driven to see what the matter was. Sport does not reach the human soul that way. ("The Crucible," unpublished typescript of early version of the play, Billy Rose Collection, New York Public Library, Lincoln Center, p. 6.)

Betrayal and Blessedness

13. The earlier version of "The Crucible," available in typescript in the Billy Rose Collection, New York Public Library, Lincoln Center, may explain more clearly the problems faced by Proctor as he makes his choices, because it presents a more complex depiction of the pressures acting on and within Puritan society.

14. Ronald Hayman, "Interview" [1970], in Conversations with Arthur Miller, ed. Matthew C. Roudané (Jackson: University of Mississippi Press, 1987), pp. 191–92.

15. Arthur Miller, "Introduction" to A View from the Bridge (New York: Viking Press, 1960), pp. vi–vii.

16. Miller, Timebends, p. 356.

17. Arthur Miller, "Introduction" to Collected Plays (New York: Viking Press, 1957), p. 48. Subsequent references are cited parenthetically by page number in the text.

18. Arthur Miller, "On Social Plays" [1955], in The Theater Essays of Arthur Miller, ed. Robert A. Martin (New York: Viking Press, 1978), p. 66.

19. Ibid., pp. 66–67.

20. Ibid., p. 66.

21. Miller, "Introduction" to A View from the Bridge, pp. viii–ix.

22. In the original one-act version of A View from the Bridge (New York: Viking Press, 1955), Catherine is a far more knowing figure, even consciously flirtatious in her relationship with Eddie. This particular dialogue that emphasizes Catherine's innocence does not appear.

23. In the original one-act version, Eddie's sexual failure within marriage and Beatrice's willingness to question him about that loss of desire is absent.

24. Although Quentin's mother's name is "Rose," she is called that rarely and under moments of great stress. In referring to her, I have called her "mother," because that seems to be the way Quentin has characterized her.

25. Arthur Miller, After the Fall, in Collected Plays, vol. 2 (New York: Viking Press, 1981), p. 157. Subsequent references are cited parenthetically by page number within the text.

26. With the publication of Miller's Timebends, there is little question that Maggie is based on Marilyn Monroe, despite Miller's defensive responses over the years. Often, the rhetoric describing Marilyn, her behavior, and Miller's reactions echo the language of After the Fall.

27. As it is a liberating recognition for Miller when he writes of Marilyn's decline in Timebends; see pp. 460–85 passim.

28. Miller, Timebends, pp. 526–27.

29. Arthur Ganz, Realms of the Self: Variations on a Theme in Modern Drama (New York: New York University Press, 1980), p. 124.

30. Ibid.

PART 3
TENNESSEE WILLIAMS

AUTHORIZING HISTORY
Victimization in A Streetcar Named Desire

Anca Vlasopolos

In a remark characteristic of judgments passed on modern drama, a critic notes that had Shakespeare written *A Streetcar Named Desire*, it would have been called a "problem" play.[1] Like Elizabethan and later problem plays, so dubbed because "the term gives least offence," *A Streetcar Named Desire* raises questions about genre and ethics, as well as about performance and audience response.[2] Although ideology of dramatic genre dissimulates the victimization inherent in tragic and comic form, both the problem plays of earlier centuries and "crisis" plays of the twentieth century tend rather to unmask the violence involved in victimization. This unmasking has disturbed critics and audiences alike. The problem comes from the strategies that these plays use to implicate the viewer in their violent processes of historiography—the processes of constructing a narrative of the characters' past—instead of purging the viewer of emotions associated with crises. *A Streetcar Named Desire* makes explicit an issue announced, but still undeclared, in earlier problem plays, namely, the narrative authority of history-makers and story-tellers versus the dramatic representation of the victim of that authority.

Academic criticism of *A Streetcar Named Desire* has been directed primarily toward the ethical and generic aspects of the play and has focused on whether the play can be classified as a tragedy. In general, critical interpretations that take generic forms as normative attempt to contain the disturbances produced by generically liminal plays like *A Streetcar Named Desire*, plays in which the values that lead to the installation of genre as norm come into question. For instance, in a sweeping indictment of

---

This essay originally appeared in *Theatre Journal* 3, no. 8 (October 1986): 322–38. It is reprinted by permission.

twentieth-century drama, Raymond Williams argues that the "rhythm of tragedy"—which in the classical age made the sacrifice of the hero regenerative—is gone; what we have instead is a resignation to general guilt among audiences who identify with a victimized hero.[3] This nostalgia for the regenerative sacrifice of classicism overlooks the hypocrisy of catharsis both on stage and off: the crisis on stage resolved by murderous unanimity, the audience purged of the very emotions that might lead to rejecting violence as a means of regeneration.

Most of the criticism of *A Streetcar Named Desire* concerns itself either with Tennessee Williams's failure to achieve a unified generic tone or, more obsessively, with the main character as a separately functioning unit of the performance. The generic and ethical yardsticks used to measure the play's success show that *A Streetcar Named Desire* fails either because it has no ethics (i.e., no moral instruction for the audience) or because it is a "modern tragedy," in Raymond Williams's terms, rather than an Aristotelian tragedy.[4] Critics who regard the play neither as typical of the failure of tragedy in the modern age, nor as an anomaly among modern plays, nor yet as a successful tragedy, attempt to domesticate the violence at the center of *A Streetcar Named Desire* by treating the play as realistic drama. They propose that the course of history makes the main character's displacement inevitable and that her violation and expulsion are "natural."[5]

Apart from the generic unintelligibility ascribed to the play, the portrayal of the hero, Blanche, has led to readings based on standards other than aesthetic ones, judgments which, although violently opposed in their reactions to Blanche, concur in their exclusive focus on the hero as the moral key to the play.[6] Perceptions of Blanche as the sole representative of sensibility destroyed by a callous society stand beside descriptions of her as sexually immoral or as a prostitute and nymphomaniac.[7] Some critics feel so strongly about Blanche that they envision her death at the end of the play, even if the plot only allows the audience to see her carried off to the asylum.[8] Responses to performances, as reported by directors and reviewers, are not as one-sided as the academic responses to the text because they contain a deep ambivalence: the savage rejection of Blanche combines with the discomfort of identifying with her destroyer and accepting the circumstances that make him triumph.[9]

Although purists unquestionably differ from audiences who enjoy the play "for the wrong reasons," the responses of both groups point to certain deficiencies in the generic and ethical approaches that have been taken toward *A Streetcar Named Desire*. If generic criticism has tended to remain neo-Aristotelian, it has conveniently discarded Aristotle's caution about the limitations of women heroes and the implications of his remarks.[10] Consequently, the single-minded concentration on the personality of the hero and the search for a flaw that explains his/her downfall—which have been applied to *A Streetcar Named Desire* since its first performance in 1947—and the Aristotelian focus with its constricted view of women have emphasized only certain aspects rather than the central concerns of the play. The larger context of the ethics represented by the play has also suffered from a critical standpoint dominated by a firm faith in the progress of history. Therefore, instead of being examined critically, the violence in *A Streetcar Named Desire* becomes symbolic of the necessary and inevitable evolution from past to present.

By bringing literary applications of anthropology as well as deconstructionist and feminist methods of reading to *A Streetcar Named Desire*, criticism can move beyond the urge to classify the play generically toward a questioning of the desire for control of the canon that underlies such urges.[11] The play's generic indeterminacy results not in a distancing but rather in an inability, almost a refusal, to crystallize emotions on either side of the issues raised. Although the oppositions set up in *A Streetcar Named Desire* between past and present, soul and body, and death and life have been examined exhaustively, the conflict between two versions of history struggling for authority should be salient for us in the light of twentieth-century historical experience. Williams's lucid representation appears in the impartial view of the combat that he presents between two antagonists and in a resolution that does not sentimentalize the victimization of the loser as an ascendance to a more glorious world. Swayed by alternating sympathetic identifications, audiences arrive at an arbitrariness involved in history-making and its attendant victimization. They perceive that historical discourse depends on power, not logic, for its formation.

Despite the struggle for authority over the interpretation of past and future that occurs in the more generically normative *Oedipus Rex*, the plot has been determined by the Delphic oracle, and no amount of Sophoclean subversion could shake his audience's faith in the divinely authorized version of the story, and hence in its predisposition to pity and terror. Williams, on the contrary, predisposes us for nothing so much as uncertainty.

Some may argue that Blanche's Southern accent and plantation origin mark her inescapably for victimization, given the turns taken by American history, as does Oedipus's name. Yet the hidden determinism uncovered ultimately by Williams's play has less to do with the history of the South as we now have it than with gender-determined exclusion from the larger historical discourse.

1

From the perspective of a conflict between different versions of history, scrutinizing Blanche at the expense of the other characters and of the theatrical context gives as lopsided a picture as would looking for Oedipus's flaw without regard to the oracle. The ultimate measure of the struggle represented in *A Streetcar Named Desire* is the opposition of reason to unreason, of sanity to lunacy. Blanche's fall from authority, her subjection, is masterfully captured by Williams in her being turned over to the supreme authority in charge of language, in charge of interpreting the past and predicting the future in the twentieth century: psychiatry, the scientific judgment of the soul's soundness. Yet, unlike the gods and their decrees, this final arbiter does not overtly envelop or determine the plot, so that the weight of authority oscillates throughout the play from Blanche to Stanley, giving it the seeming incoherence or generic indeterminacy that has troubled critics and audiences. Critics have noted astonishing similarities between these two antagonists, such as their love of costume, their charged sexual presence, and their tendency to aggrandize themselves.[12]

In the crisis precipitated by questions of ownership—of Belle Reve, of Stella's loyalty, most importantly of oneself—the shifts of authority from one character to another carry the audience's sympathy, so that perhaps the most disquieting revelation of the play is the audience's willing submission to a character's mastery of a situation and in the end to that character's version of events. But Williams intends to subvert the history-makers, an intention that becomes clear in the stage business, such as the backdrop that becomes transparent at crucial moments and the contest between types of music and jungle noises. The visual and aural effects contradict the triumph of the narrative version accepted by all the characters except the one who is dispossessed of authorship.

A Streetcar Named Desire seems to be made up of acts of "reading," of interpretations of texts that range from documents and inscriptions—the Belle Reve papers and the words on Mitch's cigarette case—to pictures and people. As they contest each other's interpretive authority, Blanche and Stanley resort to similar emotional and linguistic strategies to gain ascendancy. Why does Stanley's act of reading win out over the more literate Blanche's? Only here perhaps does Williams provide a clue about the outcome of the play: the name Blanche. Both "white" and "blank," the name seems predetermined to succumb to inscription, to be made other than itself. Not surprisingly, at the point at which the authority seems clearly to have shifted to Stanley, he declares that Blanche is "no lily." The pun, of course, does not explain but merely foreshadows Stanley's ultimate triumph. Having been shown in the beginning as incapable of telling the difference between real and fake among Blanche's remaining possessions, Stanley is finally given complete authority over his sister-in-law's true colors.

Within the scope of the readings performed by characters in the play and by the audience, Stanley Kowalski moves from being a text, even a cipher for Blanche, to being the author of history. Blanche, who is an equally unknown quantity to Stanley, enters with limited authority, which she alternately enlarges and loses throughout the first scene and then regains in the second during her confrontation with Stanley about Belle Reve. Although the mediating character, Stella, presents herself as an authority on both Stanley and Blanche, her passionate assertions about the true nature of each are disregarded by both and are disproved at least in one instance by the plot. The other characters function as a chorus, a fairly undifferentiated unit that is swayed by the exercise of authority. Although more fully characterized, Mitch nevertheless serves as a normative measure of the gain and loss of ascendancy of the two rivals.

Stanley's first appearance is mediated by two "readings": his wife's gentle reprimand for his manners and the explicitly sexual interpretation that his throwing raw meat at Stella elicits from the two neighbor women. Blanche, by contrast, remains to be read by the audience. (Unlike the spectator, the reader is presented with Williams's stage directions that shape a perception of Blanche as a stage presence.) In the first scene, Blanche reveals more directly than Stanley her strengths and weaknesses and thus the source of both her authority and her eventual loss of it. She comes inappropriately dressed, and because she seems unable to merge the information written on a slip of paper with the place in which she finds herself, she seems lost.

Throughout the play, Blanche's displacement isolates her. Her confidence is undermined by a setting in which she is unsure of the social conventions, the successful manipulation of which is indispensable for gaining and maintaining authority. Not only does Stanley dismiss her genteel protest, "Please don't get up," with "Nobody's going to get up, so don't be worried," but Stella, who has warned her about the inapplicability of her customs to the present setting, finds her sister's "superior attitude" "out of place."[13] In effect, Blanche's relation to place resonates from the first scene, in which "this place," owned by Eunice and Steve, is contrasted with Blanche's "home-place, the plantation" (248, 249), the picture of which is variously interpreted by Eunice and Stanley. Blanche's affair with Mitch centers on her needing a place away from Stella and Stanley, and Mitch's rejection of her expresses itself in a refusal to bring her "home." Stanley's birthday present to her, the bus ticket to Laurel, serves only to underline his declaration "She's not stayin' here after Tuesday." Like Stella, he knows Blanche can return to no home.

If Blanche's displacement leaves her at a tremendous disadvantage when it comes to establishing her authority, her strengths are equally apparent. Her wit and learning allow her to express bewildered merriment over the names of New Orleans streetcars and their destination, Cemeteries and Elysian Fields. She situates herself within Stella's "place" by expanding the literary allusions when she refers to the L & N tracks as Poe's "ghoul-haunted woodland of Weir!" (252). Her insistence on defining the "conditions" according to which Stella has agreed to live gives her enough authority to put Stella on the defensive: "It's not that bad at all. New Orleans isn't like other cities" (252). Like some of Stella's other assertions, this one is disproved in the plot, in which New Orleans is shown to be very much like other cities and other towns, and notably like Laurel, Mississippi.

Nowhere do Blanche's strengths have greater weight than in her confrontation with Stanley over the loss of Belle Reve. Having forced Stella to accept her story of how she lost the plantation by pitting her privations ("I . . . bled for it, almost died for it" [260]) against Stella's sensual satisfactions ("In bed—with your Polack" [262]), Blanche remains offstage for the first part of scene 2, in which Stella feebly attempts to convince Stanley of the truth of Blanche's account. Blanche's absence from the stage is less damaging than her presence in scene 1, which closes with her becoming ill in the presence of Stanley. In scene 2, Stella repeatedly cautions Stan against making Blanche ill again: "she'll go to pieces" (273). Once more, Stella's assertions are disregarded by the other characters, and she is disproved by plot developments. While Blanche is absent from the scene except as a singing voice, her physical being is replaced by her wardrobe trunk. It occasions the dispute about Blanche's veracity that continues throughout the play. Curiously, it also defends itself against Stanley's attacks as successfully as Blanche does when she comes on stage, chiefly because it contains more than Stanley can fathom and resists his attempts at reduction. Blanche declares, "Everything that I own is in that trunk" (281), and, for the time being, both owner and object successfully tell *their* story.

The violence against inanimate objects foreshadows the later victimization of the hero. In answer to Stella's warnings about Blanche's health, Stanley forces the trunk open and ravages its contents in an attempt to convince Stella that his suspicions about Blanche's fraud are well founded. But his mere physical strength is useless at this point, because his authority is undercut by his obvious and avowed ignorance of anything outside the immediate sphere of his experience. Twice Stanley is forced to invoke the authority of "acquaintances" who can appraise Blanche's furs and jewelry, already recognized as "inexpensive" and old by Stella. The third time, Stanley acknowledges directly to Blanche his incompetence in legal matters by announcing that he will consult a "lawyer acquaintance" about the Belle Reve papers.

Having begun as a stranger who is being discussed behind her back and whose possessions are being rifled for a clue about her criminality, Blanche rises in scene 2 to a position of authority vis-à-vis both Stella and Stanley. She rejects Stella's protection and invents an errand for her so she can confront Stanley on her own. Despite Stanley's attack on her trunk, she remains indisputably its owner, because while she places the Belle Reve papers in Stanley's "big, capable hands" (284), she proves to be the sole possessor of Belle Reve's history and of its end. More importantly, instead of going "to pieces," she manages to regain the integrity that she herself has felt slipping away from her ("I've got to keep hold of myself" [250]) and that has been assaulted by Stanley and been ill-defended by her sister.

The struggle for mastery between the two rivals begins as soon as they share the stage. Blanche attempts to subdue Stanley using her Southern-belle flirtation, a convention he does not entirely understand but through which he cuts easily. She uses even more provocative behavior when he begins his speech about the Napoleonic code, and again Stanley counters her move with the crude but effective "Don't play so dumb" (281). Because Stanley's experience with flirts, women who overvalue their good looks, and with those who give men "ideas" about them seems vast, Blanche's tactics fail. She begins to gain ascendancy over him only when she uses a language to describe her past and the history of Belle Reve that takes her out of Stanley's ken, that makes her the woman about whom Mitch confesses, "I have never known anyone like you" (343).

The two levels of discourse, Blanche's evocative, diffuse, evasive language and Stanley's direct, seemingly factual speech, point to a distinction based on gender and class that for a time works in Blanche's favor but ultimately defeats her. In scene 1, Stanley admits that he "never was a very good English student," but he immediately tries to erase that failing by making Blanche feel its irrelevance to his dominant position versus his higher-class, English-teaching sister-in-law: "How long you here for, Blanche?" (267). In scene 2, Stanley's interpretation of the contents of Blanche's trunk attempts to reduce them to the swindle that he suspects Blanche to have perpetrated on Stella—and, more importantly, on him. Each item he examines becomes another piece of evidence in the case against Blanche: "a solid-gold dress," "Genuine fox fur-pieces, a half a mile long," "The treasure chest of a pirate," "Pearls! Ropes of them!" "And diamonds!" (274–75). Stanley's conclusion is that "there's thousands of dollars invested in this stuff here," and that "Here's your plantation, or what was left of it, here" (274–75). Neither Stella's expertise (rhinestone is "next door to glass" [275]) nor her repeated protests ("Don't be such an idiot," "you have no idea how stupid and horrid you're being" [274–75]) have any effect on Stanley because they merely counter his propositions instead of changing the level of discourse.

Blanche, however, almost inadvertently seizes the mastery from Stanley during their confrontation about Belle Reve. Her fierce defense of her "love-letters, yellowing with antiquity, all from one boy" (282) brings in a complexity that Stanley is at a loss to fathom and hence to reduce. Instead of the cold facts of legal papers into which Stanley thinks he will instantly read an indictment of Blanche, he is faced with scattered "poems" from the dead, texts of such evocative power that Blanche articulates directly the terms of their relationship: "I hurt him the way that you would like to hurt me, but you can't!" (282). Compared with this passionate defense of her inmost core, the "intimate nature" of which cannot permit another's touch, the exchange of the legal papers becomes an anti-climax. Blanche is very much in control of Stanley as she relates the history of Belle Reve, one which he cannot hope to encompass as a comprehensible text: "There are thousands of papers, stretching back over hundreds of years" (284). This text, like the New Orleans streetcar, leads, as Blanche puts it, to the "graveyard, to which now all but Stella and I have retreated" (284). To Stanley's avowal of incompetence—"I have a lawyer acquaintance who will study these out"—she responds with grim humor, "Present them to him with a box of aspirin tablets" (284), thereby deflating whatever remains of Stanley's accusations. The dignity with which Blanche concludes this climactic confrontation with her antagonist makes Stanley later refer to her, repeatedly and enviously, as a "Queen."

Stanley moves from bafflement over the love letters to sheepishness about his suspicions and attempts to retrieve lost ground by introducing another history, another ending, to Blanche's account of Belle Reve—one to which he knows Blanche as a woman cannot remain insensible. He excuses his attack on her as the necessary action of the provider, because he and Stella will have a baby, who presumably will continue the story of Belle Reve beyond the graveyard. The respite following his announcement represents the harmony of an authority equally poised, for the moment, between the two rivals.

Blanche's vying with Stanley for Stella, for a "place," for the authority by which to assess life's worth becomes more explosive in scene 3 (The Poker Night) and scene 4, as each perfects his and her reading of the other and tries to enlist supporters for his or her own version of history. Just as Blanche's anticipation of courtesy—"Please don't get up" (290)—appears ridiculous and antiquated when applied to Stanley's poker buddies, so Stanley's exercise of authority over the women of the household seems irrationally excessive. Yet Stanley's loss of self-control in the violent break-up of the poker game merely concludes the gradual seepage of authority from him to Blanche throughout the scene. When he orders Stella to "hush up," she replies, "This is my house and I'll talk as much as I want to!" (294). Soon after, as he perceives Mitch's possible defection to Blanche's side and becomes enraged by it, Stanley orders Blanche to turn off the radio. Even his remaining allies protest, "Aw, let the girls have their music," "Sure, that's good, leave it on!" (295).

As with Blanche's trunk, physical violence becomes the response by which to subdue the female adversary. The increasing dissent makes Stanley try even harder to keep control over Mitch and the women. He bellows repeatedly for Mitch to take his place in the poker game, while Mitch is magnetized by the feminine sphere of the bedroom, so defined by Stella and Blanche's retreat to the inner room where they exchange confidences and laughter. When his commands to Mitch and Blanche fail and Blanche turns the radio on again, he throws the radio out the window. Despite the earlier slap that served both as warning and as a reminder to Stella of Stanley's rights to her, her defiance of Stanley, by calling him *"animal thing, you"* and by demanding that the poker players leave (302), provokes him into striking her in earnest. Contrary to Blanche's lament that "There's so much—so much confusion in the world" (309), his explosion restores his authority. His male friends make amends to him and take care of him, respectful of his capacity for violence, and Stella returns to Stanley, accepting his mastery over her. Blanche's reading of the night's events, "Lunacy, absolute lunacy" (303), is easily set aside by the others. Eunice even makes it clear that this night has ended less dramatically than similar nights in the past: "I hope they do haul you in and turn the fire hose on you, same as the last time!" (306). To Blanche's "I'm terrified!", Mitch replies, "Ho-ho! There's nothing to be scared of. They're crazy about each other . . . don't take it serious" (308). For the characters who are at home in the Quarter, the explosion is merely a crisis peak in a cycle in which crises lead to reconciliation and temporary harmony and, eventually, to other crises that are easily contained.

In the continuing struggle for authority, Blanche must impose her reading of reality on her sister or lose all. Whereas before the poker night Blanche's historical revisionism seems almost unconscious and motivated largely by affection, in scene 4 it becomes emphatically intentional. When Blanche first comes to New Orleans, she asks for "my sister, Stella DuBois," then corrects herself, "I mean—Mrs. Stanley Kowalski" (246). She frequently refers to Stella as the "baby" sister and as a "child." The morning after Stella and Stanley's passionate reconciliation, she attempts once more to place Stella back into the past they share, a past that excludes Stanley, by throwing herself on the bed next to her sister *"in a rush of hysterical tenderness"* and addressing her as "Baby, my baby sister!" (310). Her tenderness proves no match for Stanley's embraces, and Stella distances herself from her. Blanche then tries to awake Stella to her past, to the tradition of gentility in which they were both raised and which she cannot possibly find in her present life: "I take it for granted that you still have sufficient memory of Belle Reve to find this place and these poker players impossible to live with"; "You can't have forgotten that much of our bringing up, Stella, that you just *suppose* that any part of a gentleman's in his nature!" (320, 322).

Because Stella remains insensible to these appeals, Blanche moves from an interpretation of their particular circumstances to an overview of the history of humanity and its hope for progress. Just as Stanley tries to reduce Blanche to a criminal, she tries to reduce him to a beast. Yet whereas Stella openly rejects Blanche's reading through gesture more than speech, Stanley, who overhears Blanche's attempted coup, plots secretly to make Blanche's historical revisionism boomerang against her.

Escalating the rivalry for the authority of the historical voice, Blanche launches into her reading, reducing Stanley to a specimen from a primitive phase of evolution that must be abandoned in order for humanity to move forward. She begins by calling him *"bestial"* (322), and she supports her interpretation with the authority of anthropology:

> There's even something—sub-human—something not quite to the stage of humanity yet! Yes, something—ape-like about him, like one of those pictures I've seen in—anthropological studies! Thousands and thousands of years have passed him right by, and there he is—Stanley Kowalski—survivor of the Stone Age! Bearing the raw meat home from the kill in the jungle! (323).

Although she has seen the inefficacy of her caresses in light of Stanley's lovemaking and heard from Stella about her loyalty to the man who makes "things . . . happen . . . in the dark" (321), Blanche proclaims the superiority of "tenderer feelings" over "brutal desire." She places her sister among the "apes," subject to their will: "And you—you here—*waiting* for him! Maybe he'll strike you or maybe grunt and kiss you! That is, if kisses have been discovered yet!" (323). On the opposite side stands all that is best in humankind, "art," "poetry and music," "new light" in the "dark march" of progress. Her final plea to Stella has reduced Stanley to those who need to be left behind for the sake of culture: *"Don't—don't hang back with the brutes!"* (323).

If Blanche's argument, her view of Stella's life with Stanley, and especially her reduction of Stanley to an evolutionary throwback seem self-serving and cliché-ridden, Stanley Kowalski's language, if more direct, is also more impoverished, and his version of history is equally distorted by clichés and his desire for mastery. Because the play's action undermines her discourse rather than Stanley's, we tend to fall under the spell of the language of power, of the discourse that wins out, regardless of its poverty.[14] As late-twentieth-century intellectuals become uneasy about the privileges that Blanche's speech claims for art, poetry, and music as the light guiding humanity in its dark march, so an increasing number of people have begun questioning the clichés that help Stanley triumph over Blanche in *A Streetcar Named Desire.*

Only when Stanley taps into the dominant discourse of patriarchy and is thus able to reduce Blanche's story to an all-too-common denominator can he triumph over her. From the end of scene 4 to the climax of scene 10, Stanley proceeds to gather the evidence he needs for an interpretation of Blanche that is as reductive of her as her evolutionary claims have been of him. Evidence that Stanley begins to discredit Blanche even before he gets "proof from the most reliable sources" (359) is seen in Mitch's hesitation to give Blanche a hint about how Stanley discusses her. In scene 7, in which Stanley comes home with the "dope" on Blanche, he has already won Mitch to his side. It remains for him to win Stella and the "place" indisputably back from Blanche, for, despite Stella's seeming rejection of her sister when the latter attacks her husband, Blanche has made inroads into Stella's loyalty in the same way that she has partly redecorated the Kowalskis' apartment to suit her own "dainty" tastes. Clearly, Blanche's presence has made Stella feel a small sense of displacement as well. She declares, for instance, that she likes to wait on Blanche because "it makes it seem more like home" (333)—the lost Belle Reve rather than the New Orleans flat. Stanley notes Blanche's rise in status: "you run an' get her cokes, I suppose? And serve 'em to Her Majesty in the tub?" (358). Stella's reproof of her husband contains precisely that sense of a shared past with Blanche from which Stanley is excluded that Blanche was earlier seeking to revive in her sister: "Blanche is sensitive and you've got to realize that Blanche and I grew up under very different circumstances than you did." Stanley's reply, "So I been told. And told and told and told!" (358), emphasizes his sharpened sense that he is being supplanted, hence the necessity that his version of history fill in the "true colors" of the "lily-white" Blanche.

Stanley's "most reliable sources" prove as authoritative as the "anthropological studies" Blanche has gleaned. Stanley repeatedly assures Stella, who resists the "lies," that he has checked his sources carefully, but he offers no evidence, and his success with her is that she asks for none. In fact, she haltingly corroborates his story by indicating that there may have been problems with Blanche's behavior in the past. Yet Stella attempts to round out his account by taking a larger view of history, one that would at least partly exculpate Blanche. She tells Stanley the story of Blanche's marriage and of her husband's homosexuality, and she questions implicitly the reliability of Stanley's source: "Didn't your supply-man give you that information?" Stanley proclaims the supremacy of his version: "All we discussed was recent history. That must have been a pretty long time ago" (364).

Whereas Blanche wants to write Stanley out of history by relegating him to savage pre-history, Stanley is not satisfied with a reductive reading of Blanche; he moves to inscribe and author not only her past but her future. He has already selectively authored her past by choosing only her "recent history," the reductive anecdote of the "lily" sullied by her insatiable sexual appetite. He then blocks her escape to Mitch's home at the same time he presents her with a bus ticket not to send her back to Laurel, where he himself has acknowledged that she cannot return, but to exile her from his home. When Stella asks, "What on earth will she—do," extending Blanche's exile to a planetary scale, Stanley responds, "Her future is mapped out for her" (367). The passive construction of that sentence masks Stanley's active part as cartographer. In scenes 8 and 10, he strips Blanche of her disguises and the illusions given her by the costumes that he had overrated when he raided her trunk. But even that seems insufficient, because Blanche still manages to retain something of the strange dignity that makes Stanley refer to her as "royalty." Because she refuses to become the woman in the traveling salesman joke, the stereotype of the nymphomaniacal upper-class girl, he rapes her. His famous line rationalizing the rape, "We've had this date with each other from the beginning" (402), summarizes both the struggle for mastery in which he and Blanche have engaged, leading to the crucial combat, and his ultimate reduction of her to the whore of his history, who provokes and enjoys yet another encounter.

2

The struggle over history in which the two main characters of *A Streetcar Named Desire* are locked lifts the play above domestic drama. If it ended with the rape, the play might justifiably be regarded as representing post-war life in the South, where the most provocative problem was the shift from the aristocratically dominated tenor of social intercourse to the first-generation, lower-middle-class urban mores brought to the fore by the returning soldiers. But the troubling focus of *A Streetcar Named Desire* is not that a drunken man, left alone in a two-room flat of the French Quarter with his drunken sister-in-law, subdues and violates her, but that the act becomes public and the woman is punished. She is taken away under the consenting gaze of all the characters on stage, who constitute most of the characters in the play. The sense of unanimity is partly broken by Mitch's momentary resistance and by Stella's qualms, but in effect the unanimity about Blanche's destruction prevails.

The shift from the private, readerly quality of the contest for textual authority to the public nature of societal victimization places *A Streetcar Named Desire* in the context of sociopolitical crisis. The audience watches the sentencing of Blanche to the asylum that is to be her "home" while sharing her perception that she has been victimized by Stanley's—and implicitly patriarchy's—historical discourse. In addition to making Blanche's expulsion public by having almost the entire cast on stage in the final scene, Williams prepares subtly for the climax by introducing elements of sacrificial rituals into the text. Following the pattern of ritual, Williams has Blanche the victim be both exalted and defiled, so that both her greatness and her ignominy remove her from the range of common experience and dehumanize her, making her seem a monster. Even before Stanley's getting the "dope" on her, Blanche's past contains details that lift her life above that of an ordinary being and into the realm of myth.

First, in her account of the loss of Belle Reve, Blanche sets herself up as the besieged antagonist of the "Grim Reaper," who "had put up his tent" on the doorstep (262). The deaths she recounts acquire mythical dimensions; there seems to be a great deal of bleeding, on Blanche's part as well as on the part of those dying. None of the old people seems to have had an easy death. They died "that dreadful way," one of them even in a grotesque inversion of Stella's pregnancy: "So big with it, it couldn't be put in a coffin! But had to be burned like rubbish!" (261). Blanche herself declares she "fought and bled" and "took the blows on my face and my body!" (260, 261) while keeping death and the dissolution of the inheritance at bay. Stella accepts the mythical dimensions drawn by Blanche, because she tells Stanley that the plantation "had to be—sacrificed or something" (270).

In the second place, Blanche is associated with the mythical Daphne. She clings to her maiden name, describing it as "an orchard in spring" (299) (was Williams thinking of Chekhov's ill-fated cherry orchard since, for an unaccountable reason, Blanche, the widow of Allan Grey, is known as DuBois?). She also comes from a town called Laurel. But Williams inverts the myth of the chaste Daphne by having Blanche tell yet another story about her past, this time after Stanley has firmly established his narrative authority. Knowing she has lost Mitch, Blanche tells him another variant of her fight with Death, the death chosen by her young husband and desperately fought off by her old relatives. This time she invokes an image of herself as votary of Aphrodite, satisfying the desire of multitudes gathered before the temple at night. With admirable irony, the text reminds us that these worshipers at Aphrodite's shrine are themselves fighting death. They are young soldiers, gathered up "like daisies . . . the long way home" (389). One cliché recalls another; many of these young men are destined to push up daisies a long way from home, and their escapes, drink and sex, are as ephemeral as those of Blanche the moth. Yet by means of her myth of limitless sexual fulfillment, Blanche attempts to reshape for the future the uncontrollable decay and deaths of the past and fuse them with their opposite, "desire." Thus she envisions an easeful death, caused by an almost insignificant pollution, "an unwashed grape." At her side will be the ship's physician, "a very young" and "nice-looking" one. The struggle for breath, the bleeding, the soiled bed clothes, the head blown away, the "it" that couldn't fit in a coffin and had to be burned—all are purged in her vision of the "clean white sack," the "blaze of summer," and the ocean "blue as . . . my first lover's eyes" (410).

If Blanche exalts herself in her encounters with death and sex, Stanley's debunking of her myth as priestess of Aphrodite—he is equipped to deal with the issue of sex but not mortality—places Blanche in yet another dimension, that of the male joke about insatiable fallen women. His discourse reduces Blanche to the stature of less exalted legend among males in her home town of the chaste name:

everybody else in the town of Laurel knows all about her. She is as famous in Laurel as if she was the President of the United States. . . . the town was too small for this to go on forever! And as time went by she became a town character. Regarded as not just different but downright loco. . . . That's why she's here this summer, visiting royalty, putting on all this act—because she's practically been told by the mayor to get out of town! Yes, did you know there was an army camp near Laurel and your sister's was one of the places called "Out-of-Bounds"? (359–61)

Through their vast exaggerations, Stanley's "everybody" and his "she's practically been told by the mayor" throw doubt on the unanimity in Laurel about Blanche's reputation. Yet Stanley is close to achieving unanimity within his sphere of influence, namely Stella and Mitch, and he knows that he needs to debase Blanche thoroughly if he is to transform her from strong antagonist to victim.

Stanley's success in transforming Blanche into victim has less to do with the steady erosion of her authority than with the conventions of social discourse that discredit her speech while valuing Stanley's. Labeled as an outsider by her costume when she enters the stage, Blanche is pushed forcibly to the margins as her escape routes—to Mitch's home, back to Laurel, to Shep Huntleigh's yacht—are blocked and as her position in her sister's household becomes increasingly defined as that of an intruder. Both Mitch and Stella eventually accept Stanley's version of Blanche. The clearest signs that Blanche succumbs to Stanley's version of her, to the incomplete recent history of the traveling salesman, appear in scene 10, which fittingly culminates in her being raped. The woman obsessed with cleanliness, who takes two baths a day, who becomes hysterical when she spills a drink on her white skirt, who will not think of wearing an outfit if it is "crushed," appears in scene 10 dressed in "*a somewhat soiled and crumpled satin evening gown and a pair of scuffed silver slippers*" (391). Given Blanche's obsessive fastidiousness, one wonders where she found a soiled dress and scuffed slippers, but the stage directions deal less with the probabilities of Blanche's wardrobe than with a representation of her psyche, which has begun to allow for Stanley's assessment of her soiled lily-whiteness and for Mitch's echoing, "You're not clean enough" (390).

Bereft of any alliance with power, even an imaginary one, Blanche as a no-longer-young single woman barred from her profession, with no home, male relatives, or prospect of marriage, has her destiny mapped out for her, but not exactly as intimated

Authorizing History

by Stanley's prophecy. She joins the throng of the displaced, of whom society disposes by incarceration, expulsion, or death. Thereafter, her discourse becomes ravings and her presence an embarrassment.

To some extent, every act of victimization needs to be absolved if the crisis is to end in a particular sacrifice and not in generalized bloodshed. Anthropologists have documented the practices of looking for signs of acquiescence on the part of even an animal victim prepared for slaughter and of public lamentation after the victim's demise. In the twentieth century, when the victim is human, an arsenal of psychoanalysis is deployed to establish the complicity of the victim in its own destruction. One often hears of the fusion of Eros and Thanatos in such complicity, the union of which Blanche dreamed, but the execution of the sacrifice belies the wishful fantasy in Williams's play as it does in the sacrificial ritual itself.

Although there is no bloodletting and no actual death in *A Streetcar Named Desire*, Blanche's sacrifice is violent and ruthless. Aware of her vulnerability away from liminal times and spaces that allow her to exist outside patriarchal rule, Blanche designs her environment with extreme care. She attempts to control the lighting, the decor, and her costume, as well as that of her sister. She permits Mitch to see her only at dusk or night. She considers herself one of the "soft people," whose only power is "to shimmer and glow" (332). As she is inexorably drawn into the sphere of male judgment, the shimmering colors are bled from her: lamps are turned on in her face, colorful lanterns are torn off naked bulbs, and she is repeatedly told, "Now, Blanche." If we consider the play on *Blanche* that recurs throughout the play, we can easily hear the phrase as an imperative addressed to the woman whom we have seen clothed in a bright-red satin robe, especially as uttered both by the Matron and by the Echoes that Williams introduces into scene 11: "(*rising and falling*): Now, Blanche—now, Blanche—now, Blanche!" (416).

In scene 11, the private violence of the rape becomes the public violence of Blanche's flight from the Matron and the physical struggle with her. The "inhuman voices" and "lurid reflections" (399) on the walls link the victimization of Blanche in scenes 10 and 11 in a way that dismisses Blanche's complicity in the rape and that gives a sinister, not an erotic, slant to Stanley's claims about his "date" with Blanche.[15] Yet in this final scene, while the characters gathered on stage significantly mark Blanche's passing, they also accept their complicity in her expulsion by witnessing it without protest. Unlike the opening of scene 3, in which none of the men at the poker table intends to stand to greet the returning women, the men are standing when Blanche enters in scene 11, despite her customary protest, "Please don't get up." Moreover, they stand "awkwardly" (413), fully alerted to her presence and her fate. When Stanley rips off the lantern in the bedroom and Blanche screams, the men "*spring to their feet*" (416). Mitch ends up sobbing at the table, and Stella breaks into "*luxurious*" sobs, "*with inhuman abandon*" (419). Stanley, the inveterate poker player, leaves the game to console his wife while the others return to it. Combined with Stella's "*luxurious*" sobs, Stanley's "*sensual murmur*" (419) and sexual caresses suggest the ultimate indifference of participants in the forcible expulsion of Blanche, and hence the hypocrisy of their laments. As Eunice explains to Stella when the latter declares that she couldn't believe Blanche's "story" and go on living with Stanley, "Life has to go on. No matter what happens" (405–6).

But what happens to the viewers and the readers of Williams's play? Why is there no unanimity of response to Blanche's expulsion? If Stella can't believe Blanche's "story" and if some critics express doubts about it, the audience nevertheless sees the backstage wall become transparent to expose the sordid violence of the streets that parallels the stage action in which Stanley overpowers Blanche, and it hears the jungle sounds that take over and drown out the blues piano. In the last two scenes especially, Williams forces the audience to participate in Blanche's mental life by hearing the music, noises, and echoes that she and no one else on stage hears. These stage effects should evoke enough sympathetic identification with Blanche to make us repudiate the little world of characters left behind.

But no such identification occurs, or at least not conclusively. Although few readers and viewers side with Stanley, many agree with Eunice's assessment: life must go on, and the trinity of Stella, Stanley, and baby at the end represents life.[16] This pragmatic posture turns away from the uncomfortable issues raised by the play. In comparing the "mad" Blanche of Jessica Tandy with Uta Hagen's portrayal of a thoroughly sane Blanche, Bentley asks: "What is this? Can a sister just send someone to an asylum without medical advice? If so, which one of us is safe?" He concludes, undoubtedly for our safety, that an interpretation of Blanche as mad throughout is preferable.[17] But the play proposes precisely what Bentley, along with others, rejects: that we are not safe so long as the measure of insanity depends on the powerlessness of the individual. What makes Stanley triumph over Blanche? If Blanche appears evasive and shady in her use of lanterns and make-believe, Stanley, too, despite his protestations of simplicity, needs the magic of colored lights, smashed bulbs, and red silk pajamas to get things going. If Blanche lies about her past, about her "ideals," about who owns the liquor, Stanley also lies by omitting all but the wildest rumors from Laurel and, most damningly, by denying his "date" with Blanche. Unlike Blanche's lies, which she uses to secure for herself a place in the world and to displace, not destroy, Stanley, his lies force Blanche not only out of his "place" but out of normal society and into the asylum.

Stanley's authority derives ultimately from the same sources that most of us are forced to acknowledge in one way or another all our lives: physical violence, intimidation, and, above all, economic domination. In the quest for authority, Stanley profits from staying within the parameters set for him by his sex and class, and Blanche loses because she fails to conform. Stanley is perceived as normal: his pleasures are sex, bowling, drinking, and poker. His loyalty is to his family, for which he is a good provider. Except for his rape of Blanche, nothing Stanley does threatens the social fabric. Blanche, on the other hand, is deviant in regard to her class and sex. Although she maintains the trappings of the aristocrat in her expensive and elegant tastes, she has allowed the rest to slip, like Belle Reve, away from her. In seeking emotional fulfillment, she has disregarded the barriers of "normal" female sexuality and of class. Her actions subvert the social order: she remains loyal to the memory of her homosexual husband, she fulfills the desires of young soldiers outside the very walls of her ancestral mansion, she is oblivious to class in her promiscuity, and she seduces one of her seventeen-year-old students. Thus having overstepped the boundaries of class and profession, she arrives in New Orleans and attempts to split up the Kowalskis, even after she learns of Stella's pregnancy. She explicitly makes plans to take Stella away from Stanley, to have Shep Huntleigh set the two of them up in a "shop" in which they can earn their living together, and apart from Stanley.

Although Blanche only represents an illusory threat to the Kowalski union while Stanley's rape has the power to destroy the marriage, the man's act is more easily forgiven than the woman's desire.[18] Thus, Williams musters the most cliché-ridden conventions about sexuality and makes them work in *A Streetcar*

Named Desire, demonstrating that not only in the theater but in our lives we recognize the hierarchy of historic discourse selected on the basis of those same conventions. Which "story" do we believe in the end—the action seen on stage at the end of scene 10 or Stanley's off-stage denials? The fact that audiences feel ambivalent about Blanche is not the problem Williams raises; the problem is rather the audience's pragmatic shrug at the end of the play: life must go on, even if only for those who escape victimization, who are "safe" for now.

Unlike generically pure tragedy, *A Streetcar Named Desire* leaves us unpurged of the emotions it elicits. We resist being sucked in by Blanche's stories, for that way madness lies; although Williams makes us see and hear like Blanche, and perhaps feel like her, the authority of history is on Stanley's side. The force of *A Streetcar Named Desire* rests in our experiencing the ability of that authority to redact history and, therefore, to determine the future. The force of this "problem" play is to disquiet us so that we might hear, if not speak for, those whom history has silenced.

Notes

1. John M. Roderick, "From 'Tarantula Arms' to 'Della Robbia Blue': The Tennessee Williams Tragicomic Transit Authority," in *Tennessee Williams: A Tribute*, ed. Jac Tharpe (Jackson: University Press of Mississippi, 1977), p. 116.
2. E. M. W. Tillyard, *Shakespeare's Problem Plays* (Toronto: University of Toronto Press, 1949), p. 3.
3. Raymond Williams, *Modern Tragedy* (Stanford: Stanford University Press, 1966), pp. 157–58.
4. See Joseph Wood Krutch, *The Modern Temper* (New York: Harcourt Brace, 1929), p. 14; Orrin E. Klapp, "Tragedy and the American Climate of Opinion," *Centennial Review of Arts and Sciences* 2 (1958): 396–413, reprinted in *Two Modern American Tragedies: Reviews and Criticism of* Death of a Salesman *and* A Streetcar Named Desire, ed. John D. Hurrell (New York: Charles Scribner's, 1961), pp. 28–36; Signi Falk, "The Profitable World of Tennessee Williams," *Modern Drama* 1 (December 1958): 172–80; Kenneth Tynan, "American Blues: The Plays of Arthur Miller and Tennessee Williams," *Encounter* 2 (May 1954): 13–19, reprinted in *Two Modern American Tragedies*, ed. Hurrell, pp. 124–30; David W. Sievers, *Freud on Broadway: A History of Psychoanalysis and the American Drama* (New York: Hermitage House, 1955), pp. 376–80, reprinted in *Twentieth Century Interpretations of* A Streetcar Named Desire, ed. Jordan Y. Miller (Englewood Cliffs, N.J.: Prentice-Hall, 1971), pp. 90–93; John T. von Szeliski, "Tennessee Williams and the Tragedy of Sensitivity," *Western Humanities Review* 20 (Summer 1966): 203–11, reprinted in *Twentieth Century Interpretations of* A Streetcar Named Desire, ed. Miller, pp. 65–72; Britton J. Harwood, "Tragedy as Habit: *A Streetcar Named Desire*, in *Tennessee Williams: A Tribute*, ed. Jac Tharpe (Jackson: University Press of Mississippi, 1977) pp. 104–15.

Authorizing History

5. See Jacob H. Adler, "Tennessee Williams' South: The Culture and the Power," in *Tennessee Williams: A Tribute*, ed. Jac Tharpe (Jackson: University Press of Mississippi, 1977), pp. 30–52; Leonard Quirino, "The Cards Indicate a Voyage on *A Streetcar Named Desire*," in *Tennessee Williams: A Tribute*, ed. Tharpe, pp. 77–96; Joseph N. Riddell, "*A Streetcar Named Desire*—Nietzsche Descending," *Modern Drama* 5 (February 1963): 421–30; even Kathleen Hulley, who argues that "context-making" is at the forefront of the play's meaning, regards Blanche as uncontrolled desire that must equal death in "The Fate of the Symbolic in *A Streetcar Named Desire*," in *Drama and Symbolism: Themes in Drama 4*, ed. James Redmond (Cambridge: Cambridge University Press, 1982), pp. 89–99.

6. My use of the word "hero" rather than heroine emphasizes the active centrality of Blanche Dubois to *A Streetcar Named Desire*.

7. For defenses of Blanche's moral character, see Leonard Berkman, "The Tragic Downfall of Blanche DuBois," *Modern Drama* 10 (1967): 249–57; Bert Cardullo, "Drama of Intimacy and Tragedy of Incomprehension: *A Streetcar Named Desire* Reconsidered," in *Tennessee Williams: A Tribute*, ed. Jac Tharpe (Jackson: University Press of Mississippi, 1977), pp. 137–53; Harold Clurman, "Tennessee Williams," in *Lies like Truth: Theatre Reviews and Essays* (New York: Macmillan, 1958), pp. 72–80; Durant da Ponte, "Tennessee Williams' Gallery of Feminine Characters," *Tennessee Studies in Literature* 10 (1965): 7–26, reprinted as "Williams' Feminine Characters" in *Twentieth Century Interpretations of* A Streetcar Named Desire, ed. Jordan Y. Miller (Englewood Cliffs, N.J.: Prentice-Hall, 1971), pp. 53–64. For condemnations of Blanche, see Robert Emmet Jones, "Tennessee Williams' Early Heroines," *Modern Drama* 2 (December 1959): 211–19; Philip Weissman, "A Trio of Tennessee Williams' Heroines: The Psychology of Prostitution," in *Creativity in the Theater: A Psychoanalytic Study* (New York: Basic Books, 1965), reprinted in *Twentieth Century Interpretations of* A Streetcar Named Desire, ed. Miller, pp. 57–64; George Jean Nathan, "The Streetcar Isn't Drawn by Pegasus," *New York Journal-American*, 15 December 1947, reprinted in *Twentieth Century Interpretations of* A Streetcar Named Desire, ed. Miller, pp. 36–38; Howard Barnes, "O'Neill Status Won by Author of 'Streetcar,'" *New York Herald Tribune*, 14 December 1947, reprinted in *Twentieth Century Interpretations of* A Streetcar Named Desire, pp. 34–36.

8. Jordan Y. Miller, "Introduction" to *Twentieth Century Interpretations of* A Streetcar Named Desire, ed. Jordan Y. Miller (Englewood Cliffs, N.J.: Prentice-Hall, 1971), writes of Blanche's end, "the destruction of one whose rich humanity can only be recognized in death" (p. 12); in a 1947 review entitled "Masterpiece" (*New Republic* 117 (22 December 1947), reprinted in *Twentieth Century Interpretations*, ed. Miller, Irwin Shaw writes, "she [Blanche] is as real to us as if she were a living woman put to the torture and done to death in our own front parlor" (Miller, p. 45).

9. In a statement of remarkable moral ambiguity recorded in his "Notebook for *A Streetcar Named Desire*," in *Directors on Directing: A Sourcebook of the Modern Theater*, ed. Toby Cole and Helen Krich Chinoy (Indianapolis: Bobbs-Merrill, 1976), Elia Kazan, the famous first director of the play, writes that audiences first identify with Stanley in wanting to tell Blanche off but then realize that "they are sitting in at the death of something extraordinary" (p. 367); Clurman, *Lies Like Truth*, who considers Stanley a protofascist figure, detects a more sinister attitude on the part of the audience when he suggests that Stanley triumphs "with the collusion of the audience, which is no longer on the side of

the angels" (p. 78); Falk, "The Profitable World of Tennessee Williams," reports that during the rape scene "waves of titillated laughter swept over the audience" (p. 175).

10. Aristotle, *Poetics*, trans. Gerald F. Else (Ann Arbor: University of Michigan Press, 1973), p. 43.

11. Specific critical texts by several authors have been of great use to me in my analysis of *A Streetcar Named Desire*: René Girard, *Violence and the Sacred*, trans. Patrick Gregory (Baltimore: Johns Hopkins University Press, 1977); Victor Turner, *From Ritual to Theatre: The Human Seriousness of Play* (New York: Performing Arts Journal Publications, 1982); Robert Scholes, "Uncoding Mama: The Female Body as Text," in *Semiotics and Interpretation* (New Haven: Yale University Press, 1982); Susan Gubar, " 'The Blank Page' and Female Creativity," in *Writing and Sexual Difference*, ed. Elizabeth Abel (Chicago: University of Chicago Press, 1982), pp. 73–93; Sandra Gilbert, "Costumes of the Mind," in *Writing and Sexual Difference*, ed. Abel, pp. 193–219; and Page duBois, *Centaurs and Amazons* (Ann Arbor: University of Michigan Press, 1982), as well as Sigmund Freud, *Totem and Taboo: Some Points of Agreement between the Mental Lives of Savages and Neurotics*, trans. James Strachey (New York: Norton, 1950).

12. Normand Berlin, "Complementarity in *A Streetcar Named Desire*," in *Tennessee Williams: A Tribute*, ed. Jac Tharpe (Jackson: University Press of Mississippi, 1971), pp. 97–103; and June Schlueter, "Imitating an Icon: John Erman's Remake of Tennessee Williams's *A Streetcar Named Desire*," *Modern Drama* 28 (March 1985): 139–47.

13. Tennessee Williams, *A Streetcar Named Desire*, in *The Theatre of Tennessee Williams*, vol. 1 (New York: New Directions, 1971), p. 290. Subsequent references are from this edition and are cited parenthetically by page number within the text.

14. For instance, Ruby Cohn, in "The Garrulous Grotesques of Tennessee Williams," in *Dialogue in American Drama* (Bloomington: Indiana University Press, 1971), pp. 97–129, reprinted in *Tennessee Williams: A Collection of Critical Essays*, ed. Stephen S. Stanton (Englewood Cliffs, N.J.: Prentice-Hall, 1977), pp. 45–60, argues that Blanche "is trapped by the poverty of her imagery" and that linguistically Stanley is "a strong antagonist" (Stanton, p. 49).

15. It is no doubt the sense of Blanche's complicity in Stanley's rape of her that prompts Gore Vidal to put quotation marks around the word *victim* in his discussion of *A Streetcar Named Desire*, "Immortal Bird," *The New York Review of Books*, 13 June 1985, pp. 5–10.

16. See Krutch, *The Modern Temper*, p. 137; Adler, "Tennessee Williams' South," pp. 40–41; Vivienne Dickson, "*A Streetcar Named Desire*: Its Development through the Manuscripts," in *Tennessee Williams: A Tribute*, ed. Jac Tharpe (Jackson: University of Mississippi Press, 1977), p. 161.

17. Eric Bentley, "Better than Europe?", in *In Search of Theater* (New York: Alfred A. Knopf, 1953), p. 88.

18. For instance, Cardullo, "Drama of Intimacy," strenuously argues that Blanche is the victim of "an act of incidental, *inadvertent* cruelty," an act, therefore, more forgivable than a premeditated attack (p. 138).

"WEAK AND DIVIDED PEOPLE"
Tennessee Williams and the Written Woman

John Timpane

Like much of Tennessee Williams's public image, the tradition that he was sympathetic to women began with Williams himself. In his essays, memoirs, and letters, throughout his compulsive project of self-exploration, he took pains to delineate how his experience of women surfaced in his drama. Mothers and sons war continually; brothers and sisters suffer adoration. Nancy M. Tischler has written well about the succession of predatory mother figures in Williams, ranging from Flora Goforth of *The Milk Train Doesn't Stop Here Anymore* and Alexandra of *Sweet Bird of Youth* to Amanda of *The Glass Menagerie*, Violet Venable of *Suddenly Last Summer*, and Maxine of *Night of the Iguana*.[1] Further, in one of the most public of his many public games, Williams toyed with the name Rose and the image of roses in play after play. Williams even suggested that his early adoration of his mother and sister had contributed to the development of his homosexuality. In a letter to Kenneth Tynan, he wrote, "I used to have a terrific crush on the female members of my family, mother, sister, grandmother, and hated my father, a typical pattern for homosexuals."[2] That last phrase strikes a familiar Williams tone. Aspiring to the detachment of scientific observation, it amounts to a claim that the writer is knowledgeable and candid enough to be at once analyst and analysand.

Yet when we reread a number of Williams's plays, we might well question the nature of his "identification" with women. It will not be enough to say that Williams's women are like Williams himself—American, Southern, liminal, "mutilated," sexually compulsive, given to drugs and alcohol, mendacious, and so forth. Nor will it be enough to let pity speak for itself, to repeat with many critics that the typical Williams plot involves "the defeat or destruction of a highly pitiable protagonist."[3] The call on the audience to pity the female protagonist is very strong. But the quality of this pity is strained; it is not pity because of what we know but pity in spite of what we know. Nor is it enough to say simply that Williams's characters simultaneously excite both sympathy and antipathy.[4] They do, but they excite a range of other feelings as well. Those characters, especially his women, call on the viewer to regard a true pluralism of possibilities—which almost always includes ambivalence and repulsion. Female characters in Williams's drama are deliberately constructed to arouse these two feelings in the audience. This remarkably consistent technique suggests a great deal about the construction of a female character, as well as about "feminist" approaches to both drama and criticism.

Here I must pause to define what constitutes a worthy characterization of a woman. First, it does not seem necessary that she be written to a program—that is, that she have any required attributes at all. What does seem necessary is that there be a wide range of "play" in the character. I mean "play," for the viewer or reader, is the kind of ambivalent play that Mikhail Bakhtin sensed in the comedy of Rabelais and the novels of Dostoevski. The object of this play will be the feelings the written woman evokes. She should not be subject to complete consumption—that is, some of her attributes should escape paraphrase or easy reconciliation. To insist on such play is to insist that the written woman not be prejudicially reduced, oversimplified, or idealized. Such play can exist even in stereotypical characters; we find it, for example, in Falstaff. The few truly interesting female characters in canonical works (my list includes Emma Bovary, Anna Karenina, and the Duchess of Malfi) benefit from this play. Their polytonality, which forces viewers or readers to take a judgmental stance—or a stance from which they *presume* to judge without actually being able to do so—is part of what produces the particular effect of Emma or Anna, Blanche or Alma, or Catharine or Amanda on the reader or viewer.

This ambivalent play is evoked by many Williams women, especially in those he claimed he "liked" best. Williams often named either Blanche DuBois, Alma Winemuller, or Maggie the Cat as his "favorite" character. Of Alma, he said, "You see, Alma went through the same thing that I went through—from puritanical shackles to, well, complete profligacy."[5] Maggie the Cat was the subject of a celebrated debate between director Elia Kazan and Williams, partly over how the audience was to interpret her. As Williams told it, Kazan "felt that the character of Margaret, while he understood that I sympathized with her and liked her

"Weak and Divided People"

myself, should be, if possible, more clearly sympathetic to an audience."[6] It is significant that a character with Williams's avowed sympathy—he wrote that "Maggie the Cat [became] steadily more charming to me as I worked on her characterization" (168)—should be so ambiguous as to prompt the director to ask for a revision. Further, the so-called "Broadway Version" of act 3, although it gives Maggie the last word, is not successful in editing out the ambivalence. In this version, her last speech reads

> Oh you weak, beautiful people who give up with such grace. What you need is someone to take hold of you—gently, with love, and hand your life back to you, like something gold you let go of—and I can! I'm determined to do it—and nothing's more determined than a cat on a tin roof—is there? Is there, baby? (215)

It is startling to realize that this revision is supposed to make Maggie "more clearly sympathetic to an audience." The original version had ended with Maggie crying "I *do* love you, Brick, I *do!*" and Brick canceling her avowal with "Wouldn't it be funny if that was true?" In the revision, this dialogue is replaced by Maggie's lyric determination to mold someone else's life—"with love," certainly, but also with inheritance, "gold," in mind. Indeed, it has been claimed that once the audience knows her background, all her actions become ambiguous.[7] The revision of *Cat* emphasizes that Maggie will succeed through manipulation and mendacity; she will not transcend her conditions but rather will feed off them.

Williams was similarly vocal about his admiration of Leona Dawson of *Small Craft Warnings*: "She is the first really whole woman I have ever created and my first wholly trimphant character. She is truly devoted to life, however lonely."[8] Presumably, the modifiers "whole," "triumphant," and "devoted" are meant to be positive. Yet all of them belong to the explosively ambiguous Williams vocabulary. As a character, Leona is a descendant of Hanna Jelkes of *Night of the Iguana*. She is "whole" in the sense of being mentally sane and possessing moral integrity. She insists on "respect" and "responsibility," inveighs at "CORRUPTION," and at one point screams "LET ME SET YOU STRAIGHT ABOUT WHAT'S A LADY!"[9] When Doc, drunk and drugged, leaves to perform an illegal delivery, Leona tries to prevent him out of a well-founded fear for the lives of mother and baby. Events in the play leave no place for Leona, however. Her strong moral code, out of place at Monk's Place, clashes with her drunken soliloquies, penchant for violence, and petty neuroses. She is forced to leave her present lover, job, and circle of acquaintances, all because of Violet, a woman with no integrity or respect. Leona's emphatic physical and moral presence contrasts with Violet's lack of both. The "amorphous" Violet "has a sort of not-quite-with-it appearance" (12), and she speaks of her present life as "a temporary arrangement" (39). To drive home the impression of Violet's not quite being there, her rope-bound suitcase is on stage during the entire action. Yet it is Leona who is forced to leave and Violet who is allowed to stay. Leona packs up her trailer, and her plans for the future are "triumphant" only in a most equivocal way: "What I think I'll do is turn back to a faggot's moll when I haul up to Sausalito or San Francisco." In the same speech, the confidence she projects is stripped bare: "it scares me to be alone in my home on wheels built for two . . ." (71). Violet's incompletion earns her at least a temporary stay in someone's bedroom; Leona's completion earns her a nighttime escape into the fog on the highway.

Other women—we may call them tragic protagonists—advertise their own ambiguity. Alma of *Summer and Smoke* says of herself,

> Oh, I suppose I am sick, one of those weak and divided people who slip like shadows among you solid strong ones. But sometimes, out of necessity, we shadowy people take on a strength of our own.[10]

Alma and other of Williams's tragic women are in transition, from youth to age, from integrity to degradation, from illusion to disillusion, from sexual certainty to sexual confusion. Violet of *Small Craft Warnings* is described as "Amorphous. . . . Something more like a possibility than a completed creature" (12). Jim, Doc, Chance, Stanley Kowalski, Brick, Val, and other Williams's men are very often set or decided in some important way, with a corresponding loss of scope. The women, by virtue of their weakness and lack of closure, have greater mobility. Weakness and division, the propensity of having "two natures" or more, give the women a surplus of possibility, which makes them more productive, less exhaustible as characters.

In constructing a tragic woman, the literary artist faces a paradoxical task: to create a character with whom the audience finds something in common and yet to compel that audience eventually to take a critical distance from that character. Both sides of the task are essential. If the audience finds nothing recognizable in the character, no ground to share, then her fate is not likely to mean very much. Meaning also will be lost if the audience is not prompted to take a critical stance on the character—if the audience never feels the urge or the necessity to judge.[11]

As soon as we recite these requirements, we can see why it has been so difficult to construct the tragic woman. For reasons I will address later, both the misogynist/gynephobe writer and the advocate will have trouble achieving the ambivalence and ambiguity required for tragedy. In contrast, Williams's women are defeated or destroyed not by male dominance, patriarchy, or misogyny but by their own predilection for destruction—that is, by their own desires. Laura of *Glass Menagerie* is awkward partly because of her self-enforced virginity; Alma of *Summer and Smoke* chooses to take up with the young man at the end of the play; Lady of *Orpheus Descending* chooses both to have Val's baby and to throw herself in front of the bullet that kills her; Catharine of *Suddenly Last Summer* refuses to let go of Sebastian or her version of what happened to him. Male dominance is of little interest; Williams's plays feature some of the most inert male protagonists in drama. Instead, the emphasis falls on something literature needs: an authentic and authoritative depiction of female foolishness, limitations, and error. What worries so many critics about Shakespeare's treatment of Ophelia, Desdemona, and Lady Macbeth is here, too—indeed, much more consistently than in Shakespeare—the insistence that it is necessary, cathartic, and therefore healthy to suspect, hate, or despise certain women, especially those one "likes" best; to measure their failings, even when these failings are attractive; and to watch them destroy themselves by their own free wills, even when that freedom is an illusion.

A case in point is that of Catharine Holly of *Suddenly Last Summer*, whose "destruction or defeat" is predicted from the beginning of the play. The terms of Catharine's oppression are not dictated by men but by the rich, powerful Mrs. Venable, who tries to bribe Dr. Cukrowicz into giving Catharine a prefrontal lobotomy. Audience repulsion toward Mrs. Venable is carefully crafted: in the stage directions ("*She has light orange or pink hair*"[12]); in stage setting, a surreal jungle of viscid flora that is to resemble "*organs of a body, torn out*" (349); and in her attitude toward her inferiors, including Catharine: "Most people's lives—what are they but trails of debris, each day more debris, more debris, long, long trails of debris" (363). Thus Catharine has been denigrated before she even appears before the audience, and by an extremely unsympathetic character. Yet one of her first actions is to stub the burning end of her cigarette into Sister Felicity's hand—and suddenly Catharine shares in the repulsion.

That burst of senseless violence ignites a series of ambifying changes. The distinct (or indistinct) possibility of Catharine's madness is a standard appeal for audience ambivalence in that madness compels distance as well as pity: "How can you hate anybody and still be sane? You see, I still think I'm sane!" (396). Catharine and her relatives may share in Sebastian's inheritance if she agrees to stop telling her version of Sebastian's death. Her justified fear of Dr. Cukrowicz initially attracts pity, but later she all but cooperates with him, almost inviting the needle. Her account of her first sexual experience and its possible implication in her possible madness similarly arouse both pity and distance. The former arises from the disastrous social and emotional consequences of her encounter at "the Duelling Oaks at the end of Esplanade Street" (398) and the latter from the neurotic compulsiveness revealed in Catharine's character. She is given one of the play's most direct appeals for pity—"It's lonelier than death, if I've gone mad, it's lonelier than death" (404)—and the play's bleakest, most repulsive pronouncement: "Yes, we all use each other and that's what we think of as love, and not being able to use each other is what's—*hate*" (396).

Although near the end Catharine says that "I think the situation is—clear to me, now . . ." (390), the closing ellipses resonate with the opposite possibility. At the end of the play, the audience knows very little for certain about her or the truth of her account of Sebastian's death. Her truthfulness is questionable from the start because she tells her story under compulsion and under the influence of thiopentone, widely believed in 1958 to be a "truth drug." Dr. Cukrowicz's last line, which closes the play, adds to the ambiguity: "I think we ought at least to consider the possibility that the girl's story could be true" (423). This is a sentence divided against itself in an effort both to recognize and to deny the truth of Catharine's story. He has every reason to claim she has lied, yet he himself has administered the truth drug. Still, if he wants Mrs. Venable's bribe, he will refute the story and give himself grounds for ordering Catharine's lobotomy. His sentence is a timid attempt to buck the horror of Catharine's story and his own impulse to pity her. Yet it does suggest that Catharine may be lying—and she has reasons enough to do so. Her relatives can profit if she lies; she may wish to protect the sanctity of her relation with Sebastian. In the end, the truth of Catharine's story is only a "possibility." That possibility, the conflicting motives of all who surround Catharine, and her own conflicting motives add to the imminence of her destruction. She has sought her own undoing in a classical fashion, just as she had insisted on returning to the ballroom and ruining her reputation, had agreed to accompany Sebastian on his travels and then later had procured for him, and had followed him up the white hill of his destruction.

In short, the audience is not allowed to draw any conclusions about Catharine. In place of what the audience expects—a clear, unambiguous view of her there is instead a range of possibilities. To choose one way of interpreting her would be to deny the equal plausibility of other ways. As Williams knew, the standard bourgeois audience takes its first refuge in standard, bourgeois reactions. To deny such reactions or to mix them inextricably with more complex reactions forces members of the audience to play ambivalently with their repulsion. To use, hesitantly, a cant term, I might say that Williams has deconstructed his audience's response.

It is easy to see why ambiguity was dear to Williams. After all, ambiguity is a form of control. If an audience can consume a character completely, exhaust the possibilities of the character's meaning, the audience has exerted its power over the play, perhaps decisively so. If the playwright has designed the characters for the express purpose of being consumed, the playwright is playing to the audience, being a whore for the public. However, if inexhaustible characters and situations can be created, if there is always something that escapes paraphrase or immediate understanding, the play retains its power to arouse and perplex. (And, we might add, the playwright retains his or her power over the audience—the power of the originator, the privileged source.) Williams brooded constantly over such issues. His most spirited defense of ambiguity appeared in a note to *Cat on a Hot Tin Roof*:

> Some mystery should be left in the revelation of a character in a play, just as a great deal of mystery is always left in the revelation of a character in life, even in one's own character to himself. This does not absolve the playwright of his duty to observe and probe as clearly and deeply as he *legitimately* can: but it should steer him away from "pat" conclusions, facile definitions, which make a play just a play, not a snare for the truth of human experience.[13]

Williams's main plea here is for the superior verisimilitude of ambiguity, but, in his essay "The Timeless World of a Play," he drives toward what might have been his main motivation:

> Whether or not we admit it to ourselves, we are all haunted by a truly awful sense of impermanence. I have always had a particularly keen sense of this at New York cocktail parties, and perhaps that is why I drink the martinis almost as fast as I can snatch them from the tray. This sense is the febrile thing that hangs in the air. Horror of insincerity, of *not meaning*, overhangs these affairs like the cloud of cigarette smoke and the hectic chatter. This horror is the only thing, almost, that is left unsaid at such functions.[14]

It is as if the playwright took refuge in ambiguity—a surplus of meaning, a refusal to eliminate interpretations—out of this horror of not meaning. In a way, ambiguity is a hedge against annihilation.

Williams's achievement is one of the most notoriously uneven in western drama. But, as suggested above, his method of writing women has advantages over both traditional and feminist methods. Writers who fear or hate women cannot allow the object of hatred or fear to be ambiguous; it must be idealized, stylized, trivialized. The written women must be made consumable, located on a pedestal, immobilized. Advocacy poses other obstacles. Women that undergo a programmatic fate cannot be tragic because their tragedy is largely external to the women themselves—theirs is supposed to be every woman's tragedy, being the inevitable effect of the male quest for dominance. The advocate writer thus will be ill-equipped to portray the truly ambiguous female because a clear brief must be carried for the plaintiff. (Advocacy has made it difficult to make one's women culpable.) A well-ground axe cuts too sharp, and the necessary tension between sympathy and judgment is lost. Both the misogynist writer and the advocate will have reasons for eliminating competing ways of reading the written woman. Neither kind of writer will allow the written woman to escape—and neither one wants that woman to escape the reader either. But, as seen above, Williams, perhaps out of his "horror of not meaning," seeks to place his women beyond reduction, to make sure they escape.

So we are driven to other possibilities, most of which carry us beyond standard questions of gender expectation. One early criticism was that Williams's women actually lost "universality" because their stories were too unique, not applicable to all humanity because they were individual case histories.[15] But Williams's treatment of women does not admit of anything else. Of course one's women will refer to other women and other men, just as women do in the world outside the theater. But questions of "gender expectations" verge on the specious and banal because individual women differ so widely in their behaviors. What set of expectations could possibly hold for Alexandra del Lago, Blanche Dubois, Leona, Catharine, and Serafina? In the end, little of much importance. (What set of gender expectations would hold for Timon, Othello, Hamlet, and Macbeth?) Williams's women find themselves in circumstances that demand that they take on as many roles—psychological, sexual, and class—as they need to achieve the failure they desire. Thus, rereading Williams exposes the current hunt for such expectations as a reverse form of prejudice, a project of construction doomed by its own assumptions. Construction of the female must be largely idiographic—that is, the individual character must be built up on her own, out of continuities and disruptions specific to her. It is of women as Williams writes of drama: "By a sort of legerdemain, events are made to remain *events*, rather than being reduced so quickly to being mere *occurrences*."[16] Women should be represented as events, as special, unrepeatable happenings in time; they are not replicas or occurrences of any other events. Otherwise, the woman we write will be the woman we wish to write, and, worse, the woman that everyone else has always written.

Notes

1. Nancy M. Tischler, "A Gallery of Witches," in *Tennessee Williams: A Tribute*, ed. Jac Tharpe (Jackson: University Press of Mississippi, 1977), pp. 502–7.

2. Tennessee Williams, letter to Kenneth Tynan, in *Tennessee Williams' Letters to Donald Windham 1940–1965*, ed. Donald Windham (New York: Holt, Rinehart and Winston, 1977), pp. 301–2.

3. Norman J. Fedder, "Tennessee Williams' Dramatic Technique," in *Tennessee Williams: A Tribute*, ed. Jac Tharpe (Jackson: University Press of Mississippi, 1977), p. 798.

4. See, for example, Robert Brustein, "America's New Culture Hero," *Commentary* 25 (February 1958): 123–25, and the discussions of Williams in Eric Bentley, *The Dramatic Event: An American Chronicle* (New York: Horizon Press, 1954). Brustein's influential article was one of the earliest articulations of ambiguity in Williams, although Brustein is concerned with a single male character, Stanley Kowalski.

5. Jim Gaines, "A Talk about Life and Style with Tennessee Williams" [1972], in *Conversations with Tennessee Williams*, ed. Albert J. Devlin (Jackson: University Press of Mississippi, 1986), p. 216.

6. Tennessee Williams, "Note of Explanation," in *The Theatre of Tennessee Williams*, vol. 3 (New York: New Directions, 1971), p. 168. Subsequent references to Williams's "Note" and to *Cat on a Hot Tin Roof* are cited parenthetically by page number within the text.

7. Jeanne M. McGlinn, "Tennessee Williams' Women: Illusion and Reality,

Sexuality and Love," in *Tennessee Williams: a Tribute*, ed. Jac Tharpe (Jackson: University Press of Mississippi, 1977), p. 518.

8. Gaines, "A Talk about Life and Style," p. 216.

9. Tennessee Williams, *Small Craft Warnings* (New York: New Directions, 1972), p. 20. Subsequent references are cited parenthetically by page number within the text.

10. Tennessee Williams, *Summer and Smoke*, in *The Theatre of Tennessee Williams*, vol. 2 (New York: New Directions, 1971), pp. 244–45.

11. Williams took seriously the Aristotelian requirements for tragedy. His essay "The Timeless World of a Play" [1951], in *Where I Live: Selected Essays*, ed. Christine R. Day and Bob Woods (New York: New Directions, 1978), is remarkable in its emphasis on the therapeutic nature of catharsis:

> Yet plays in the tragic tradition offer us a view of certain moral values in violent juxtaposition. Because we do not participate, except as spectators, we can view them clearly. . . . Our hearts are wrung with recognition and pity, so that the dusky shell of the auditorium where we are gathered anonymously together is flooded with an almost liquid warmth of unchecked human sympathies, relieved of self-consciousness, allowed to function. . . . (53)

12. Tennessee Williams, *Suddenly Last Summer*, in *The Theatre of Tennessee Williams*, vol. 3 (New York: New Directions, 1971), pp. 349–50. Subsequent references are cited parenthetically by page number within the text.

13. Tennessee Williams, "Critic Says 'Evasion,' Writer Says 'Mystery'" [1955], in *Where I Live: Selected Essays*, ed. Christine R. Day and Bob Woods (New York: New Directions, 1978), p. 72.

14. Williams, "The Timeless World of a Play," pp. 51–52.

15. John Gassner, *Dramatic Soundings* (New York: Crown, 1968), p. 327.

16. Williams, "The Timeless World of a Play," p. 52.

PART 4
EDWARD ALBEE

WHAT'S NEW AT THE ZOO?
Rereading Edward Albee's American Dream(s) and Nightmares

Mickey Pearlman

1

To reread Edward Albee's one-act play *The Zoo Story* (1958) is to reexperience the caustic, cryptic vision of an angry playwright thirty years after the play was performed (1959), in German, in Berlin.

The Zoo Story is a two-character dialogue of male strangers, both locked in rigidly defined "male" roles, with the resonately Christian names of Jerry (Jeremiah?) and Peter, whose chance encounter on a bench in Central Park provokes a clash of dichotomous visions of power, space, and society. Jerry is an antagonizing but isolated vagrant, whose life has been, in his opinion, short-circuited, if not exploded, by women. He lives in a West Side rooming house populated by "a colored queen" in a Japanese kimono, "who always keeps his door open ... when he's plucking his eyebrows,"[1] a Puerto Rican family in "the two front rooms" (22), a "lady ... on the third floor [who] ... cries all the time," and a landlady who is a "fat, ugly, mean, stupid, unwashed, misanthropic, cheap, drunken bag of garbage" (27). He is a man out of society and out of control. Peter is Albee's archetypal insider, insulated but vacuous, who "wears tweeds, smokes a pipe, carries horn-rimmed glasses" (11), and lives in the East Seventies with "one wife, two daughters, two cats and two parakeets" (23), a fifties man who predates the culture clashes and role definitions of the sixties.

The women in this play appear only through the twisted memories of Jerry or the innocent reflections of Peter. All stereotypical characterizations of women, however, do appear, and, filtered largely through the mixed-up memories of Jerry, they emerge full force, tumbling into the hostile atmosphere of Albee's anti-female universe. That has been described as the product of a homosexual tirade, an American absurdist tableau, or a fragmented conversation about the inability of humans to communicate, locked as they are in racial, social, economic, and gender no-exit zones. As in Albee's later plays, these women are powerful and pathetic, damaging or deranged, vulgar and vicious, impinging on the spaces of men with damaging regularity.

Jerry speaks first about his now dead "good old Mom" (23) who "embarked on an adulterous turn of our southern states," the anti-earth mother as slut and alcoholic, whose "most constant companion . . . among others, among many others . . . was a Mr. Barleycorn" (24). She is the prototypical Albee female—a symbol of betrayal, lust, and debasement—always the victimizer even when she seems helpless. The characterization is made more vicious and inexorable by its implied contrast to the usual explication of mother figure as dependable, sacrificing saint, a role usually created and then derogated by male writers. The strong implication is that she is responsible for Jerry's preoccupation with whores, the "pretty little ladies" whom he never sees "more than once" since he's "never been able to have sex with, or, how is it put? . . . make love to anybody more than once." And, he adds, "puberty was late . . . I was a h-o-m-o-s-e-x-u-a-l- . . . queer, queer, queer" for "eleven days . . . with the park superintendent's son" (25). Mother love, in American fiction and drama frequently the source of emotionally crippled and childish or brutal heroes, is, in its absence, the genesis of a character similarly crippled who deserts his prostitutes as his mother deserted him. American literature is littered with the corpses of men who have been smothered by affection; here we are presented with the unmothered vision. "Good Old Mom" has a sister "who was given neither to sin nor the consolation of the bottle," who "did all things dourly: sleeping, eating, working, praying. She dropped dead on the stairs to her apartment . . . on the afternoon of my high school graduation. A terribly middle-European joke . . ." (24) The untainted saint who never strays replaces the tainted sinner who always strays, but she also betrays Jerry by her emotional absence and inconvenient death. She is in attendance, but absent, and proves to be a disappointing mother figure who disappears in a dramatic and arbitrary moment, as did "Good Old Mom." The aunt is Albee's stereotypical version of the enervated, long-suffering woman as silent sufferer whose most lasting legacy is an unloved and empty male victim who feels betrayed, in different ways, by her sacrificial approach to reality.

And Jerry is annoyed by her, and hostile to her memory, because her role as sacrificer and saint figure is part of his emotional powerlessness and his sense of social impotence. "Good Old Mom" and her sister are followed by the previously mentioned "lady living on the third floor, in the front." Her crying is "muffled, but . . . very determined. Very determined indeed" (27), an unnamed Greek chorus of one, ostensibly helpless, because her response to life is unexplained weeping. She evokes in the reader neither pity nor pathos, nor is Jerry interested in finding out the source of her pain. In fact, her helplessness annoys him and reminds him of his own pain. But she serves as direct contrast to Jerry's central antagonist, the landlady (and her dog), "the gatekeeper[s]" (27) of rooming house as Hell, whose trademark is vulgarity and who does not conveniently keep her pain behind closed doors. Jerry tells Peter that after "she's had her mid-afternoon pint of lemon-flavored gin she always stops me in the hall . . . presses her disgusting body up against me to keep me in a corner . . . The smell of her body and her breath . . . you can't imagine it." The landlady is a comic figure who lusts not only after Jerry but also after recognition, contact, and acceptance. In her daily, self-induced stupor, she cannot distinguish between reality and illusion. Jerry says that he has "found a way to keep her off. When . . . she presses herself to my body and mumbles about her room and how I should come there, I merely say: but, Love; wasn't yesterday enough for you, and the day before? . . . a simple-minded smile begins to form on her unthinkable face, and she giggles and groans as she thinks about yesterday and the day before; as she believes and relives what never happened. Then, she motions to that black monster of a dog she has, and she goes back to her room. And I am safe until our next meeting" (28). The landlady is one of Albee's most unattractive women (she has plenty of competition for this dubious honor), and it is difficult to sympathize with her in a culture in which we are socialized to detest the licentious, out-of-control female. Actually, her out-of-control behavior is less damaging than Jerry's, but it is perceived as more detestable because it emanates from a woman.

When Jerry mixes rat poison into the hamburgers with which he tries secretly and unsuccessfully to neutralize the dog's power over him and to increase his power over the dog, the landlady turns from obnoxious aggressor to a "sniveling" antagonist who begs Jerry to "pray for the animal" (33). The dog, which Jerry calls "malevolence with an erection" (32), eventually recovers its former malicious state, having learned nothing about power. The landlady "recovered her thirst, in no way altered by the bow-wow's deliverance" (33). The dog returns to his previously vicious state, the landlady to her bottle, and Jerry to his nether-nether world where "neither kindness nor cruelty by themselves, independent of each other, creates any effect beyond themselves . . . the two combined . . . are the teaching emotion. And what is gained is loss" (35–36).

The stereotypical woman as materialist and manipulator surfaces in Jerry's allusions to Peter's wife. She is unnamed, but in Jerry's eyes she is both powerful and incomplete. ". . . you're not going to have any more kids, are you?" says Jerry. "Is it your wife?" "That's none of your business!" Peter replies in fury, but adds: "Well, you're right. We'll have no more children" (16). She is another woman who has failed, having produced two daughters but no sons. Peter points out that this is determined genetically, but he absorbs Jerry's accusatory point of view, although he knows that, scientifically, it is a ridiculous charge. They do have two cats. "But, that can't be your idea. No, sir. Your wife and daughters? (*Peter nods his head*)" (18).

Peter's wife is in charge of one of the three demarcated spaces, or zoos, that Albee creates. She serves as zookeeper of the East Side apartment, a civilized institution of children, family, and jobs that marks the parameter of Peter's world. The landlady guards the gates of one rooming house-as-zoo that symbolizes the lonely, entrapping spaces of the societally displaced, most of whom are females or male homosexuals. The park becomes a symbolic microcosm of society as zoo, where dissimilarly caged animals, including the human variety, exist guardedly in an antagonistic state. All space delineations are limited and defined—the East Side apartment, the West Side rooming house, and the park bench over which the final, fatal fight occurs. The bench represents both safety and freedom to Peter; it is his space away from space. As he says, ". . . I see no reason why I should give up this bench. I sit on this bench almost every Sunday afternoon, in good weather. It's secluded here; there's never anyone sitting here, so I have it all to myself." For Jerry, the bench is initially an object of power and control ("Get off this bench, Peter; I want it") (41), a concrete symbol of his attempt to manipulate and dominate Peter and to become the chief zookeeper of the park as society. He sees the bench as part of his effort to make contact, to communicate, to be acknowledged at any cost. His efforts to jar Peter into acknowledging him and the encounters over the bench are replicated in his encounters with the dog. The setting changes—Jerry in the rooming house, the zoo, the park—but the common denominator of all three encounters is violence and encoded brutality. He is fierce and friendless, but there is something here that feminists who examine the silent loneliness of brutalized women will recognize—the desperate and pathetic need to be heard and to have that pain assuaged. How Jerry forces Peter to listen is part of what Emory Lewis called a "masochistic-sadistic interplay . . . [which reflects] a murky, homosexual milieu,"[2] with Jerry as the male partner and Peter playing the part of diffident, nonaggressive female, moving at Jerry's insistence into a smaller, more limited space (the end of the bench). Then he is trapped, defenseless, furious, and helpless. He says: ". . . I'm a responsible person, and I'm a GROWNUP. This is my bench, and you have no right to take it away from me" (45). Similarly, the landlady's dog has been appropriating the space of the hallway, making Jerry into a defenseless, furious, and helpless victim.

The play ends as Jerry impales himself on his own knife that Peter is holding "with a firm arm, but far in front of him, not to attack, but to defend" (47), and with Jerry's words: "Peter . . . Peter? . . . Peter . . . thank you. I came unto you (*He laughs, so faintly*) and you have comforted me. Dear Peter," and his final assurances to Peter that "you're not really a vegetable . . . you're an animal" (48, 49). These words have evocative New Testament and sexual overtones intertwined. The new designation was won apparently through Peter's inadvertent involvement with violence. What Jerry is saying is that Peter is no longer acting like a woman—at least an Albee woman—who deserts ship (bench), drops dead, silently weeps, or lives in a hermetic or fantasy world.

This play has often been said to be about alienation and the noncommunication that signifies the mechanized, urbanized, supposedly civilized western world. But in a feminist rereading, it is also an American absurdist work that, in its anger, displays all the usual stereotypical visions of women and enlarges the endless canon of plays, stories, and novels that agonize over the predicaments of men by further diminishing the emotional, sexual, and spiritual needs of women.

2

The American Dream, first performed in 1961, is a showcase for the four characters who also appear in *The Sandbox* (1960), a fourteen-minute sketch. Both plays are "an examination of the American Scene, an attack on the substitution of artificial for real values in our society, a condemnation of complacency, cruelty, emasculation and vacuity; it is a stand against the fiction that everything in this slipping land of ours is peachy-keen" (53).

Twenty-eight years later, in 1989, American society is still not "peachy-keen," having endured, if not improved, through decades of Vietnam scar tissue, a generation of yuppies, and thirty years of ardent consumerism. America as marketplace has recently been elevated to an art form by eight years of a Washington glitzkrieg defined more by style than substance. Because it is American society in the fifties that Albee marks as "vapid, barren, and sterile . . . absurd and meaningless,"[3] *The American Dream* is both current and dated. For example, Albee would undoubtedly find plenty of material for act 2 in the hostile takeovers, Love Canals, AIDS epidemic, bridges falling down across America, insider trading scams, and drug-infested streets of the eighties to make the point again that noncommunication, artificiality, and false values are corruptive and destructive. But almost thirty years later, in a feminist rereading, it is doubtful that any audience will so blithely accept Mommy, Mrs. Barker, and Grandma, an odious triumvirate, as the matriarchal Murder, Inc. of the family and its natural legacy, society.

Mommy, who is emasculating, efficient ("I can get satisfaction, but you can't" [62]) and cruel, is Albee's bad (American) dream, reducing Daddy, with snarls and sarcasm, to pathetic impotence. She is invested by Albee with tremendous power; Daddy is divested of energy and masculinity. Daddy is vague, respectful, and boring ("I *am* paying attention, Mommy" [58]), like an overdisciplined child: rich but not powerful, an unlikely specimen in the U.S.A., where money and options are natural soulmates. He has been reduced by Mommy to the role of supplicant and cipher. As Mommy announces blatantly, "I have a right to live off of you because I married you, and because I used to let you get on top of me and bump your uglies; and I have a right to all your money when you die." "And aren't you lucky all I brought with me was Grandma. A lot of women I know would have brought their whole families to live off you. All I brought was Grandma" (67). Daddy's role now is to put up with "it" and to shut up *about* it.

The problem with Mommy as female victimizer figure for the eighties is that few women in the audience want or expect to earn a gold Bloomingdale's charge card for thirty years of sexual service, and there are happily few, if any, men who would make this unspeakable, if unspoken, contract. In the eighties, Mommy's exaggerated power and manipulative skills would not be wasted on an unattractive wimp like Daddy but would most probably find their natural outlet on the playing fields of Wall Street, in board rooms of America, or in Silicon Valleys coast to coast. Woman as bloodsucking vampire figure is passé, although mothers, wives, and matriarchs are still suspect.

Mrs. Barker, a hermaphroditic screamer, "the chairman [sic] of your woman's club" (78), is presented as an amoral pimpette who delivers "bumbles." (". . . I'm such a busy girl, with this committee and that committee, and the Responsible Citizens Activities I indulge in" [90]. The "bumbles," i.e., male babies, represent innocence and love and are delivered by her from the "Bye-Bye Adoption Service" to the Mommys and Daddys of America. Mrs. Barker is deeply committed, of course, like Mommy, to the unimportant non-issues—like the color of her hat. She is a veritable chargé d'affaires of the triviality and insensitivity of women à la Albee. ("What an unattractive apartment you have!" [77], etc.) To quote Mommy, "She's a dreadful woman, you don't know her; she has dreadful taste, two dreadful children, a dreadful house, and an absolutely adorable husband who sits in a wheel chair all the time . . . She's just a dreadful woman, but she *is* chairman of our woman's club, so naturally I'm terribly fond of her" (60).

Grandma, who is "feeble-headed" and "cries every time she goes to the johnny as it is" (62), has spent the last twenty years of widowhood as an unpaid live-in servant to Mommy and Daddy. She is buried alive in *The Sandbox* and is immured in a sea of boxes in *The American Dream*. Grandma is a pitiful figure. ("Old people are very good at listening; old people don't like to talk; old people have colitis and lavender perfume.") She is waiting for the arrival of the imaginary "van people" (72) for a journey to an unnamed oblivion, the natural repository of the aged in Albee's U.S.A. They are expendable, dispensable, and disposable. As she says, "Old people aren't dry enough, I suppose. My sacks are empty, the fluid in my eyeballs is all caked on the inside edges, my spine is made of sugar candy, I breathe ice . . . old people are gnarled and sagged and twisted into the shape of a complaint" (82–83). Her life, which consists of "some old letters, a couple of regrets . . . Pekinese . . . blind at that . . . the television . . . my Sunday teeth . . . eighty-six years of living . . ." (120), is packed in boxes in the smaller, confined spaces almost always associated with women in American literature, and the spaces get smaller and more confining as her victimization nears completion.

The three women, therefore, epitomize the worst stereotypes of American females—Mommy is the evil, all-powerful emasculator; Mrs. Barker is the déclassé, intellectually vacant instigator; and Grandma is the pathetic, ill-used, and nameless saint figure—Albee's offering of a treacherous trinity of female fates fatale.

The two men, of course, are victims, and more importantly they are innocents. ("You're the American Dream, that's what you are" [108].) They are not party to the materialism and tawdriness that Albee is trying correctly to deride. Daddy's worst sin is that he has turned into an incompetent vegetable who "has tubes now, where he used to have tracts" (90). This is hardly a surprising turn of events in an Albee Mommy-world dominated by an egregious stereotype, the Rambo of domesticity gone wrong. The Young Man, who represents what Albee believes America most adores—youth, beauty, and a modicum of brainpower—who will "do almost anything for money" (109), recalls the sensory potential lost in the same way that a money-maddened, commercialized society devalues whatever cannot be arbitraged or sold short. The "bumble," we are told, had its eyes gouged metaphorically right out of its head; it cried its heart out, its eyes, heart, tongue, and hands were sacrificed, but "first, they cut off its you-know-what" (100), and "it finally up and died" (101). The Young Man is the twin of his castrated, blind, and adopted brother, the empty American ideal, the "bumble of joy" provided by Mrs. Barker. "I no longer," he says, "have the capacity to feel anything. I have no emotions. I have been drained, torn asunder . . . disemboweled . . . I am incomplete . . . I can feel nothing . . . And it will always be thus" (115).

The point is that there is no mattress beneath the American dream, and the sleeper is caught in an unending nightmare of vulgarity and crassness. For many theatergoers, that part of Albee's vision may still ring true. His implicit idea, however, is that the malignancies ("I do wish I weren't surrounded by women . . ." [86]) that pervade the American experience stem from the confused, craven, or contemptible influence of women. Women as enemies of the Dream is merely empty bombast, an outdated, outlandish vision of an angry young man of the sixties. In a feminist rereading, Mommy, Grandma, and Mrs. Barker seem to be only overblown cartoon characters who predate what has been learned in the last twenty-eight years about the victimization of women and the pain of men. The American Dream is only a familiar, if painful, artifact of the historically long-lived vision of women as the progenitors and perpetuators of the end of Paradise and the decimators and destroyers of the potentially utopian ideal.

Notes

1. Edward Albee, The Zoo Story, p. 22. Quotations from The American Dream and The Zoo Story are from Edward Albee, The American Dream and The Zoo Story (New York: New American Library, 1963). Subsequent references are cited parenthetically by page number within the text.

2. Emory Lewis, quoted in Instructor's Manual, Anthology of American Literature, ed. George McMichael (New York: Macmillan Publishing, 1986), p. 362.

3. Laurence Perrine, ed., Instructor's Manual, Literature: Structure, Sound, and Sense (New York: Harcourt Brace Jovanovich, 1983), p. 302.

MAGNIFIED AND SANCTIFIED
Tiny Alice Reconsidered

Naomi Conn Liebler

Critical efforts to comprehend *Tiny Alice* usually result in a shoulder-shrugging acquiescence to the play's complexity that would have it be a dramatic representation of all that troubled American (and European) audiences two decades ago. The play, said the critics, was about our relation to God or the lack thereof,[1] a modernized mystery/morality play concerning the temptations of world, flesh, and devil,[2] a "grand reunion fantasy" about family life,[3] about "man's tragic struggle in an equivocal and enigmatic universe,"[4] "about the triumph of a strong woman over a weak man," and "a homosexual day-dream,"[5] about all the spiritual crises of the first two-thirds of the twentieth century. Alternatively, it was a mean-spirited author's trick, a theatrical rip-off of concerns properly left to the psychiatrist's office or the university's department of philosophy. It was all manner of things; most of all, it was or became a Rorschach test for the critics themselves. Albee was not giving anything away outside of the theater. A review today of the assessments of *Tiny Alice* is like a trip down memory lane to visit and perhaps to smile at those issues we once considered *angst*-worthy.

Current readers, therefore, should not be surprised to note that the nature of Alice, represented but not necessarily embodied in Miss Alice, causes the greatest *angst* of all—even more than the inner/outer realities of the castle library, Julian's past and present, the societal twin pillars of the law and church figured by Lawyer and Cardinal, the mouse in the model, and all the other puzzling trademarks of this tricky play. Whatever Alice is—God, devil, the ineffable pressures of modern life—she is female, and for followers of Albee's drama, she is particularly interesting. She may be a killer, but she is not the castrator that Mommy (*The American Dream*), Nurse (*The Death of Bessie Smith*), and Martha and Honey (*Who's Afraid of Virginia Woolf?*) are. Her function is

Magnified and Sanctified

close, although not identical, to that of Albee's other women, invisible or nearly invisible in the first three plays: Peter's wife and the ugly, isolated landlady in Jerry's narrative (*The Zoo Story*); Grandma (*The American Dream*); the spirit of Bessie Smith, who, like Alice, never appears in her own play. In these antecedent works, Albee was moving toward the explosive expression that became Tiny Alice. The castrators got most of the critics' attention: a misogynist representation was something they understood and readily identified. But what could be made of the unseen woman who moves but is not herself moved, who exerts a force that "temp—test[s]," in Julian's words,[6] but cannot be encompassed?

Alice's invisibility, like that of Mrs. Peter, the Landlady, and Bessie Smith, forces a response. Our reactions to the women who are not present depend entirely on what the audience is told about them, and we are told mostly by male characters who have their own failures to cope with. Because we cannot know Alice—and that is the point of both her invisibility and her surrogate's representation—we can only react to and through what Julian needs her to be. He, the deliberate martyr, defines his needs clearly to Lawyer, Butler, Cardinal, Miss Alice, and the audience by narrating his past, dreams, fantasies, and own uncertainty. Such eager victims, like Kafka's Joseph K., lead their executioners to the killing place, all the while protesting that they are victims. Passive aggression is aggression nonetheless.

It is easy to see and perhaps to identify with Julian's inability to assume responsibility for his life up to and including the moments presented in the play. Like Peter, Daddy, and George, he meant well, tried to cooperate, wanted to be of service to others, whether or not they needed serving: "I would serve! (*Clenches his fist*) I would serve, and damn anyone or anything that stood in my way. I would shout my humility from the roof and break whtever rules impeded my headlong rush toward obedience. . . . I was impatient with God's agents, and with God, too, I see it now. . . . And I was blind to my pride, and intolerant of any who did not see me as the humblest of men" (119). Julian confesses in act 2, scene 3, to the sin of pride committed in the past, as if he were now beyond such transgressions. Miss Alice, who listens to this, cuts through the "set paragraph" with "Pride still," but Julian cannot see his structured self-effacement as irresponsible. We see it, however, because a moment before he hurls this confession" at Miss Alice, he attacks her with a different kind of innocence:

Julian. What's being *done* to me. Am I . . . am I being temp—tested in some fashion?
Miss Alice. . . . Tempted?
Julian. Tested in some fashion?
Miss Alice. TEMPTED?
Julian. BOTH! Tested! What! My . . . my sincerity, my . . . my other cheek? You have allowed that . . . that *man*, your . . . lover, to . . . ridicule me. You have *permi*tted it.
Miss Alice. I? Permit?
Julian. You have allowed him to abuse me, my position, his, the Church; you have tolerated it, and *smiled*. (116–17)

Julian thinks that martyrdom will have the design he gave it in the dream of sacrifice he had as a little boy, the dream about the Christian and the lion that he tells to Miss Alice as act 2 closes. As this act closes, Miss Alice enfolds him in the wings of her outstretched gown and invites him to marry Alice. The narrated dream blends into the physical enfolding in a moment of intense religious, sexual, and mystical union. Miss Alice's language is very clear: it is Alice, not Miss, who will marry Julian, but Julian of course does not hear the difference and cannot understand beyond what his rapture tells him. In case we also fail to get the crucial distinction, it is analyzed by Lawyer in the beginning of the next act: "Give me *any* person . . . a martyr, if you wish . . . a saint . . . He'll take what he gets for . . . what he wishes it to be. AH, it is what I have always wanted, he'll say, looking terror and betrayal straight in the eye. Why not: face the inevitable and call it what you have always wanted. How to come out on top, going under" (148). Julian's martyrdom must not be as mundane as ridicule or the abuse of position; it must have the romance of the Roman arena. Julian insists upon that; perhaps all deliberate martyrs do. But Albee makes it clear that we do not get to choose, that choice itself is an illusion born of arrogance. To Butler's question, "When you're locked in the attic, Julian, in the attic closet, in the dark, do you care who comes?" he answers, "No. But . . ." (139). "But" is the operative word. Julian wants to retain the privilege and power of choice, an option the function of service or martyrdom by definition precludes. "Dear Julian," says Lawyer, as the truth of service begins to unfold:

we all serve, do we not? Each of us his own priesthood; publicly, some, others . . . within only; but we all do—. . . . Predestination, fate, the will of God, accident . . . All swirled up in it, no matter what the name. And being man, we have invented choice, and have,

Magnified and Sanctified

indeed, gone further, and have catalogued the underpinnings of choice. But we do not know. Anything. End prologue. (160)

Having invented choice, we then demand it: choice becomes an inalienable right, whether it backfires or temporarily satisfies. Miss Alice attempts to explain it: "Julian, I have tried to be . . . her. No; I have tried to be . . . what I thought she might, what might make you happy, what you might use, as a . . . what? . . . We must . . . represent, draw pictures, reduce or enlarge to . . . to what we can understand" (161). In the end, "There is no choice here, Julian" (168); just before he shoots Julian, Lawyer charges Cardinal: "Don't you teach your people anything? Do you let them improvise? *Make their Gods? Make them as they see them?* . . . [To Julian] Resign yourself to the mysteries . . ." (169). As he dies, Julian gradually comes to accept the God Alice, manifested in a shadow spreading across the stage and a heartbeat that fills the whole theater. His acceptance is slow, as painfully slow as the four-and-a-half pages of monologue that end the play, and, in fact, his reluctance or inability to acknowledge God as Alice is sustained up to the moment of his death. Until then, Julian clings to the traditional distinction between God—the masculine "Lord"—and Alice: "How long wilt thou forget me, O Lord? . . . Consider and hear me, O Lord, my God . . ." (189). The masculine "Lord" remains Julian's choice of apostrophe up to the play's last line: "The bridegroom waits for thee, my Alice . . . is thine. O Lord, my God, I have awaited thee, have served thee in thy . . . ALICE? . . . ALICE? . . . GOD? . . . I accept thee, Alice, for thou art come to me. God, Alice . . . I accept thy will" (190).

Julian's invocation of and appeal to God at the moment of his death, which also happens to be the end of the play, is not new to Albee's audiences. *The Zoo Story* ends the same way, in a pair of "Oh my God"s uttered, respectively, by Peter who has run offstage and by Jerry as he dies. What has changed between 1958 and 1964 in Albee's vision is how his characters use such invocations. In the earlier play, the phrase expresses Peter's gut-wrenching horror at what he has done and what he has become: a killer, "an animal, too"; Jerry's *"combination of scornful mimicry and supplication"*[7] reminds the audience of his previous identification of God as "A COLORED QUEEN WHO WEARS A KIMONO AND PLUCKS HIS EYEBROWS, WHO IS A WOMAN WHO CRIES WITH DETERMINATION BEHIND HER CLOSED DOOR . . . who, I'm told, turned his back on the whole thing some time ago" (35). The scornful mimicry is not of God but of what we decide and then insist God is, and the supplication is to whatever God is, in case God is still listening. By the time Albee writes Julian's ending, God is Alice: the horror, scorn, and mimicry are gone; the supplication to Whatever remains. And Whatever has become female, very much present in the shadow and heartbeat and still acceptable, embraceable, only at the moment of the protagonist's death. Until that moment, Albee's characters think they have the power to make choices and to make their choices into truth. *The American Dream*'s ending puts the same point a little differently when Grandma closes the play with "Well, I guess that just about wraps it up. I mean, for better or worse, this is a comedy, and I don't think we'd better go any further. . . . So, let's leave things as they are right now . . . while everybody's happy . . . while everybody's got what he wants . . . or everybody's got what he thinks he wants. Good night, dears" (127). Comedies can end that way: Grandma's conspiratorial interruption makes it clear that the author has chosen only for the moment to give "everybody . . . what he thinks he wants"; neither life nor the rest of Albee's drama does that.

Julian wants God, wants Miss Alice, wants to be of service, wants martyrdom—and, like most people, he hasn't the slightest understanding of what those desires involve, what their fulfillment costs. He has an idea of what he means when he admits to them, but it's his idea, and it does not compel God, Alice, or service to be as he thinks they are. So Albee puts the question to his audience: what if we got what we wanted, or what we said we wanted, and it turned out to be something other than what we specified in our design? Does it matter who comes to open the attic closet door? What if the power, the mystery, the great algebraic variable X looks like what men are accustomed to mastering? If Julian has been mistaken in identifying what he would serve, does that void the contract to serve? Does it matter if God is a woman or a colored queen?

Much has been written about the psychological underpinnings of *Tiny Alice*, notably in regard to its exposure of Julian's repressed unconscious. In "Staging the Unconscious: Edward Albee's *Tiny Alice*," Mary Castiglie Anderson explores the connection between Julian's conscious quest for martyrdom and his repressed sexuality. In this essay, she notes almost casually that "Albee is hardly offering us any profound insight when he suggests that religious fanaticism is often based upon sexual repression. If his play sought only to uncover Julian as a fraud at the end, after having uncovered institutional religion as a fraud right from the start, *Tiny Alice* would simply be a social statement against all the spiritual trappings, even the most strenuous, with which we surround ourselves. There is certainly that statement made in the play, but it is not the central issue [because] . . . Julian is far too attractive a character. . . . He is sincerely confused in regard to this area of his life, but in other respects he is open, intelligent, flexible, genuinely simple, and, unlike his Cardinal, without conscious ulterior motives."[8]

One could argue about Julian's openness that one so out of touch with his own real needs is not in a position to be genuinely open and certainly that he is anything but simple; nevertheless, it is his very "attractiveness" that makes Albee's point. Because we are inclined to like Julian, even to identify with his most appealing personal characteristics, as audiences and readers tend to do, we cannot dismiss his surrogate relation to us, and his specific role in regard to the church is analogous to the ones we have, individually and universally, with whatever structures we attach our lives to for definition and support. Although the play is not "simply . . . a social statement against all the spiritual trappings," it is nonetheless a strong and complex statement about trappings, both accoutrements and harnesses, with which we do surround ourselves without troubling to be rigorously honest about the extent to which we "improvise. *Make* [our] Gods. *Make* them as [we] *see* them."

Anderson's essay approaches the play from the perspective of Jungian psychoanalytic criticism, and it is a very good, very convincing exemplar of that perspective. As such, however, it also enters the critical cul de sac to which such analyses tend. "It must be made very clear," she writes, "that on one level Lawyer, Miss Alice, and Butler function as full, three-dimensional characters with independent motivations and psychologies. But on another level, they are projections of Julian's mind. It is because of this dual function that she assigns to them in the first place, they would not be confusing at all, and perhaps in that case she might be able to accommodate Cardinal, missing from the list of "projections," in the lineup. A further problem with such psychoanalytic approaches is that they take the play or the character beyond the plot into a future it never has. Anderson makes the point that, when Julian enters Miss Alice's enfolding embrace at the end of act 2, the moment "is a point of initiation for Julian, necessitating the loss of innocence . . . he undergoes a symbolic death and an entrance into experience resulting in the sacrifice of rigidly idealistic (and, by implication, immature) beliefs. Thus, as the hero, Julian experiences a kind of initial rebirth into a more autonomous individualism, enabling him to continue on his quest to penetrate the mysteries of life and death."[10] But Julian never becomes that autonomous individual, never penetrates the mysteries; there is no sense by the play's end that he has been reborn or that he will be. If Julian is to be seen as a Jungian analysand, his transformation is cut off by his death at the end of the play, and although the juxtaposition of "God, Alice" in his last words indicates an *acceptance* of the identity, it does not tell us what, if anything, Julian understands by it. "It may be," says Miss Alice in act 1, scene 3, "I am . . . noticeable, but almost never identified" (59).

The utility of an analysis of Jungian emblems in the play is its bringing forward and focusing attention on what Anderson identifies as projections of the *anima*, the female principle, of which there are a remarkable number in this play. Anderson notes the traditional appellation of "Mother Church" as "an archetypal anima—the female counterpart to Christ" and the castle itself as "the symbol of Julian's unconscious (as well as a female archetype)."[11] For good or ill, the critical perspective that is most often employed to illuminate the role of the feminine seems to be some version of the psychoanalytic, which suggests that the female principle, where it operates as a significant energy in a play, is an adjunct or a cause of some male neurosis. It is important to see that, for all of Julian's suffering and perhaps despite our own, we know no more about Alice at the end of the play than we did throughout. It is not necessary to subscribe to a Jungian or any other psychoanalytic reading to value the reminder of how much of the play's elusive subject—Tiny Alice—is rendered in terms of female identity or, more precisely, in terms identified as female.

Julian N. Wasserman's essay, " 'The Pitfalls of Drama': The Idea of Language in the Plays of Edward Albee," calls Albee's abiding concern with precision in language

> essentially Zen in nature. That is, language as a temporal creation is rooted in the phenomenal while the ideas which it attempts to convey find their source in the ontological. The result of this paradox is that definitions are futile attempts to cast the infinite in the garb of the finite and are of necessity doomed to failure. Such exercises ultimately obscure more than they reveal because of a mistaken notion of their completeness and an ill-placed faith in their ability to capture completely the essence of the subject being defined.[12]

And yet, words and other representative signs are the only means human beings have for mediating between ideas and things and

Magnified and Sanctified

for expressing such mediation. To illustrate Albee's interest in the problem, Wasserman focuses considerable attention on the discussion of the model/replica in *Tiny Alice*: it

> present[s] the limitations of language as a mediating instrument between the abstract and the concrete, [it] simultaneously present[s] the argument for the necessity of the linguistic medium, despite its imperfect status. . . . the model and the artifice are the only means by which the Abstraction and its relationship to the concrete may be observed and known. Ironically, the very imperfections of language may be said to be the source of its attraction for Albee since its failure to capture completely the Abstract, as it is termed in *Tiny Alice*, is what renders the Abstract comprehensible to the human intellect. Language, as the "glorious imperfect," allows the imperfect to know glory if not perfection.[13]

The Abstract, or the ineffable, is by its very nature incapable of translation into language. Language, on the other hand, together with the human mind that makes it, insists by *its* nature on such a translation (literally, a "carrying across"). The perversity of human intellect is that it stubbornly attempts to do by means of language what cannot be done: to express the inexpressible, to bridge the gap between the abstraction and the concrete so that we can make use of the idea:

> *Julian.* I could not reconcile myself to the chasm between the nature of God and the use to which man put . . . God.
> *Butler.* Between your God and others', your view and theirs.
> *Julian.* I said what I intended: *(Weighs the opposites in each hand)* It is God the mover, not God the puppet; God the creator, not the God created by man.
> *Butler. (Almost pitying)* Six years in the loony bin for semantics?
> *Julian. (Slightly flustered, heat.)* It is not semantics! Men create a false God in their own image, it is easier for them! . . . (44)

Men make God in their own image because it is easier for them to use the idea of God; Julian, who has always sincerely "fought against the symbol" (162), wants to reject the notion that the distinction between the "real" God and the popular one, between the mover and the puppet, the creator and the created, is a matter of language. As Wasserman observes, "The passage is the key to Julian's thinking as it clearly shows that to Julian the difference between the First Cause and its emanations, between an object and the perception of that object, is both real and irreconcilable. Furthermore, the movement is essentially Neo-Platonic since the contrasting movement from experience to abstraction, namely man's creation of God, is rejected out of hand. Because the distinction is real, it is not in Julian's eyes 'semantic,' that is, without substance. Julian then is rejecting what he believes to be the relative in favor of the Absolute."[14] Albee tests his protagonist's need to know the difference by casting God as Alice, female, not made in *man's* image, and as Tiny, the mouse in the model, not the overarching immanence. If the image of God is not man-made, then God's name and gender will not much matter. The extent to which they do matter reflects the importance of knowing, of possessing clear knowledge, of owning the expression of the idea in order to pass it along. If God is Alice and Alice is female, then she will not be Julian's male-constructed possession any more than Miss Alice is after the "wedding."

Wasserman's analysis of the model/replica dialectic helps to clarify the issue of relativity and, eventually, by extension, that of naming and gender designation. The castle in whose library room the characters stand and move throughout most of the play is a reconstruction of one that once existed somewhere in England, "every stone, marked and shipped." To Julian's "Oh; I had thought it was a replica," Lawyer answers, "Oh no; that would have been too simple. Though it *is* a replica . . . in its way . . . *(Pointing to the model)* Of that" (85). Julian thinks he is being teased; asked to distinguish the model from the room by applying the appropriate term, he evades answering: "I mean the . . . I mean . . . what we are in." Lawyer cuts off the game: "You needn't accept his alternative . . . that since we are clearly not in a model we must be in a replica," to which Julian responds, "I will not accept it; the problem is only semantic" (86). Wasserman says about this exchange:

> To Julian the relationship between the model and the replica, as opposed to the relationship between God and the world, is semantic. The difference between idea and event is absolute; the differences between the various emanations of that idea are not. Language is, to Julian, part of the phenomenal. It is not . . . a bridge from one realm to the other, for Julian would reject . . . artifice . . . as an Aristotelian movement from the concrete to the abstract, since that is the movement which Julian wishes to avoid. Julian's reaction is to resolve the tension of that duality not by transcendence of the oppositions or by accepting their existence and arranging them hierarchically but rather through a complete dismissal of the phenomenal. Because Julian sees the use of symbols as a lessening of the Abstract, he rejects it out of hand. The Lawyer replies,
>
>> I have learned . . . Brother Julian . . . never to confuse the representative of a . . . thing with the thing itself.

Magnified and Sanctified

In other words, the corruption of the Cardinal . . . in no way diminishes the God for which he stands. The manipulation of the symbol does not affect the idea which it represents. Again, that is why the fire, although first seen in the model, must be extinguished in the replica. The destruction of the chapel must be reflected in the model for its purpose is to reflect the replica as it is, not as it was. The fire, of course, has no effect on the original which exists only in memory and is no longer affected by events in the real world. Thus, Julian's fear that symbols constitute a lessening of the Abstract is proven to be groundless.[15]

Julian's fear is groundless precisely because it is based on several assumptions: that symbols are what they stand for, that he can and does comprehend truth by apprehending the symbols, and that he can gain direct knowledge of the Abstract by rejecting the mediation of symbols, whether embodied in persons, objects, or language. As Wasserman points out,

> The problem . . . is that the Abstract is, as Julian claims, unknowable and ineffable. Julian is correct to that extent, and yet like everyone else Julian has continued to pursue that unattainable knowledge. What sets Julian apart is his refusal to accept the necessary compromise or mediation that such a paradox demands. By refusing to accept mediation which others accept, Julian has only placed the Abstract farther beyond his reach. By rejecting symbols, Julian is abandoning all that may be known of the Absolute on the non-mystical, conscious level. . . .
> He is, until the final lines of the play, a man who will not understand because he rejects language and symbol as an unnecessary, even unacceptable compromise.[16]

Julian thus stands at the pole of willfulness opposite that of such Albee characters as Peter and Nick, those who think they understand the way the world works because they think they can read the signs: "What were you trying to do?" Jerry asks early in *The Zoo Story*, "Make sense out of things? Bring order? The old pigeonhole bit?" (22). Throughout his work, Albee repeatedly presents the failure and persistence of that human effort. Although Julian readily admits the inadequacy of his sign-reading, he is unwilling to accept that inadequacy as the best we can do; instead, he wants to reject the signs, which he cannot do because it cannot be done. In *Tiny Alice*, as in other plays, Albee tells us that human history is the record of intellectual assignment, of charting and categorizing and systematizing the observed as well as the unobservable *as if* such assignment were productive. That record is incorporated into *Tiny Alice*, although it is easily missed in reading the play, as Richard Davison points out, because it is embodied in certain stage properties that remain in full audience view in all the library scenes. Across the room from the model of the mansion is "a huge reading table" (23) on which is a phrenological head. Davison recognizes the imagistic significance of the head as analogous to the model itself:

> In the last scene the phrenological head is placed diagonally across from the sectioned globe of the world [not in the original text of the play], visually reinforcing the microcosm-macrocosm relation of the castle and its models, of Brother Julian and all men. The human brain is seen to be departmentalized, as the castle is sectioned into rooms, as the world is divided into countries. The scientific certainty of the divisions makes an ironic contrast with Julian's final view of the universe as a conglomeration of uncertainties about everything except death.[17]

The irony is not only about Julian's uncertainty; it is also about the universal and perennial human effort to know representatively: maps and globes of the world antedate actual circumnavigation and geographic verification; the phrenological model is similarly based on speculation. The model of the mansion *is* an exact and verifiable replica of the mansion that houses it, but it is subject to unverifiable speculation nonetheless:

> *Butler.* You don't suppose that within that tiny model in the model there, there is . . . another room like this, with yet a tinier model within it, and within . . .
> *Julian.* . . . and within and within and within and . . .? No, I . . . rather doubt it. It's remarkable craftsmanship, though. Remarkable. (25–26)

Implicit by extension is the equal possibility that the library in which they converse is itself a model of a larger one without, and that of yet a larger one, and so on. Julian, and most of us, would "rather doubt" that, and of course we will never know. But we will continually create charts and models and representations of what we insist we do know (and historically have been wrong about: recall the archaic errors of the phrenological head and the historical revisions of cartographers), as if the chart, map, or model were proof of what it purports to represent. Albee's cautionary lesson about our understanding of the phenomenal world is that it is tenuous at best. As Anne Paolucci observes, "The mystery of the replica hangs over our consciousness from the beginning. . . . We sense from the start the hidden life in it; the provocative notion of a never-ending series is compressed in the airtight, Chinese-box arrangement of smaller and smaller replicas . . . down to an infinitesimal question. . . . A new dimension is thus created before our eyes; we feel—and Julian's restraint is our cue—that ordinary logic no longer applies and ordinary experience can no longer reassure us."[18] There *could* be a tinier model within the one we see, and there *could* be a larger one surrounding our physical rooms, and the power that breathes and engulfs everything in shadow at the end of the play can be enormous and outside everything, or it can be tiny, the mouse in one of the models. We don't know, and, in the absence of knowledge, we usually choose to make it enormous. When Lawyer warns Julian, "Don't personify the abstraction. Julian, limit it, demean it. Only the mouse, the toy. And that does not exist . . . but it is all that can be worshipped" (107), he is trying to make him see the arbitrariness of choosing what is to be exalted, and also to see that, consequently, miniaturization has the same value as expansion. Later, Miss Alice attempts the same kind of illustration: "We must . . . represent, draw pictures, reduce or enlarge to . . . to what we can understand" (161). The play seems to say that it doesn't matter any more than it matters who opens the attic closet door.

The model on the table is "sealed. Tight. There is no dust" (26); when Julian committed himself to the asylum, which "was deep inland, by the way . . . and had . . . sections—buildings, or floors of buildings—for patients in various conditions" (58), it was because he had "declined. I . . . shriveled into myself; a glass dome . . . descended, and it seemed I was out of reach, unreachable, finally unreaching . . ." (43). These congruences suggest a vision of the universe as an infinite set not of boxes within boxes but of sealed bell jars containing versions of themselves. Bell jars are more challenging than boxes because we can see through the glass to what is within, which makes us think we have contained and controlled it: the old pigeonhole bit. The play continually presents an array of enclosure images: the little boy locked in the attic closet, the caged cardinals that Lawyer in the opening scene and Julian in the end address for companionship in their mutual isolation—these lead imagistically to the "caged Deity" to whom Julian kneels in his final prayers.[19] The effect on the audience is more than an appeal to the intellect to notice the parallels, the microcosm-macrocosm connection. I recall my own uncertainty, as the sound of the heartbeat at the end of the play grew steadily louder in the Billy Rose Theater in 1965, about whose heartbeat I heard. As the sound filled the stage and spilled over into the audience, the beat could not after a while be distinguished as belonging to the stage. It could have been mine. Readers of the play can only take an auditor's word for that. Audiences, like Julian, the birds, and the mouse in the model, are situated likewise in a hierarchically structured, divided, and sealed showcase. Not surprisingly, the audience's experience at the performance of this play, or any play, is closely analogous to Julian's predicament, because in both cases the experience requires the choice of belief, the deliberate decision to comprehend the observed phenomenon as representing something we call reality. As Bigsby remarks, "While it is clear that Plato's idea of reality differs in kind from Albee's one feels that they would both concur in Plato's statement that the function of knowledge is 'to know the truth about reality.' . . . It is hardly surprising, therefore, to find that Alice, who finally becomes identified with the forces of reality, derives her name from the Old German word for 'truth.' "[20]

Identifying the meaning of Alice's name satisfactorily explains Albee's choice, although it does not immediately account for the difficulties critics have with both the feminization and the diminution of what she is. In the often-noted play-within-a-play in act 2, scene 2, Butler stands in for Julian while Lawyer rehearses how they will present the truth to their subject:

> *Butler.* But there is something. There is a *true* God.
> *Lawyer.* There is an abstraction, Julian, but it cannot be understood. You cannot worship it.
> *Butler.* There is more.
> *Lawyer.* There is Alice, Julian. That can be understood. Only the mouse in the model. Just that. . . . accept it. (107)

The abstraction cannot be understood; the name Alice, "truth," can be. Julian's guides believe what they say to and about him; they believe in Alice, talk to her, embedded in the model, at the end of each scene in the central act of the play: Miss Alice at the end of act 2, scene 1, Lawyer at the end of act 2, scene 2; Miss Alice again as Julian's seduction is completed at the end of act 2, scene 3. Julian joins their community of belief at the end of the play; although he dies in the moment, the play makes it clear that his murder could have been avoided if he had come to his epiphany sooner, more willingly:

> Miss Alice. Poor Julian. *(To the Lawyer)* You did not have to do that; I could have made him stay. . . .
> Butler. Do you want a doctor for him? . . . Because he will bleed to death without attention? . . .
> Lawyer. *(After a pause)* No doctor. (171–72)

But Julian requires extreme crisis for his acceptance. Only at the point of death, when he contemplates again who might come to open the attic door, does he understand that "no one will come" (176). "The play concludes with his realisation that reality is not an aspect of a defined role or an extension of individual desires but rather the immediate result of choices made in the context of a concrete world whose only premise and conclusion is ultimate death. . . . Used to the projections of his own sensibilities he has come to accept a diminution of his concept of reality."[21] Perhaps what is most alienating for audiences and readers in the play's presentation is this matter of choice when it comes to God. Mardi Valgemae quotes from an interview between Paul Gardner and Albee taken shortly after the play opened: "Once Julian accepts the existence of what does not exist, his concept (his faith) exists for him. Or, if one does not accept God, then there is nothing. Since Julian accepts Tiny Alice, his God becomes real."[22] Julian's faith is his choice, his truth; it is not necessarily, and certainly not demonstrably, *the* truth.

One point that the play makes repeatedly is that what people call Truth has a way of changing from time to time. This point is made most obviously in the change Miss Alice makes from a disguised old crone when Julian first meets her to an attractive and relatively young woman; the crone's wig becomes an important prop, a reminder of how quickly we take what we see for reality. The point is made again, less obviously but nonetheless forcefully, in the sustained presence of a prop discussed earlier, that is, in the phrenological head on stage throughout the library scenes. Not much is done with this head during the play, although it ultimately serves as a stand for the wig, and during his death scene Julian crawls to it and addresses it as if it were Alice: "Thou art my bride? Thou? For thee have I done my life? Grown to love, entered in, bent . . . accepted? . . . Art thou the true arms, when the warm flesh I touched . . . rested against, was . . . nothing? And *she* . . . was not real? Is thy stare the true look? Unblinking, outward, through, to some horizon? And her eyes . . . warm, accepting, were they . . . not real? Art thou my bride?" (188). Any wig stand, a bust of Minerva, or even of Miss Alice herself might have held the hair or received Julian's ironic revelation. By using the phrenological head, Albee reminds us that at one time phrenology was thought to reveal the workings of the mind, to illuminate another mystery of inner workings by recourse to outward formations. It didn't, of course, do so with any verifiable accuracy, but that did not stop many people from believing that it did. The point is that when people seek certainty regarding the unseen, there is a significant chance that we will be wrong in our assessments, as we were about phrenology. But we take our best shot, go with our selected beliefs during any period of time. Although history records necessary changes in those beliefs from age to age and decade to decade, it rarely prompts people to hold their present constructs more tentatively. We believe absolutely because we need to act out of greater certainty than life gives us.

The challenge that Alice puts to Julian and to Albee's audience is to relinquish the need for certainty in framing a system of belief and release the requirements of proof and logic. In *Tiny Alice*, "the efforts of the dramatist are concentrated in the heightening of the irrational, the intuitive, the emotional,"[23] in other words, of what is traditionally thought of as the feminine; this feminine encompassing of the idea that is called Alice remains outside the characters of the play "as catalyst and final cause."[24] The traditional western concept of deity is masculine and implacable, but Alice is a welcoming, embracing, and, only when necessary, deadly force. Her feminine identity is not specified as maternal or sexual (although *Miss* Alice is explicitly both of those); she remains indefinite, identified only as *power*. To a male celibate like Julian, such female power is most threatening, most challenging to his assumptions about faith. It is not necessary to select specific symbolic attributes; what is important about Alice's femaleness is that it is totally *other* for Julian, as different as it could be from his initiate's concept of God.

The central question of the play is mirrored in Julian's acceptance of Miss Alice for Alice. It is an acceptance rather than a confusion; the crucial distinction tests our attentiveness to detail, and we can hardly fault Julian for failing to distinguish more than at least one of the play's critics has done.[25] As Paolucci notes about Julian's wedding, "He has married Alice, not Miss Alice. And there has been no deception. He chose to hear what he wanted to hear."[26] As the play draws to a close, what is accepted changes from error to accuracy, through the agency of questions put first to the phrenological wig-stand, then to Julian's original idea of God, and finally to Alice. In his last words, Julian gives up his own self-created and self-reflecting image of God: "I accept thee, Alice, for thou art come to me. God, Alice . . . I accept thy will" (190). In letting go his ego's primacy, he learns the nature and strength of choice.

One way to think of the female nature of deity in this play, and the way that virtually all critics have embraced, is as an outlet for Julian's neurosis. The relation between the lay brother and Miss Alice, and between his ideas of martyrdom and sexual experience, has been noted in almost every analysis and review of the play. Many of those analyses are illuminating and convincing, especially Paolucci's. But the premise that the celibate yet uncommitted Julian, susceptible to illusion and especially to erotic hallucination, should find his apocalypse in the image of a woman tends to skew the reception of the play's central issue: the responsibility we have for our choices and the degree of choice we have in identifying the icons we live by, for, and through. It is easy to cast Alice as the female nemesis, an ironic comeuppance of a sympathetically drawn, unwitting hypocrite. But Alice also rules over the relatively unsympathetic Lawyer and over Butler, Cardinal, and Miss Alice. These characters, whatever else they may be, appear to be mentally healthy. They cannot be dismissed as neurotic, although the intertwinings of their relationships with each other, past, present, and continuing, are complicated. Their relation to Alice is comparatively simple; they know and accept her, even the Cardinal, whose submission strikes Julian as unthinkable: "In the sight of God? You dare?" (172). In the case of Miss Alice, particularly, Alice cannot be explained as the expression of a psychosexual martyr complex. Miss Alice is as much Alice's servant as the others are. Albee's choice of the feminine, therefore, becomes the ground upon which the audience must assess its own notions, particularly its notions about forces, deic or otherwise, we choose to define our lives' purposes. In the "ceremony of Alice," Julian raises his glass in a toast "To the wonders . . . which may befall a man . . . least where he is looking, least that he would have thought; . . . To all that which we really want, until our guile and pride . . . betray us?" (157). In these words, Julian speaks for everyone, although he does not yet fully understand the truth of his own words. Paolucci identifies the paradox inherent in the words: "we see, in the willing renunciation of his conscious choice, acquiescence to a higher will. Chance thus becomes design and willful action the instrument for accomplishing what is already preordained and irrevocable. It is the paradox of Christ's last words on the Cross (echoed by

Julian), the divine awareness of complete and eternal separation from God."[27]

The paradox also belongs to the audience, which is perhaps why so many critics have had trouble coming to terms with this play. (The most petulant response I have read comes from Philip Roth, who "would like to know who this Alice is that she can and will cause such miracles of nature" [the simultaneous fires in castle and model chapels].[28]) Although the play invites theological interpretations like Paolucci's, it does not require them. If we try to identify Alice and what she demands of Julian, we get caught in our own hermeneutic nets. And yet we are at best reluctant, and probably unable, to think about this play without some kind of interpretation. Abstraction cannot be defined or expressed, because it is abstract. But to discuss what the play puts before us, we must use limits and definitions, which Albee enables us to do by casting his inquiry in terms of specific plot and characters. Alice is God *for Julian*, appropriately because God is the goal of Julian's self-definition and identity, which for him is synonymous with faith: "My faith and my sanity . . . they are one and the same" (45). Not all of us are as devout and dedicated as Julian is (and even he had set limits to his commitment, having refused ordination into priesthood). To think of Alice purely in Julian's terms is to delimit understanding or circumscribe it in a way that brings it within ken. Alice can be called anything we like so long as our relationship to her is similar to Julian's with God. Near the end of the play, Lawyer asks Cardinal, "*Who* are the Gods?" The Cardinal does not answer; the next line is Julian's, and the stage direction *(Pain)* preceding Julian's reply, "God in heaven!" (173), lends ambiguity to his response: it may be an answer, or it may be an agonized expletive. In any event, the answer is Julian's; he gets no support from his clerical superior. Thus, Alice can be love, profession, home, country—any terms by which we define ourselves, by which we say we live and for which we say we would die. If the honesty of our claims were to be tested, as Julian's is, would we come any closer than he does to knowing what we identify with? If *it* turned out to be other than what we swore to, as in this case of feminine identity, would it make a difference? The best answer Julian could make, we remember, was "No. But."

Writing about post-surrealist drama, Maurice Valency says:

> In these plays, all ostensibly realistic in their setting and handling, the poetic effect is derived from the tantalizing manner in which

meaning is suggested or withheld, that is to say, from the manipulation of the mystery. In these plays a good part of the dramatic effect derives from the skill of the writer in suggesting and obscuring motive and meaning. Plays written after this manner make use of a very special sort of showmanship. It depends largely on teasing the audience with intimations that are never substantiated and are probably incapable of substantiation without some risk of banality. Unquestionably this sort of play, when properly written, justifies itself on the stage, if only because it deals openly with the sort of mystery that the greatest drama conceals.[29]

Aiming toward that kind of theater in Tiny Alice, Albee asks his audience to confront difficult questions whose answers, if there are any, require a most rigorous open-mindedness. The possibility that answers do not exist to the questions the play presents intensifies its complexity and frustrates its critics. The questions concern the ways we define ourselves through our professed faiths. These faiths are not necessarily religious in the traditional sense, but they are fundamentally spiritual. Such choices ultimately govern behavior, but Albee's concern in this play moves beyond (or before) the social hypocrises played out in his earlier drama. Undoubtedly the mystery of Alice configures the challenge in feminine terms, because in 1964—and perhaps still—spiritual submission, more threatening than social or political submission, to a female power poses the greatest difficulty for the greatest number of people. The problem is more than semantic. In the earlier plays, the invisible women (Mrs. Peter, Jerry's landlady) were dismissed in favor of the men who were the audience's focus; Bessie Smith died. Alice continues to breathe and beat while the house lights come up; her presence follows the audience out of the theater and into their lives.

Notes

1. See, for instance, C. W. E. Bigsby, "Curiouser and Curiouser: A Study of Edward Albee's *Tiny Alice*," *Modern Drama* 10 (Winter 1968): 258–66, and Mardi Valgemae, "Albee's Great God Alice," *Modern Drama* 10 (Winter 1968): 267–73.
2. Mary E. Campbell, "The Tempters in Albee's *Tiny Alice*." *Modern Drama* 13 (May 1970): 22–33.
3. Lucina P. Gabbard, "Unity in the Albee Vision," in *Edward Albee: Planned Wilderness*, ed. Patricia De La Fuente (Edinburg, Tex.: Pan American University, 1980), p. 24.
4. Richard Allan Davison, "Edward Albee's *Tiny Alice*: A Note of Re-examination," *Modern Drama* 11 (May 1968): 56.
5. Philip Roth, "The Play That Dare Not Speak Its Name," *New York Review*

of Books 4 (25 February 1965): 4, reprinted in *Edward Albee: A Collection of Critical Essays*, ed. C. W. E. Bigsby (Englewood Cliffs, N.J.: Prentice-Hall, 1975), pp. 105, 108.

6. Edward Albee, *Tiny Alice* (New York: Atheneum, 1965), p. 116. Subsequent references are cited parenthetically by page number within the text.

7. Edward Albee, *The Zoo Story*, p. 49. Quotations from *The American Dream* and *The Zoo Story* are from Edward Albee, *The American Dream and The Zoo Story* (New York: New American Library, 1963). Subsequent references are cited parenthetically within the text.

8. Mary Castiglie Anderson, "Staging the Unconscious: Edward Albee's *Tiny Alice*," *Renascence: Essays on Value in Literature* 33 (1979), reprinted in *Modern Critical Views: Edward Albee*, ed. Harold Bloom (New York: Chelsea House, 1987), p. 87.

9. Ibid., p. 93.

10. Ibid., p. 92.

11. Ibid., pp. 90, 89.

12. Julian N. Wasserman, "'The Pitfalls of Drama': The Idea of Language in the Plays of Edward Albee," in *Edward Albee: An Interview and Essays*, ed. Julian N. Wasserman (Houston: The University of St. Thomas, 1983), pp. 34–35.

13. Ibid., pp. 42–43.

14. Ibid., p. 47.

15. Ibid., p. 48.

16. Ibid., pp. 50, 51.

17. Davison, "Edward Albee's *Tiny Alice*," p. 57.

18. Anne Paolucci, *From Tension to Tonic: The Plays of Edward Albee* (Carbondale: Southern Illinois University Press, 1972), p. 71.

19. Davison, "Edward Albee's *Tiny Alice*," p. 59.

20. Bigsby, "Curiouser and Curiouser," pp. 260, 261.

21. Ibid., p. 265.

22. Valgemae, "Albee's Great God Alice," p. 273 (Paul Gardner, "*Tiny Alice* Mystifies Albee, Too," *New York Times*, 21 January 1965, p. 22).

23. Paolucci, *From Tension to Tonic*, p. 72.

24. Ibid., p. 79.

25. Davison repeatedly refers to Miss Alice as "Alice" and "Tiny Alice," failing to distinguish the representative from the represented.

26. Paolucci, *From Tension to Tonic*, p. 95.

27. Ibid., p. 101.

28. Roth, "The Play That Dare Not Speak Its Name," p. 108.

29. Maurice Valency, *The End of the World: An Introduction to Contemporary Drama* (New York: Oxford University Press, 1980), pp. 435–36.

PART 5
SAM SHEPARD

SAM SHEPARD'S SPECTACLE OF IMPOSSIBLE HETEROSEXUALITY
Fool for Love

Lynda Hart

Sam Shepard's one-act play *True Dylan* ostensibly records an actual conversation cut between the playwright and one of his earliest idols, Bob Dylan. Sam and Bob discuss whether or not men can have a "pact" with women. "So, you don't have much hope for women," Sam says to Bob. "On the contrary," Bob replies, "Women are the *only* hope. I think they're a lot more stable than men. Only trouble with women is they let things go on too long."

> *Sam.* What things?
> *Bob.* The whole Western sense of reality. Sometimes women have a tendency to be too lenient. Like a kid can go down and bust some old man in the head, rob a buncha old ladies, burglarize his brother's joint, and blow up a city block, and his momma will still come down and cry over him.
> *Sam.* Yeah, but that's just nature, isn't it? The nature of being a mother.
> *Bob.* Yeah, I guess so. Nature.[1]

Notice how "women" slide almost imperceptibly into "mothers" in this dialogue, the same elision that occurs when man sets himself apart from Woman and Nature by posing them as equivalents—Woman *is* Nature in patriarchal logic, and nature is reproduction. Women thus carry the burden of responsibility for "western reality," yet they are disempowered by their "natures." This patriarchal logic not only reduces women to functionary vessels, but it also inevitably locks Shepard into a fatalistic conception of hetero-social and sexual relationships.

Shepard's work, as it has developed, reflects a growing concern for and fascination with male violence. His nuclear family trilogy—*Curse of the Starving Class*, *Buried Child*, *True West*—and *Fool for Love* and *A Lie of the Mind* are intensively Oedipal dramas that represent escalating destructiveness within nuclear family politics. Women in these plays are powerless spectators to the enduring, eternal, and inevitable battle between father and son. In her article, "Men Without Women: The Shepard Landscape," Florence Falk argues that in Shepard's plays the landscape is "pervasively a Man's world, run according to a frontier ethic that recruits women as handmaidens." In the Shepard dramatic frontier, the hero is the "violent male-as outlaw," man's preferred world is "essentially homoerotic," woman are "a straggling group of camp followers, and men treat these 'bitches,' 'broads,' and 'stupid fucking cunts' as recalcitrant and dangerous possessions." Shepard's plays reside in the domain of "Male Homo Erectus." But Falk finds "Shepard himself . . . an unlikely defender of the patriarchal system and sexual asymmetry."[2]

On the other hand, Don Shewey describes Shepard as an exemplary patriarchal hero. Shewey thinks of Shepard as "an archetypal American male," a "unique combination of Ernest Hemingway and Gary Cooper," a man who "rather enjoyed" being confused with Dr. Sam Sheppard, the infamous wife murderer. Shewey delights in anecdotes that emphasize Shepard's machismo, like the time he pissed in a prop toilet during a playwriting course at the University of California, Davis—a "very butch gesture, showing what a downhome guy he was." Shewey links Shepard's association with both Theater Genesis and the San Francisco Magic Theatre as evidence of Shepard's "aggressive heterosexuality." Shewey quotes Ralph Cook's description of Theatre Genesis—within the off-off Broadway circuit noted for "an almost conspicuous heterosexuality." Shepard joined the Magic Theatre, Shewey says, because it was a place where "the masculine ethos was unquestionably championed." The book contains a photograph of Shepard with Shewey's caption: "The greatest American playwright of his generation and the thinking woman's Beefcake."[3]

Shewey is not alone in reporting such anecdotes and opinions. Shepard was on the cover of the November, 1985 *Newsweek* featuring an interview in which he reported on his adventures in the East Village in the early sixties. "As for women," he says "I rode everything with hair." Clearly the cowboy bronco-buster as Shepard hero is in concert with his own self-image and is less than incidentally connected with his attitude toward women. In the same interview, Robert Altman talks about directing Shepard as Eddie in the screen version of *Fool for Love*. As critics have noticed, Shepard's screen roles blend with his public image; either he selects roles that appeal to his own self-perception, or he plays the roles offstage as well as on. In either case, roles blend with his reality. Altman talks about one striking example of this merging. One day on the set of *Fool*, Shepard played a scene in a surprising way: "It was aggressive, it was hostile, and really shocked me." Altman was delighted because it was just what he wanted from Shepard for that scene. Then he realized that Jessica Lange was on the set and that Shepard was "doing this for her." "What I had been watching on the set was his behavior in reality: I wasn't mistaken in what lit the fuse, but what exploded was real dynamite."[4]

As a public figure, Shepard suffers from the kind of defamation in reporting that most "stars" endure eventually. Nevertheless, Shepard deliberately enhances this public image. In response to a reporter's question about how he handles the congestion of New York City, Shepard quips, "I got a 38, that's my escape hatch."[5] He fully exploits his image as a cowboy, frequently appearing in western gear and scuffling with reporters. Why, then, does Falk find Shepard an unlikely supporter of patriarchy? Her essay was published in 1981, slightly before Shepard had gained the public recognition and popular mystique that he has today. Critics like Falk who are familiar with Shepard's earlier work before the domestic dramas and his early involvement with Joe Chaikin's Open Theater might indeed be surprised by his later development.

Shepard took the now-famous Open Theater-developed concept of "transformations" and extended it into his plays primarily through a revised concept of characterization—from fixed and psychologically associative to multiple, shifting, and fluid. In his own words, he preferred a concept of character that was "constantly unidentifiable, shifting through the actor, so that the actor could almost play anything, and the audience was never expected to identify with the character."[6] Shepard seemed to have been rejecting two cardinal tenets of realism: coincidence of actor/character identity and spectator's identification with characters. Like his teacher Chaikin, Shepard seemed to be searching for an alternative to the naive mimesis of realism. In Chaikin's words, "the theater . . . seems to be looking for a place where it is not a duplication of life. It exists not just to make a mirror of life."[7]

The Open Theater was dedicated to demystifying the process

of artistic creation. In their movement away from verisimilitude and mimesis, they were attacking the realistic theater's suppression of the ideological processes at work in representational structures. By dismissing realism's aesthetic of unity of character, their transformational strategies could foreground shifting and plural cultural constructions of identity. By denying the spectators the pleasure of identification, their productions could insist on the spectators' self-perception as active, critical subjects. The effect of such methods might have been a critical foregrounding of the language of representation, an elevation of the signifier over the signified. Similar goals are constitutive of some feminist theater. As Helene Keyssar points out, "Drama that embraces transformations inspires and asserts the possibility for change; roles and role-playing, not hidden essences, merit attention; we are what we do and what we become, and no one, neither woman nor man, is restricted from becoming other."[8] The Open Theater's strategies seemed to hold out possibilities for redressing the relegation of the feminine to the repressed or suppressed term in patriarchal ideologies. But like many postmodern performers who are flourishing in the ground broken by groups like the Open Theater, they failed to utilize these strategies to disrupt sexual difference. As Jill Dolan argues in reference to the work of the postmodernists Elizabeth LeCompte, Richard Foreman, and Robert Wilson, "through deconstruction and formal invention, they might subvert the aesthetic values of text and authority once held sacred, but the political values inherent in the cultural mirror of their representation remain firmly intact . . . [they] continue to tell the story of desire that perpetuates the paternal law of sexual difference."[9]

A primary method for the Open Theatre was "display," which was intended to disrupt the "logic of domination" by turning from "representation to presentation."[10] Chaikin's group recognized that realism does more than reflect; it perpetuates the past by reproducing it. The feminist critic interested in disrupting sexual difference approaches the drama with an awareness that "Woman," as Teresa de Lauretis articulates, "is the very ground of representation, both object and support of a desire which, intimately bound up with power and creativity, is the moving force of culture and history."[11] Shepard not only failed in his early plays to use the transformational strategies he learned from the Open Theater to deconstruct sexual difference, he regressed to a naive realism (however "heightened," "modified," or "super" realistic it may be). His dramatic aesthetic, beginning with *Curse of the Starving Class* in 1976, which marked his adoption of the realistic mode, could be called reactionary, as Bonnie Marranca, who first acknowledged Shepard's oppressive representations of women, has recently suggested.[12] It is significant that his recuperation of realism coincides precisely with his rise to critical acclaim and the concomitant, coterminous, full blown expression of his misogyny and gynephobia.

Although Shepard's work is often frankly and transparently autobiographical, the contemporary critical marketplace has it that the author is dead and that my reference to Shepard's personal attitudes toward women are naive and/or irrelevant. But the critical text that has emerged in relationship to his work has not been separated from Shepard the individual who has been valorized, mythologized, and seen as legendary. Shepard has been described as "an American fantasy," "the inkblot of the 80's," an "American original," and the "New American hero."[13] He has been constructed as the "leading man," who has it all—fame, fortune, sex appeal, mystery, and power. The critical discussion of Shepard that has made him a spokesman for America is intimately bound up with the man as an individual. It has been, to borrow Michel Foucault's words, "more than a gesture, a finger pointed at someone; it is to a certain extent the equivalent of a description." In the critical discourse that hovers around the man and his work, Shepard and "Shepard" oscillate between the poles of description and designation, and, granting that they are linked to what they name, they are not totally determined either by their descriptive or designative functions." Foucault's conception of the "author-function" seeks the revelation of "the manner in which discourse is articulated on the basis of social relationships."[14] This is the question I explore through examining the texts that are created by and about Shepard. It is not what his plays reveal about him as much as what his plays and his immense popularity and success reveal about contemporary American social relationships. As a feminist reader of Shepard's texts, I focus on how women are positioned in his narratives and what function they serve. Just as women imperceptibly elide into mothers in the Dylan/Shepard dialogue, women become coincident with Woman in Shepard's plays.

Shepard's family trilogy firmly established him as a preeminent voice in American theater. This trio of nuclear family plays set the terms and conditions that lead to the violence against women overtly marked in his gender conflict plays. Elsewhere, I have discussed the pornographic vision in Shepard's latest play,

A Lie of the Mind (1985) and his screenplay *Paris, Texas* (1984).[15] Here I look at the play that made the transition from his trilogy of Oedipal narratives to these more recent violently misogynistic plays.

Fool for Love was the first of Shepard's plays that addressed the question of heterosexual "love" as a central theme. In 1981, Marranca pointed out that Shepard seemed to have no interest in relationships between men and women: "He writes as if he is unaware of what has been happening between men and women in the last decade. . . . his female characters are much less independent and intelligent than many of those created by [his literary] forefathers a hundred years ago."[16] Shepard says that he had always believed that there is "more mystery to relationships between men." Just before he wrote *Fool for Love*, he decided that he could find "the *same* mystery between men and women" (emphasis mine). *Fool for Love*, then, became his first conscious effort to create a fully autonomous female character, one who could "remain absolutely true to herself."[17] A year later, Shepard described the "true relationship" between men and women as "terrible and *impossible*" (emphasis mine).[18] Taking Shepard literally, the relationship between men and women is *impossible*, and men and women relate in the *same* way that men relate to men. Is he saying that the relationship between the opposite sexes is thinly disguised male homoeroticism? That men and women's relationships are really veiled male relationships? *Fool for Love* is the play that purports to realize a fully developed relationship between a man and a woman. My reading of the play supports Shepard's contention that heterosexual relationship is impossible; I take the man at his word.

Fool for Love has not been Shepard's greatest critical success despite winning an Obie award. It puzzled critics like Walter Kerr, who saw it as evidence of Shepard's growing reputation as a "cult dramatist" who played to a coterie audience.[19] But *Fool for Love* is essentially a realistic play, like the domestic trilogy that preceded it: the characters are searching for an identity that is gradually revealed through dialogue and action; a character (Martin) functions as an outsider who facilitates exposition; dialogue alternates between concealment and revelation; recognition scenes uncover a secret that explains the main characters' problems. Although Shepard bends and stretches these conventions, they are recognizable structural patterns in the play. The one distinctive deviance from this realistic pattern is the father's presence outside the onstage illusion—an anti-illusionistic device that Shepard does not use in his earlier realistic plays. Although gender conflict and heterosexual relationship appear to be the play's central concerns, paternal control and manipulation frames the play and determines its onstage action. Unlike the family trilogy, in which the father was either realistically absent (*True West*) or center stage (*Buried Child* and *Curse of the Starving Class*), the father in *Fool for Love* moves in and out of the narrative, physically as he crosses the proscenium boundary and psychologically as he invades and is erased from his children's memories. He is thus both omnipresent (like Pirandello's absent author) and missing. The father in the drama is then like the father in his children's narrative as they remember his pervasive and controlling influence in their lives that was characterized by a series of appearances and disappearances.

Although May and Eddie did not meet each other until they were teenagers, their experiences coincided as children of the same man who alternately cohabited with their respective mothers. Because the old man fathered each of them with different mothers, they are half-sister and brother; thus, incest is their fearful secret, the bond that holds them together and the shame that tears them apart. Eddie has "inherited" his father's proclivity for disappearance. As we find out in the first scenes, for fifteen years he has left May many times and returned to her. His most recent disappearance was taken to have a fling with an enigmatic "countess." As the play opens, May is sitting limply on the bed, Eddie is working resin into a leather bucking strap, and the old man watches them from his rocking chair outside the frame. Shepard's play enacts the sad spectacle of patriarchy's determination of sexual difference that prescribes the dominance of one sex over the other and the father's control over the narrative.

May and Eddie are exemplary characterizations of Luce Irigaray's "obsessive" and "hysteric." Eddie, "the 'obsessive' . . . who wants and demands and repeats, and turns around and around in his original desire, which he claims to master in order, finally, to establish his omnipotence," and May "the 'hysteric' . . . who drifts aimlessly, wanting nothing, no longer knowing her own mind or desire, acting 'as if' or 'as you like it,' her body the only reminder of what has been. . . ." The structure of *Fool for Love* plays out the inevitability of their imposed roles—"the game seems to have got off to a bad start. At best, a mournful pleasure seems in store. Sadly repetitive, painstakingly, or infinitely fragmenting things, rambling on with pauses only for explosions." This description from Irigaray's close rereading of

Freud's "Femininity" is taken from a section she calls "mimesis imposed."[20] Shepard's play reproduces that imposition through re-presentation.

The scenario is pornographic: Eddie, like the pornographer, is obsessed, "chained and enslaved, not to a real woman, nor to a body, but to the past and his image of the past, which he must recreate again and again."[21] Eddie's primary relationship is not with May but with the past and its representative—the father. He shares with his father a desire that constructs reality in his own image, and that image is Woman. "Take a look at that picture on the wall over there," the old man says to his son as he points at an empty picture frame in which he sees a photograph of Barbara Mandrell, his wife "in [his] mind." "That's realism," he insists.[22] Eddie and the old man share an understanding on this point, for Eddie, like his father, is a "fantasist." May is as absent as the image of Barbara Mandrell. Eddie constructs the reality of their relationship even in the face of her denial of his claims. "It's all a fantasy," she tells him, "you got me confused with somebody else," "you're gonna' erase me" (24, 23, 19), she says. Walter Kerr finds May's remarks incomprehensible,[23] but for women who have been silenced, colonized, and eradicated from history, May's remarks are straightforward.

From Eddie's dominant perspective, May's history is made up of fragments of his desire. She is his fetish. As evidence of his love for her, he hangs his head and confesses: "I missed you. I did. I missed you more than anything I ever missed in my whole life. I kept thinkin' about you the whole time I was driving. Kept seeing you. Sometimes just a part of you. . . . your neck kept coming up for some reason. I kept crying about your neck" (21). Eddie constantly wields a lasso, a less than incidental action when we consider his choice of an eroticized part of May, and he strokes and fondles a twelve-gauge shotgun. His masturbatory pleasure depends on May's presence to be subjected to his controlling look, his specularization of her, a gaze that he insists she return to validate him: "May, look. May? I'm not goin' anywhere. See? I'm right here. I'm not gone. Look" (17).

Thus within the onstage narrative, May and Eddie's relationship is clearly "terrible," a history of violence, abandonment, and possessiveness in which May has been the object of his obsessive desire. He has pursued her across country and has come to claim her again as the dramatic action of *Fool for Love* begins: "I was comin' back to get you," "I'm takin' you back" (25, 22)—such is Eddie's project. May is trapped in the motel room;

on the one occasion that she tries to escape, Eddie carries her back as she kicks and screams. At one point in the action, May circles the room crying and hugging the walls, finally sinking to her knees and crawling on the floor, much like the creeping and crawling woman in Charlotte Perkins Gilman's *The Yellow Wallpaper*, who is also reduced to these circumstances by a man who claims to be protecting and rescuing her.

Eddie can come and go from the claustrophobic set; his mobility is also emphasized in his frequent reminders of the distance he has traveled to pursue her. May, on the other hand, is immobilized; she is limp and inert when we first see her. She is alienated from her body as Shepard's telling stage direction suggests—"*face staring at floor*"—and as a recent critic unselfconsciously described—"the first stage image features her body."[24] May is, in Jurij Lotman's typological description of the "mythical text," "a function of this space" whereas Eddie is the "mythical subject":

> Characters can be divided into those who are mobile, who enjoy freedom with regard to plot-space, who can change their place in the structure of the artistic world and cross the frontier, . . . and those who are immobile, who represent, in fact, a function of this space.[25]

De Lauretis's commentary on Lotman's mythical text is supported in Shepard's representation: "As he [the mythical subject] crosses the boundary and 'penetrates' the other space, the mythical subject is constructed as human being and as male; he is the active principle of culture, the establisher of distinction, the creator of differences. Female is what is not susceptible to transformation. . . ."[26] As much as May has tried to free herself from Eddie, he always returns, and she always succumbs to his desire. Although she insists that he leave, when he attempts to do so, she becomes "hysterical," hangs onto his legs, and pleads with him to stay. Thus Shepard renders the female subject remaining "absolutely true to herself."

So far, we have seen how Shepard's play supports his assertion that the relationship between men and women is "terrible." But *Fool for Love* goes further to assert that their heterosexual union is "impossible," that it is the "same" as men's relationships with men, i.e., (hommo)erotic.[27] As I stated previously, the distinguishing feature of *Fool for Love* is the placement of the father. In the earlier family plays, Shepard represented the father as controlling the son's destiny. Wesley in *Curse of the Starving*

Class, Vince in *Buried Child*, and Lee and Austin in *True West* all succumb to their father's authority by becoming them. Despite the internal narrative of resistance to the father's power, Wesley dons his father's filthy, discarded clothing until by the end of the play his mother is unable to distinguish between her son and her husband; Vince returns to the family home and violently usurps Dodge, the patriarch, who claims Vince as his true son and heir; Lee and Austin gradually partake of their absent father's characteristics until they are both versions of him. In these three plays, the father exists within the internal narrative of the play.

In *Fool for Love*, however, Shepard places the father outside the action by initially confining him to a black-curtained space outside the proscenium. But this apparent banishment of the father only serves to foreground his (author)ity. As the dialogue moves toward recognition of the source of Eddie and May's conflict, we learn that their shared paternity is as much or more at issue than Eddie's infidelities. We can see in Eddie's actions an "inherited" repetition of his father's history. But his fundamental claim to May's love is their link with the father: "you know we're connected, May. We'll always be connected. That was decided a long time ago" (34). Although the old man resists acknowledging his paternity, "You could be anybody's. Probably are. I can't even remember the original circumstances" (49), May and Eddie fully recognize him as their mutual father. Thus, their incestuous affair does not preclude their union but establishes its inevitability. The father's power is inexorable. Paternity determines the possibility of the couple's relationship and renders it inescapable.

The project of *Fool for Love* is the abandonment of the father, a project that fails. Shepard does not keep the father outside the boundaries of the onstage narrative; he brings him onstage to demand that his story be told. When May and Eddie relate their respective versions of their history for the first time, they are incongruent. But they merge when May fills in the "detail" about Eddie's mother's suicide. "Eddie's mother blew her brains out. Didn't she, Eddie?" she asks. At this moment the father crosses the platform onto the stage and protests: "Stand up! Get on yer feet now goddamn it! I wanna' hear the male side a' this thing. You gotta' represent me now. Speak on my behalf. There's no one to speak for me now." Eddie breaks his allegiance with his father by corroborating May's story with the crucial detail: "It was your shotgun" (73). Eddie and May then meet each other's gaze. Fixed on each other, they move slowly toward each other and unite in an embrace that shuts out the father's warnings: "Keep away from her! You two can't come together! You gotta hold up my end a' this deal. I got nobody now! Nobody! You can't betray me! You gotta' represent me now! You're my son!" (75) Although the father's demands are ignored momentarily by his son, his authority is recuperated by Eddie's final action—he disappears again into the desert, under the pretext of rounding up his horses that the Countess has set loose. "He's gone," May repeats, "he's gone." The patriarch has the last words in the play. Pointing again to the empty space on the wall, he says: "Ya' see that picture over there? Ya' know who that is? That's the woman of my dreams. That's who that is. And she's mine. She's all mine. Forever" (77).

Onstage or offstage, externally or internally, the Father's vision of reality retains its authority. May and Eddie's relationship is indeed impossible. Under their father's control because of the social reality of their incestuous "love," they are bound by the Law of the Father, the patriarchal prescription for antagonism and asymmetry through the construction of gender difference. Sexuality in the play is located in May's body (emphasized when we watch her change clothes onstage, transforming from her "former tough drabness" into a "very sexy woman" [28]), a male property. Most critics agree that Shepard's family and gender conflict plays represent the demise of the family and thus the breakdown or degeneration of a social order; what they usually fail to see is that the plays exhibit a power struggle for the *maintenance* of the social order that is crumbling and that struggle is between fathers and sons, with the latter overthrowing the father only to assume his position and reinstate the old order. The sign of this struggle is violence, which is both a subject of the plays and the structural principle that activates them. Shepard is aware that violence as a subject and social reality holds special appeal for him as he reveals in an interview: "There's something about American violence that to me is very touching. In full force it's very ugly, but there's also something very moving about it, because it has to do with humiliation. There's some hidden, deeply rooted thing in the Anglo male American that has to do with inferiority, that has to do with not being a man, and always, continually having to act out some idea of manhood that invariably is violent."[28]

Shepard is indeed "touched" by violence. His plays represent the fantasy of a writer who is deeply committed to a "rhetoric of violence" and a violent rhetoric. Violence pervades the social constructs in his plays and is embodied in their discursive practices, both of which, as de Lauretis demonstrates, are "engendered in representation."[29] Shepard's return to realism was not a casual choice nor simply the selection of one structural principle over another. His realism perpetuates the power structures of the patriarchy and presents them as natural and inevitable no matter how deplorable they may seem to be. *Fool for Love* is as much an Oedipal narrative as any of the previous family plays, perhaps even more so because in this play Shepard attempts to account for the place of Woman in the narrative and demonstrates her vacancy. May's body becomes a space, "a territory in which the battle is waged." "The story of Oedipus weaves the inscription of violence (and family violence, at that) into the representation of gender."[30]

Thus, although Shepard tries to create female subjectivity in his plays, he merely returns to the struggle between men; the "mystery between men and women" in his plays is indeed "the *same*" as the mystery between men. For the feminist spectator, there is not much mystery. Women are coincident with Woman in this discourse. Shepard shares the role of "fantasist" with his father and son characters. His plays continue and perpetuate the story of male desire, (hommo)sexual desire and power. Hence his popularity, his honorary status as a mythic spokesman for America, and his penetration into the psyche of the American mind is no mystery for the feminist spectator who knows that the maintenance of the patriarchy is the collective vision of our culture's majority.

Shepard's attempt in *Fool for Love* to represent a heterosexual encounter turns out to be only his male characters' encounters with their imaginary others, "lies of their minds," monologues masked as dialogue. The rule of the Father (Phallus) renders all possibility of relation between the sexes impossible, as Shepard's controlling patriarch exemplifies. Ironically, the playwright who is portrayed as an aggressive heterosexual is fully committed to representing the same tired story of his fathers (which *is* the story of hommo-sexuality disguised as heterosexuality). Shepard may have succeeded in creating a female character who can announce her fear of being erased, but she has already been erased by the playwright's representation. *Fool for Love* is, at best, a tale of the "mournful pleasure" of failed heterosexuality.

Notes

1. Sam Shepard, *True Dylan: As It Really Happened One Afternoon in California*, Esquire, July 1987, p. 66.

Sam Shepard's Spectacle

2. Florence Falk, "Men Without Women: The Shepard Landscape," in *American Dreams: The Imagination of Sam Shepard*, ed. Bonnie Marranca (New York: Performing Arts Journal Publications, 1981), pp. 90–103.

3. Don Shewey, *Sam Shepard: The Life, The Loves, Behind the Legend of a True American Original* (New York: Dell Publishing, 1985). Shewey does not document any of his sources, including direct quotations.

4. Jack Kroll, with Constance Guthrie and Janet Huck, "Who's That Tall, Dark Stranger," *Newsweek*, 11 November 1985, p. 72.

5. Sam Shepard, as quoted by Samuel G. Freedman, "Sam Shepard's Mythic Vision of the Family," *New York Times*, 1 December 1985, sec. 2, p. 1.

6. Sam Shepard, as quoted by Pete Hamill, "The New American Hero," *New York*, 5 December 1983, p. 98.

7. Joseph Chaikin, *The Presence of the Actor* (New York: Atheneum, 1972), p. 25.

8. Helene Keyssar, *Feminist Theatre: An Introduction to Plays of Contemporary British and American Women* (New York: Grove Press, 1985), p. xiv.

9. Jill Dolan, "Is the Postmodern Aesthetic Feminist?" *Art and Cinema* New Series, 1, no. 3 (Fall 1987): 4.

10. Karen Malpede, *Three Works by the Open Theater* (New York: Drama Book Specialists, 1974), p. 26.

11. Teresa de Lauretis, *Alice Doesn't: Feminism, Semiotics, Cinema* (Bloomington: Indiana University Press, 1984), p. 13.

12. Bonnie Marranca, "The Controversial 1985–86 Theatre Season: A Politics of Reception," *Performing Arts Journal* 10, no. 1 (1986). In this dialogue with Gerald Rabkin and Johannes Birringer, Marranca brings up the possibility that Shepard is a reactionary based on her response to *A Lie of the Mind*. I discuss this dialogue and Shepard's play further in "Sam Shepard's Pornographic Vision," *Studies in the Literary Imagination* 20, no. 2 (Fall 1988), pp. 69–82.

13. These references occur, respectively, in *Newsweek*, 11 November 1985, p. 3; *American Theatre* 1, no. 1 (April 1984); *Playboy*, March 1984, pp. 90, 112, 192–93; *New York*, 5 December 1983, pp. 75–102.

14. Michel Foucault, "What Is an Author?", in *Language, Counter-Memory, Practice: Selected Essays and Interviews*, ed. Donald F. Bouchard, trans. Donald F. Bouchard and Sherry Simon (Ithaca: Cornell University Press, 1977), pp. 121, 121, 137.

15. Lynda Hart, "Sam Shepard's Pornographic Vision."

16. Bonnie Marranca, "Alphabetical Shepard: The Play of Words," *Performing Arts Journal* 5, no. 2 (1981), reprinted in *American Dreams: The Imagination of Sam Shepard*, ed. Bonnie Marranca (New York: Performing Arts Journal Publications, 1981), pp. 30–31.

17. Sam Shepard, as quoted by Michiko Kakutani, "Myths, Dreams, Realities—Sam Shepard's America," *New York Times*, 29 January 1984, sec. 2, p. 26.

18. Sam Shepard, as quoted by Stephen Fay, "the silent type," *Vogue* 213 (February 1985): 216.

19. Walter Kerr, "Where Has Sam Shepard Led His Audience?" *New York Times*, 5 June 1983, sec. 2, p. 3.

20. Luce Irigaray, *Speculum of the Other Woman*, trans. Gillian C. Gill (Ithaca: Cornell University Press, 1985), pp. 60–61.

21. Susan Griffin, *Pornography and Silence: Culture's Revenge Against Nature* (New York: Harper and Row, 1981), p. 60.

22. Sam Shepard, *Fool for Love* (San Francisco: City Lights, 1983), p. 27. Subsequent references are cited parenthetically by page number within the text.

23. Kerr, "Where Has Sam Shepard Led His Audience?", p. 3.

24. William Herman, *Understanding Contemporary American Drama* (Columbia: University of South Carolina Press, 1987), p. 67. Herman uncritically accepts and perpetuates the pornographic representation of May, whom he describes as Shepard's first "life-sized young female character" (p. 66). No wonder he finds the couple's distorted love "hilarious" (p. 67).

25. Jurij Lotman, "The Origin of the Plot in the Light of Typology," trans. Julian Graffy, *Poetics Today* 1, no. 1–2 (1979): 161–84.

26. Teresa De Lauretis, *Technologies of Gender* (Bloomington: Indiana University Press, 1987), pp. 43–44.

27. I write (hommo)erotic this way to emphasize that it is *male* sexuality that is being represented, from the Latin "homo" = man. Luce Irigaray puns on the French word for man, "homme," and makes the distinction between "homosexuality" and "hommo-sexuality" in *Speculum of the Other Woman*, pp. 101–3. In *This Sex Which Is Not One*, trans. Catherine Porter (Ithaca: Cornell University Press, 1985), Irigaray writes: "Psychoanalytic discourse on female sexuality is the discourse of truth. A discourse that tells the truth about the logic of truth: namely, that *the feminine occurs only within models and laws devised by male subjects. Which implies that there are not really two sexes, but only one. A single practice and representation of the sexual*" (p. 86) (author's emphasis).

28. Kakutani, "Myths, Dreams, Realities," p. 26.

29. De Lauretis, *Technologies of Gender*, p. 33.

30. Ibid., p. 44.

SELF AS OTHER
Sam Shepard's Fool for Love and A Lie of the Mind

Rosemarie Bank

For the last twenty years, the same period that saw the rise in the United States of what is generally identified as poststructuralist or postmodernist criticism and historiography,[1] scholars have consistently analyzed plays from a gender perspective. There is disagreement concerning both the extent and nature of the analyses because some feminists have argued that poststructuralist criticism, with its concentration on white, male perspectives, has distracted attention from the initial impulse to open and reread the canon in terms of gender.[2] Other critics discern a depoliticization of gender issues caused by deemphasizing or personalizing the differences between women and men and among women, arguing that postmodern performance—elitist, complacent, racist, and sexist in its "deconstructed but not dethroned" stagings of the status quo—has little at stake politically.[3] The perception is that poststructuralism holds "that the two terms in a binary opposition are each other's inherent possibilities"; accordingly, a postmodern view of gender asks whether "the suppressed term in the pair [female] is elevated to subvert the dominant [male],"[4] a question that can be politicized or depoliticized. Many of these critical discourses become focused in the first of Sam Shepard's works in which women are central to the dramatic action, Fool for Love (1983) and A Lie of the Mind (1985), because these decidedly postmodern plays depict physical and emotional brutality directed against female characters, thus becoming, at the political level of discourse, as feminist critics have observed, part of the problem rather than part of the solution.

That this and other levels of discourse will continue is both certain and desirable. It is also clear that we can discern a pause in the development of poststructuralism/postmodernism during which scholars have noted the elevation of criticism over art. The virtues and vices of this elevation—for pure criticism is itself an art, yet art presses insistently toward the foreground—have been less dominant in the works of the theater scholars, whose study—performance—drives relentlessly toward praxis. The inexorability of action in theater may account in part for the slow appearance of postmodernism in theater scholarship—because a text is only one form of action on the performative scene—and for the widespread mistrust of postmodernism's endlessly circling language and deferred meanings. Yet the pause we perceive in the development of postmodernism may be a threshold, signalling a shift rather than a halt in the level of discourse. That shift is discernible in Shepard's recent work, which becomes both subject and object of the critical discourse, just as criticism (analyses of "truth") becomes the subject and object of the discourse of both plays.

The threshold that has been marked in postmodernist criticism and theater represents, among other things, a shift away from binary systems and their historic connections to the linear thought of modernism, with its causes and effects, direct correspondence with "life," certainty about what is "real," and its intellectual, social, and artistic investment in "truth," "sources," and "meaning." The level of discourse that now emerges in performance studies suggests a different space of representation, what Michel Foucault terms a heterotopia, embracing nearly endless doubling and transformation, which cannot be encompassed by binary critical constructs. In this view, all relationships are ambiguous, and there is no single action toward which all things tend, hence no single "story" and no single "meaning" that can be derived after the performative act is completed. The nature of transformational dramaturgy demands that dramatic action and its performance be continually displaced. In such a space of representation, gender transforms, doubles, and multiples (as do all other dramatized "binary" systems), challenging and confounding received traditions concerning sex and sexuality.

The purpose of the present discourse is to explore the doubling and transformation of gender in *Fool for Love* and *A Lie of the Mind* and the space of representation thereby created. At the end we will consider the political level of discourse, a means of weighing what a feminist rereading of these plays enables us to discern.

Self as Other

* * * *

Fool for love . . . and not just at a distance but as one who had been summoned and embraced.[5]

The attraction between May and Eddie in Shepard's *Fool for Love* is given the force of natural law. Like bodies moving through space, their "distortions" are "real" (in physics, both space and time are distorted by gravity). In May and Eddie's case, the distortion/reality results from their mutual attraction and its history. May characterizes their relationship as "all a fantasy,"[6] an assessment echoed by the absent but present Old Man, who says to Eddie, "I thought you were supposed to be a fantasist, right? Isn't that basically the deal with you? You dream things up. Isn't that true?" (19). Eddie has been summoned to this space by his desire, a combination of memory and a present action that speaks to May's current desire both to have Eddie present and have him gone.

The space of representation in *Fool for Love* is similar in many ways to Velázquez's painting "Las Meninas," which Foucault analyzes skillfully in *The Order of Things*. The seedy motel room on the edge of the Mojave Desert is also a site, like the painting, for multiple doubling, an environment in which "truth" and "reality" can have no fixed location because the space of representation, like a mirror, both reflects and distorts. In such a place, fantasy and lying are indistinguishable, "truth" ambiguous. As Eddie observes, "Lying's when you believe it's true. If you already know it's a lie, then it's not lying" (42), a perception that extends not only to the characters' absent yet omnipresent histories but to the spectators who "know" the play is a lie yet believe it to be "true," thereby becoming a part of the space of representation, mirrored players, as in Velázquez's painting.

May and Eddie try relentlessly to achieve verification, to break the mirror and establish an authoritative version of self and other, their private and shared lives. They must fail, because, as in much postmodern theater, the gaze here is fractured; the mirror is already broken, not to the end of verifying a single image, but, as Foucault observes of "Las Meninas," to substantiate that

> human nature—like the folding of representation back upon itself—transforms the linear sequence of thoughts . . . offer[ing] jumbled fragments of it, repeated and discontinuous, . . . extremes meet within it, the same things occur more than once; identical traits are superimposed in the memory; differences stand out.[7]

Yet, despite their inability to achieve verification, May, Eddie, and the Old Man continue their attempt, persisting in their independent interpretations—of the mothers' stories, of May and Eddie's love life, of the objects in a scene—ceaselessly changing yet repeating their stories, circling endlessly in their attempts at self-validation; until a major threshold ends the discourse for this time (44–48).

In this play, fantasy and lying are major aspects of macho and of love. Eddie manifests macho in his competition with Martin, his maneuvering of the discourse concerning what manliness is, and in his attempts to impress May (24, 29, 37–43). May manifests an equivalent of macho in her jealousy of the Countess (13–15). The Old Man is traditionally macho in his insistence on "the male side a' this thing," that Eddie "bring [May] around to our side" (52–53). Certainly, *Fool for Love* shows numerous examples of struggles for dominance that are gender-based—the perspective of the play itself, not surprisingly, has been identified by critics as male[8]—and May, Eddie, and the Old Man clearly attempt to control history and (re)write the record.

Fantasy, lying, and macho are most intense in love, where "truth" and "reality" are synonymous with desire. The Old Man points to an imaginary photo on a wall, identifying it as "somethin' real, okay? Somethin' actual," a photo of Barbara Mandrell to whom the Old Man is "really" married—in his mind (20). Yet love is no less ambiguous in the characters' personal histories, for as they endlessly construct, deconstruct, and reconstruct their memories, the events and feelings those memories depict become immortal and destined. Eddie casts May as the beloved from "the second we saw each other," mutualizes that attraction—"we knew we'd never stop being in love" (48)—and makes the bond eternal ("You'll never get rid of me. You'll never escape me either. I'll track you down no matter where you go" [35–36]). May lives out her mother's history as a woman possessed by love (51–52), while the Old Man possesses "reality" in his fantasies—"That's the woman of my dreams. That's who that is, and she's mine. She's all mine. Forever" (55).

The dominant dramatic mode for possessing the space of representation is storytelling, reinforced theatrically by shifts in lighting and punctuated often by noise. Storytelling leads to a major threshold in the play, a shift in the level of discourse. It occurs when Eddie verifies May's account of the death of the mother and is encapsulated in the repeated line "You were gone," just as May at the end of the play repeats of Eddie, "He's gone (52,

54). In the space between these repetitions, history is ruptured: the son refuses to stand for the father; the father reveals that he experienced love, previously described as split between two women, as complete wholeness with at least one of them; and Eddie and May come together for a second tender kiss promising a completion in the other (45, 53). But the threshold is a shift, not an ending because the Countess strikes, Eddie "can't let her get away with that" (54), and it is May this time who is figuratively kneed in the groin, as her initial fear of Eddie's leaving is at last and once again realized.

Fool for Love describes what Foucault calls a heterotopia, observing that "we do not live in a kind of void, inside of which we could place individuals and things. . . . we live inside a set of relations."[9] Heterotopia is defined as all the real sites in a culture "simultaneously represented, contested, and inverted."[10] Foucault likens heterotopia to that aspect of a mirror allowing us to identify the other, the place where we are not, making "this place that I occupy at the moment when I look at myself in the glass at once absolutely real, connected with all the space that surrounds it, and absolutely unreal, since in order to be perceived it has to pass through this virtual point which is over there."[11] In addition, a heterotopia "is capable of juxtaposing in a single real place several spaces, several sites that are in themselves incompatible,"[12] a definition of theatrical space as well. Like theater, heterotopias are linked to breaks in traditional time, accumulating time (e.g., the dramatic canon) or dispersing it (e.g., the evanescence of performance). Heterotopias are to some measure both open (penetrable) and closed (isolated),[13] much as a theater is a public space but charges admission. A heterotopia, then, may "create a space of illusion that exposes every real space, all the sites inside of which human life is partitioned," or may "create a space that is other, another real space, as perfect, as meticulous, as well arranged as ours is messy, ill constructed, and jumbled."[14]

Heterotopias reflect the concept of timespace in physics, in which one must know both how fast and where something is occurring. But the potentialities of the canvas, as with "Las Meninas," are multiplied in performance. In *Fool for Love*, the lover creates the beloved. Time (Eddie, the Old Man) is summoned and embraced by space (May, the mothers). Time dilates (slows) and expands (quickens) as it penetrates space. But traditional gender roles also reverse: May occupies the space (trailer) Eddie provides; her mother penetrates the Old Man's space in her city by city search for him; May creates her own space in the motel and occupies it, while Eddie brings both space (the horse trailer) and time (the Countess) with him. The characters continually double, displacing spaces of representation ascribed to their gender opposites, only to reassume traditional spaces, and to pass into the mirror again. In a universe in which chaos is natural, self can quickly become other, woman man, and man woman.

In *A Lie of the Mind*, gender doubling is further extended to man man and woman woman, as brothers become brothers and mothers become daughters. On an ultimate level of abstraction, both these plays could be said to fragment single selves into their component and warring parts. If the dominant sense of self is male because the playwright is male, selfhood also embraces the female: Beth is part of Jake, "right there" with him even when he believes she is dead[15] and, no less intensely, Jake, Frankie, and Sally's dead father is still "alive" inside Lorraine, their mother (86). Self is also a repository (accumulated time) of experience; thus, sons absorb the gender obsessions of their mothers (Jake and Lorraine) that daughters (Sally and Beth) reject. In this space of representation, there is only one "reality"—are you alive or dead—and "truth," as the play's title cues us, will be both a lie and (colloquially) a landscape of the mind.

Timespace is a dominant participant in the play's heterotopia. Jake is the outcast who does not know where he is, in space

> Frankie. What state?
> Jake. Some state. I don't know. They're all the same up here. (34)

or in time; as Jake reveals, "I never even saw it comin'" (5). During the play, Jake comes in from the outside—to a null place (the motel), to his childhood room (Lorraine's space), and, finally, briefly inside Beth's home—but he is no longer a feature of any scene. Jake, like Mike and the younger Baylor, fulfills Meg's description of the hunter-wanderer: "The male one goes off by himself. Leaves. He needs something else. But he doesn't know what it is. He doesn't really know what he needs. So he ends up dead. By himself" (98). By contrast, Beth takes possession of timespace, with which, as a result of her beating, she can communicate directly (e.g., how far is down, where is here, when am I) (6–7). Beth's transformation began before Jake beat her (and not for the first time [4]), a transformation via performance:

Self as Other

> *Jake.* Everything changed. She was unrecognizable. I didn't even know who I was with anymore. I told her, I told her, look—'I don't know who you think you are now but I'd just as soon you come on back to the real world here.' And you know what she tells me?
> *Frankie.* What?
> *Jake.* She tells me this is the real world. This acting shit is more real than the real world to her. (11)

Beth herself later confirms the importance of transformation: "Pretend. Because it fills me. Pretending fills. Not empty. Other. Ordinary. Is no good. Empty. Ordinary is empty" (71). Beth, perforce, must (re)invent herself, and her success in doing so is attested by her mother, Meg, who says, "She's like a whole different person . . . All I recognize any more is her body. And even that's beginning to change" (92–93). While Jake's ultimate trajectory, like Mike's (and Baylor's before he became too old), is outside and dead, Beth's is interior and alive. She will not die without Jake, does not say, as Jake does, "I'm gonna die without [you] . . . I love you more than this life" (15, 120), for the space of representation of their love is the mind and the heart, and these spaces Jake has fractured forever. In the process, he has simultaneously "killed them both" (19) (killed their love) and enshrined their love forever by freezing it in time (Beth: "Heez in me. You gan stop him in me" [20], just as the dead father is alive eternally in Lorraine). Jake's insistence at the beginning of the play that Beth is not a "thought," not a "picture," but is real(ly) present even when absent becomes, by the end of the play, a "true" memory, as Lorraine says, "All in the past. Dead and gone. Just a picture" (109). Present is transformed into past, feeling into memory.

Possession of the space of representation, of time and hence memory, of (hi)story and therefore the "true" lie, all play a part in the individuation process at work in the play. Separation enables the characters to distinguish self from other. Beth's separation is central to the action, because it is her (re)creation that causes us to see this particular mental and emotional landscape and who and what inhabits it. From the beginning, Beth insists on selfhood, that she is alive and not a baby: [to Mike] "You have a feeling I'm you! This! [Points to her head.] This didn't happen to you. This! This. This thought. You don't know this thought. How? How can you know this thought? In me" (43). Beth's separation from those around her allows her to recognize and describe essential things very clearly—that her mother is love; that

Mike's love is only pride in playing the protector and avenger; that her father (Baylor) has given up love for death; and that she, now different than she was, "knows" love (43–44, 54–55).

The clarity of perception of some things, often associated with children and forms of brain damage, also can result from experience; thus brother (Frankie) becomes brother (Jake) through the remembered sound of a voice, and brother (Jake) elects brother (Frankie) as a replacement for the betraying self (51, 120). Foucault gives an ironically gender-colored comment on the ambiguity of doubling:

> The unthought (whatever name we give it) is not lodged in man like a shrivelled-up nature or a stratified history; it is, in relation to man, the Other: the Other that is not only a brother but a twin, born, not of man, nor in man, but beside him and at the same time, in an identical newness, in an unavoidable duality. This obscure space so readily interpreted as an abyssal region in man's nature, or as a uniquely impregnable fortress in his history, is linked to him in an entirely different way; it is both exterior to him and indispensable to him.[16]

Individuation, therefore, does not indicate the elimination of the Other—which is located and functions both in space and time (that is, heterotopically)—but rather its transformation.

Transformation in the separation of child from parent is evident in the relationship between Lorraine and her daughter Sally. Lorraine elects her son Jake (the Other) over Sally (26), a rejection of self representing a displacement of power—controlling the present son as a substitute for the absent father. (This doubling of family members is a feature of both plays, as sisters and brothers and mothers and sons become "lovers" in a tangle of strategies to possess the space of representation and its inhabitants, past and present.) But Sally will not be cast out; she returns from her circular wandering to establish new relationships with her brother and mother, relationships located in the present—the past "was a whole other time" (64). As the son leaves again, Lorraine and Sally change roles, as Sally symbolically "carries on" (preserves the photograph) and Lorraine destroys the things she saved that no one ever returned to claim (107–113). The women relinquish space, a funeral pyre for memory, because place is unnecessary if you are never coming back.

The place of representation, however, is not that forgiving because it is lodged in time as well as space. As seen in *A Lie of the Mind*, time fractures memory like a broken mirror; time unknowingly changes everything while the characters doze through life (Frankie, Meg) (73, 76), until no one "recognizes" you or you yourself. Memory may accumulate or disperse time, but it inexorably displaces experience, as Beth notes: "If something breaks—broken. If something broken—parts still—stay. Parts still float. For a while. Then gone. Maybe never come—back. Together. Maybe never" (45). Memory does not fade completely, because the characters retain remembrances of everything from familiar smells and textures to ancient trespasses against them, but "the parts never come back together" as before. Yet feelings abide—Beth "knows love" and Lorraine is no less possessed by her husband now that he is dead than she was when he lived (55, 85–86)—though minds and bodies have been transformed.

The doubling of self and other in *A Lie of the Mind* is multiplied in gender. Robbed of her "right mind" by Jake's beating (but where is "mind?" In thought? In feeling?) Beth says Mike took her brain and her father told him to (74). She, the doubled self, perceives Frankie has a brain and she none, but casts herself as the man, the "big shirt," father, brother, and lover in one, playing against Frankie's "woman," characterized as "soft," "gentle," "without hate," "sweet," the Other transformed into Self (72). As a doubled self, Beth possesses space as well as time. Mike has to force her outside and dares Jake to claim Beth and her space by reviving jealousy (118–19). But Jake knows his mind is a lie and relinquishes both space (ownership) and time (memory), from which Beth has already displaced him.

Jake is doubled in Mike, who also doubles Baylor. Mike displays nurturing behavior with Beth, of which both Meg and Baylor are incapable, but, like a possessive parent, Mike wants to dictate what the space of representation—the lie of the mind—will be and control it. He cannot do this because the rest of the players refuse to cooperate: "nobody cares" (119). Jake relinquishes possession instead of fighting for ownership, and Baylor does not care about the prisoners he or his son Mike have taken, only for the symbols of remembered manliness—a rack of antlers and a correctly folded flag. Mike's victories are "out there" in the space Baylor and time have abandoned (106).

Age has placed Baylor in a new space—inside—that he populates with memories of a long-vanished frontier, a primary characterizer of gender in American history/memory. But while the hunter/wanderer has been "out there," the women have defined the interior landscape. At first, the description seems traditional:

Meg. The female—the female one needs—the other.
Baylor. What other?
Meg. The male. The male one.
Baylor. Oh.
Meg. But the male one—doesn't really need the other. Not the same way. (98)

In Meg's description, the male leaves and dies. Baylor is so shaken by Meg's words that he begins issuing orders, "trembling with rage." But Meg is not intimidated, and, instead of leaving, she puts Baylor in his place, which is the women's space:

Meg. All these women put a curse on you and now you're stuck. You're chained to us forever. Isn't that the way it is?
Baylor. Yeah! Yeah! That's exactly the way it is. You got that right. I could be up in the wild country huntin' antelope. I could be raising a string a' pack mules back up in there. Doin' somethin' useful. But no, I gotta play nursemaid to a bunch a' feeble-minded women down here in civilization who can't take care a' themselves. I gotta waste my days away makin' sure they eat and have a roof over their heads and a nice warm place to go crazy in.
Meg. Nobody's crazy, Baylor. Except you. Why don't you just go. Why don't you just go off and live the way you want to live. We'll take care of ourselves. We always have. (99–100)

Baylor does not give up easily, if ever, turning his bluster instead on the hapless, immobilized Frankie: "Don't you try and threaten me in my own goddamn house! [A man's home is his castle.] This isn't Southern California. [Effete, feminized civilization.] This is Montana, buster! [A man's world, the wild country.]" (103). Even in the presence of the wounded innocent, we smile in recognition of the lie. Yet if Frankie represents the new gender order, in many ways he seems to be the victim of the old, like Lorraine, Sally, Meg, and Beth. What he thinks of the brave new world is lost in his allegiance to the old code, where men espouse loyalty to each other in the possession of women and space: "Jake, you gotta take her with you!! It's not true, Jake! She belongs to you! You gotta take her with you! I never betrayed you! I was true to you!" (121).

Like *Fool for Love*, *A Lie of the Mind* describes a heterotopia (all the real and unreal sites of the culture), juxtaposed and often incompatible spaces accumulated or dispersed in time. The heterotopia of *A Lie of the Mind* reflects timespace multiplied by performance, both the performance of the actors and—into the

Self as Other 237

mirror—of the characters. Again, time penetrates space to be retained (Baylor, Frankie) or cast out (Jake, Mike), and traditional gender roles reverse as Lorraine and Sally relinquish ownership (if they do) and penetrate the "out there," while Meg and Beth assume possession of the experientially earned timespace. The characters double and (re)double endlessly; Self becomes Other and multiplies, displacing spaces of representation and creating a heterotopia that transforms continuously because in *A Lie of the Mind* there is no single rupture (threshold) of history but a continual passage through the virtual point. Here, memory (truth) is fractured from the play's beginning, like Beth's battered mind, fragments floating and mocking the idea of a single relationship that could be called truth. Truth lies, and lies are true, for what is absent pulls the present to it and the present mourns what has departed. The relationship is not binary but heterotopic, the universe of time and experience embraced in Meg's words, "Looks like a fire in the snow. How could that be?" (122).

The fire in the snow is both illusion and reality, self and other, not as terms of opposition but as a means of locating the level of discourse at a given instance in a relationship. Because a heterotopia may create both "a space of illusion that exposes every real space, all the sites inside of which human life is partitioned," and also a "real space, as perfect, as meticulous, as well arranged as ours is messy, ill constructed, and jumbled,"[17] the "other space" that is *A Lie of the Mind* also embraces the audience. As in "Las Meninas," the spectator is part of the performance, not as a superficial "observer" of modern art but as a participant in the space of illusion that is yet a real space. Performance in this postmodern sense is not an analogue for life; it *is* life because, as with Velázquez's painting, we pass endlessly into the mirror, alive here, there, and everywhere, at once present and absent in time. To Foucault, humanness itself is identifiable through such doubling:

> Far from leading back, or even merely pointing, towards a peak—whether real or virtual—of identity, far from indicating the moment of the Same at which the dispersion of the Other has not yet come into play, the original in man is that which . . . introduces into his experience contents and forms older than him, which he cannot master; it is that which, by binding him to multiple, intersecting, often mutually irreducible chronologies, scatters him through time and pinions him at the centre of the duration of things.[18]

* * * *

As we construct, deconstruct, and reconstruct duality in the matter of gender, it becomes both easier and more difficult to separate Self and Other: easier when critical awareness seeks the dualogue, more difficult when it behaves as though there were one level of discourse or only one that mattered. What emerges from the latter view is a constraining rather than a facilitating criticism because, as *Fool for Love* and *A Lie of the Mind* substantiate, postmodern drama is fractured in its gaze and has pulled gender into—although rarely through—the mirror. With the assumption of virtual space, forms of doubling multiply—self and other, mind and body, being and becoming, time and space, eros and thanatos—as we have seen in the plays. In such a space, relationships of dominance and suppression are subverted endlessly to such an extent and so constantly that power is always only a moment in timespace about to transform into another form of energy. Chaos is natural in the post-Heisenberg universe. All we can "know," then, is how fast and where the threshold (shift) is taking place.

The heterotopic timespace that is theater presents Self as Other, being the double, not merely recognizing it. In this sense, we are all parts of the same Self—black white, young old, rich poor, woman man, taste touch, bird fish, here there—and all parts of the Other. Not even the boundaries of life and death can be fixed, for May and Eddie's Old Man and Lorraine's dead husband are all more alive in the space of illusion than actual people are in the spectator's real space, accumulating time in the very act of dispersing it. If Self is "completed" in the Other, that completion is temporary and temporal. Presence is always defined, as in *Fool for Love* and *A Lie of the Mind*, in terms of absence: an absent person, a past time, a lost part of the self, a shattered dream, a jettisoned relationship, a place that is no place and every place. The search for and confrontation with the Other is inevitable and endless because it is the search for and confrontation with the Self.

The echoes of the shattered mirror also are endless. The significance of the sound may be clearer at the moment in criticism than in theater history, but the heterotopic timespace that is performance encompasses and erases our artificial separation of the two modes of inquiry. In the Circle Repertory's production of *Fool for Love* and in *A Lie of the Mind* at the Promenade Theater, for example, Shepard maximized a sense of suppressed energy in

Self as Other

his directing, an energy often described as menace or impending violence. In the present analysis, that "violence" can be seen as the approaching threshold (shift), the energy of ongoing transformation. Impending chaos can be frightening and violent, but it is also the heterotopic climate of postmodern drama; in this scheme, as in Artaud, life is a double for theater because both use transformation. Theater makes transformation manifest in the act and image, as well as the word. Self as Other in *Fool for Love* and *A Lie of the Mind* provokes us to explore the set of relations inside of which we live because we are both the subject and object of gender analysis. But let Foucault have the last (if gender-colored) word:

> Superficially, one might say that knowledge of man, unlike the sciences of nature, is always linked, even in its vaguest form, to ethics or politics; more fundamentally, modern thought is advancing towards that region where man's Other must become the Same as himself.[19]

And herself, as well.

Notes

1. Michèle Lamont, "How to Become a Dominant French Philosopher: The Case of Jacques Derrida," *American Journal of Sociology* 93, no. 3 (November 1987): 584–622.
2. Jane A. Gallop, in an interview/article by Karen J. Winkler, "Post-Structuralism: An Often-Abstruse French Import Profoundly Affects Research in the United States," *Chronicle of Higher Education*, 25 November 1987, p. A8.
3. See both Sue-Ellen Case, "The Personal is [Not the] Political," and Jill Dolan, "Is the Postmodern Aesthetic Feminist?", *Art and Cinema* New Series 1, no. 3 (Fall 1987): 4–5. See also Case, *Feminism and Theatre* (New York: Methuen, 1988), and Dolan, *The Feminist Spectator as Critic* (Ann Arbor: UMI Research Press, 1988), which expand the views expressed in these earlier articles.
4. Dolan, "Is the Postmodern Aesthetic Feminist?", p. 4.
5. F. Scott Fitzgerald, *The Basil and Josephine Stories*, eds. Jackson R. Bryer and John Kuehl (New York: Charles Scribner's, 1973), p. 2.
6. Sam Shepard, *Fool for Love* (Book Club Edition) (San Francisco: City Lights Books, 1983), p. 18. Subsequent references are cited parenthetically by page number in the text.
7. Michel Foucault, *The Order of Things: An Archaeology of the Human Sciences* (New York: Pantheon Books, 1970), pp. 309–10.
8. Ann Wilson, "Fool of Desire: The Spectator to the Plays of Sam Shepard," *Modern Drama* 30 (March 1987): 52.
9. Michel Foucault, "Of Other Spaces," *Diacritics* 16 (Spring 1986): 23.
10. Ibid., p. 24.
11. Ibid.

12. Ibid., p. 25.
13. Ibid., p. 26.
14. Ibid., p. 27.
15. Sam Shepard, *A Lie of the Mind* (Book Club Edition) (New York: New American Library, 1986), p. 4. Subsequent references are cited parenthetically by page number in the text.
16. Foucault, *The Order of Things*, p. 326.
17. Foucault, "Of Other Spaces," p. 27.
18. Foucault, *The Order of Things*, p. 331.
19. Ibid., p. 328.

CONTRIBUTORS

JUNE SCHLUETER, Associate Professor of English at Lafayette College, is author of *Metafictional Characters in Modern Drama* (1979), *The Plays and Novels of Peter Handke* (1981), and, with James K. Flanagan, *Arthur Miller* (1987). With Paul Schlueter, she has edited *The English Novel: Twentieth Century Criticism*, vol. 2, *Twentieth Century Novelists* (1982), *Modern American Literature, Supplement II* (1984), and *An Encyclopedia of British Women Writers* (1988). Forthcoming books include *Modern American Drama: The Female Canon*, an edited collection intended as a companion to this volume, and, with James P. Lusardi, *Reading Shakespeare in Performance: King Lear*. Schlueter has also published essays and reviews on modern drama and Shakespeare and is coeditor of *Shakespeare Bulletin*. She held a Fulbright lectureship in West Germany in 1978–79.

ISKA ALTER is Assistant Professor of English at Hofstra University. She is also author of *The Good Man's Dilemma: Social Criticism in the Fiction of Bernard Malamud* (AMS Press, 1981) and essays on Shakespeare, modern drama, and Jewish-American fiction.

GAYLE AUSTIN is Executive Director of the Southeast Playwrights Project and Literary Manager of the Horizon Theatre Company in Atlanta. She was Coordinator and Literary Manager for The Women's Project in New York for the first six years of its existence (1978–84). She has taught at Georgia State University, Hunter College, and the University of South Carolina-Spartanburg. In 1986–87, she held a grant from The Kentucky Foundation for Women to write a group of essays on women and the performing arts, and she has published articles in *Southern Quarterly*, *Performing Arts Journal*, *TheaterWeek*, and *Theater Times*. "The Madwoman in the Spotlight: Plays of Maria Irene Fornes" appears in *Making a Spectacle: Feminist Essays on Contemporary Women's Theatre*, ed. Lynda Hart (University of Michigan Press, 1989).

ROSEMARIE BANK, Associate Professor of Theatre at Kent State University, has had articles and reviews published in *Theatre Journal, Nineteenth-Century Theatre Research, Theatre History Studies, Essays in Theatre, Theatre Research International, Theatre Studies, On-Stage Studies,* and *Women in American Theatre*. She has presented numerous papers at the national meetings of the American Society for Theatre Research, the American Theatre Association, and the Association for Theatre in Higher Education, the Mid-American Theatre Conference, and the American Culture Association. A Board member of ASTR and chair of its Scholar's Prize Committee, she has also chaired the A.T.A.'s Theatre History Program and served on its Board. She has been Theatre-in-Review Editor for *Theatre Journal* and serves as an associate editor for *Theatre History Studies, Theatre Annual, Theatre Studies, Theatre Survey,* and the *Journal of Dramatic Theory and Criticism*.

SUZANNE BURR is Lecturer in English at The University of Michigan, where she teaches courses in writing and literature. Her dissertation, *Ghosts in Modern Drama*, discusses ghostly images in the work of Ibsen, Strindberg, and O'Neill. She is the author of "Students Write about Shakespeare: The Triple Play in the College Classroom," in *Shakespeare and the Triple Play: From Study to Stage to Classroom*, ed. Sidney Homan (Bucknell University Press, 1988). She presented a paper on O'Neill's influence on Sam Shepard and David Mamet at the 1989 Northeast Modern Language Association conference.

ANNE FLÈCHE, a graduate student at Rutgers University, New Brunswick, New Jersey, is writing a dissertation on Eugene O'Neill, Tennessee Williams, and mimetic theory.

LYNDA HART is Assistant Professor of English at The University of Pennsylvania. She is the author of *Sam Shepard's Metaphorical Stages* (Greenwood, 1987) and editor of *Making a Spectacle: Feminist Essays on Contemporary Women's Theatre* (University of Michigan Press, 1989).

NAOMI CONN LIEBLER is Associate Professor and Graduate Programs Coordinator, Department of English, Montclair State College. Her publications include articles on Shakespeare and Pirandello, several book reviews, and numerous theater reviews for *Shakespeare Bulletin*. Her current project is a book-length study of the ritual underpinnings of Shakespearean tragedy.

BETTE MANDL is Associate Professor of English at Suffolk University in Boston. Her articles have appeared in such publications as the *Doris Lessing Newsletter, Notes on Contemporary Literature,* and *The Eugene O'Neill Newsletter.* She is currently writing a book on O'Neill from a feminist perspective.

JEFFREY D. MASON, author of *Wisecracks: The Farces of George S. Kaufman* (UMI Research Press, 1988), has published articles on Sam Shepard, Eugene O'Neill, and Maxwell Anderson and has contributed several theater and book reviews to *Theatre Journal.* An actor and director with more than sixty productions to his credit, he has staged *The Glass Menagerie, The Contrast,* and *The Butter and Egg Man,* and in 1977 he played the role of Danforth in *The Crucible* in Nevada City, California. He teaches directing, theater history, and American theater at California State University, Bakersfield, where he is Associate Professor of Theatre, and he is currently preparing a book-length study on nineteenth-century American theater and drama as a polemic response to the mythic ideology of America.

MICKEY PEARLMAN is editor of *American Women Writing Fiction: Memory, Identity, Family, Space* (University Press of Kentucky, 1988); author of *Tillie Olsen* (forthcoming, Twayne Publishers), and *Re-inventing Reality: Patterns and Characters in the Novels of Muriel Spark* (Peter Lang Publishing, 1989); and editor of *Mother Puzzles: The Theme of Mothers and Daughters in Contemporary American Literature* (Greenwood Press, 1989).

KAY STANTON, Associate Professor of English at California State University at Fullerton, has presented more than twenty papers at professional conferences in the United States and several other countries. Among her published works are articles on Shakespeare, Marlowe, and Milton, and she is author of *Death of a Salesman's Wife,* a play that is a feminist sequel to *Death of a Salesman.*

JOHN TIMPANE has taught at Rutgers University and the University of Southampton, and is presently at Lafayette College and Princeton University, with his main interests including composition, Renaissance drama, and the theory of comedy. His composition textbook, *Writing Worth Reading* (Bedford Books, 1986), was co-authored with Nancy Packer. He also has written extensively for medical and scientific publications.

ANCA VLASOPOLOS is Associate Professor of English and Director of the Program in Comparative Literature at Wayne State University. Author of *The Symbolic Method of Coleridge, Baudelaire, and Yeats*, she has published articles on plays by Shakespeare, W. B. Yeats, Tennessee Williams, and Jean Anouilh, on film, the Romantic period, and twentieth-century literature. She is currently writing a book on anti-generic theater, starting another on women in the poetry of the British Romantic poets, and completing a poetry manuscript.

INDEX

Abel, Elizabeth, 170 n.11
Adler, Jacob H., 169 n.5, 170 n.16
Aeschylus, 35 n.13
Albee, Edward, 12, 17–18. Plays: *The American Dream*, 17, 187–91, 191 n.1, 192, 193, 196, 210 n.7; *The Death of Bessie Smith*, 192, 193, 209; *The Sandbox*, 187–88, 189; *Tiny Alice*, 17, 192–210, 210 nn. 8, 17, 19, 22, and 25; *Who's Afraid of Virginia Woolf?*, 192; *The Zoo Story*, 17, 183–87, 191 n.1, 192, 193, 201, 209, 210 n.7
Alter, Iska, 15
Altman, Robert, 214–15
Anderson, Mary Castiglie, 196–98, 210 n.8
Aristotle, 150–51, 170 n.10, 180 n.11
Artaud, Antonin, 28, 239
Austin, Gayle, 14

Bakhtin, Mikhail, 171
Banks, Rosemary, 18
Baraka, Amiri, 56 n.22. Play: *Dutchman*, 56 n.22
Barlow, Judith E., 30, 33, 35 nn. 7 and 13, 36 n.17
Barnes, Howard, 169 n.7
Barthes, Roland, 33, 36 n.25
Bates, Barclay W., 97 n.8
Beauvoir, Simone de, 12, 19 n.4
Belenky, Mary Field, 47 n.12
Bentley, Eric, 98 n.15, 166, 170 n.17, 179 n.4
Berkman, Leonard, 169 n.7
Berlin, Normand, 170 n.12
Beyer, William, 102 n.37
Bigsby, C. W. E., 204, 209 n.1, 210 nn. 5 and 20
Birringer, Johannes, 225 n.12
Black, Johnny, 113 n.1
Blackwood, Christian, 96 n.3

Blair, Mary, 48
Bliquez, Guerin, 98 n.18, 107, 114 n.5
Bloom, Harold, 18, 210 n.8
Blumberg, Paul, 97 n.11
Bogard, Travis, 55 n.7, 56 n.21
Booth, Edwin, 29–30, 32
Bouchard, Donald F., 225 n.14
Breton, André, 12
Broe, Mary L., 66 n.10
Brustein, Robert, 179 n.4
Bryer, Jackson R., 239 n.5
Burr, Suzanne, 13–14

Campbell, Mary E., 209 n.2
Cardullo, Bert, 169 n.7, 170 n.18
Carlisle, Olga, 99 n.24
Case, Sue-Ellen, 239 n.3
Chabrowe, Leonard, 35 n.7
Chalkin, Joseph, 215, 225 n.7
Chinoy, Helen Krich, 169 n.9
Circle Repertory Company, 238
Claudel, Paul, 12
Clinchy, Blythe McVicker, 47 n.12
Clurman, Harold, 112, 114 n.14, 169 n.7
Cobb, Lee J., 99 n.21
Cohn, Ruby, 170 n.14
Cole, Toby, 56 n.19, 169 n.9
Cook, Ralph, 214
Cooley, John, 52, 56 n.20
Cooper, Gary, 214
Corrigan, Robert W., 113, 114–15 n.15
Czerwinski, Edward J., 56 n.18

da Ponte, Durant, 169 n.7
Davison, Richard Allan, 202, 209 n.4, 210 n.19
Day, Christine R., 180 n.11
De La Fuente, Patricia, 209 n.3
De Lauretis, Teresa, 27, 31, 32, 33, 35 nn. 5, 8, and 12, 36 nn. 16 and 25,

216, 221, 224, 225 n.11, 226 nn. 26 and 29
de Man, Paul, 36 n.15
Derrida, Jacques, 239 n.1
Devlin, Albert J., 179 n.5
Dickson, Vivienne, 170 n.16
Dolan, Jill, 215, 225 n.9, 239 nn. 3 and 4
Dostoevski, Feodor, 172
duBois, Page, 170 n.11
Dunnock, Mildred, 99 n.20
Dylan, Bob, 213, 217

Eisinger, Chester E., 101 n.33
Eliot, T. S., 36 n.22, 50. Poem: *The Waste Land*, 32–33
Ellmann, Mary, 12, 13, 19 n.5

Falk, Florence, 214, 215, 225 n.2
Falk, Signi, 168 n.4
Fay, Stephen, 225 n.18
Fedder, Norman J., 179 n.3
Field, B. S., Jr., 99 n.22, 101 n.32
Fitzgerald, F. Scott, 239 n.5
Fjelde, Rolf, 47 n.5
Flèche, Anne, 13
Floyd, Virginia, 48, 55 n.2
Flynn, Joyce, 55 n.7
Floreman, Richard, 215
Foster, Richard J., 97 n.13
Foucault, Michel, 18, 217, 225 n.14, 228, 229, 231, 239, 239 n. 7, 240 nn. 16, 17, and 18
Freedman, Samuel G., 225 n.5
French, Warren, 97 n.7
Freud, Sigmund, 14, 59, 168 n.4, 170 n.11

Gabbard, Lucina P., 209 n.3
Gaines, Jim, 179 n.5, 180 n.8
Gallop, Jane A., 239 n.2
Ganz, Arthur, 142, 145 n.29
Gardner, Paul, 205, 210 n.22
Garland, Robert, 101 n.37
Gassner, John, 180 n.15
Gates, Henry Louis, Jr., 55 n.15
Gelb, Arthur and Barbara, 39, 47 n.6, 55 n.1
Gelb, Philip, 101 n.36
Genet, Jean, 12, 50. Play: *The Blacks*, 50

Gilbert, Sandra M., 11, 12–13, 19 nn. 1 and 7, 54, 56 n.23, 170 n.11
Gill, Brendan, 35 n.11
Gillet, Peter J., 50, 55 n.10
Gilman, Charlotte Perkins, 221. Novel: *The Yellow Wallpaper*, 221
Girard, René, 60, 170 n.11
Goldberger, Nancy Rule, 44, 47 n.12
Gora, Thomas, 35 n.2
Gordon, Lois, 97 n.7, 107, 114 n.6
Gregory, Patrick, 170 n.11
Griffin, Susan, 225 n.21
Gross, Barry Edward, 97 n.10
Gubar, Susan, 54, 56 n.23, 170 n.11
Guthrie, Constance, 225 n.4

Hagen, Uta, 166
Hamill, Peter, 225 n.6
Hansberry, Lorraine, 54. Play: *A Raisin in the Sun*, 54
Harding, Sandra, 54–55
Harshbarger, Karl, 98 n.18
Hart, Lynda, 18, 225 n.15
Harwood, Britton J., 168 n.4
Hayman, Ronald, 145 n.14
Heilman, Robert Bechtold, 115 n.16
Hellman, Lillian, 14–15. Plays: *Another Part of the Forest*, 14, 59–66; *The Little Foxes*, 63, 65
Hemingway, Ernest, 214
Herman, William, 226 n.24
Herne, James A., Play: *Margaret Fleming*, 36 n.27
Hinden, Michael, 55 n.7
Hoffman, Dustin, 96 n.3, 99 n.21
Huck, Janet, 225 n.4
Hulley, Kathleen, 169 n.5
Hume, Beverly, 100 n.26
Hurd, Myles R., 114 n.7
Hurrell, John D., 97 n.13, 168 n.4
Hynes, Joseph A., 97 n.13

Ibsen, Henrik, 36 n.27, 38, 49–50, 55 n.9. Plays: *A Doll House*, 36 n.27; *Ghosts*, 38; *Hedda Gabler*, 38; *The Master Builder*, 38; *Pillars of Society*, 38, 47 n.5
Irigaray, Luce, 219–20, 225 n.20, 226 n.27

Jacobson, Irving, 99 n.19

Index

JanMohammed, Abdul R., 50, 55 n.15
Jardine, Alice, 35 n.2
Jones, Robert Emmet, 169 n.7

Kakutani, Michiko, 225 n.17, 226 n.28
Kazan, Elia, 169 n.9, 172
Kerr, Walter, 218, 220, 225 nn. 19 and 23
Keyssar, Helene, 216, 225 n.8
Klapp, Orrin E., 168 n.4
Kofman, Sarah, 36 n.23
Kolodny, Annette, 12, 18, 19 n. 8
Koon, Helene Wickham, 96 n.2, 99 n.19, 101 n.32
Kott, Jan, 51, 56 n.18
Kristeva, Julia, 35 n.2, 36 nn. 14 and 24
Kroll, Jack, 225 n.4
Krutch, Joseph Wood, 168 n.4, 170 n.16

Lacan, Jacques, 14
Lamont, Michèle, 239 n.1
Lange, Jessica, 215
Lawrence, D. H., 12
LeCompte, Elizabeth, 216
Lévi-Strauss, Claude, 14, 59–60
Lewis, Emory, 191 n.2
Liebler, Naomi Conn, 17–18
Lotman, Jurij, 221, 226 n.25

McGill, William J., Jr., 114 n.10
McGlinn, Jeanne M., 179–80 n.7
Macgowen, Kenneth, 48
McMichael, George, 191 n.2
Madden, David, 101 n.33
Mailer, Norman, 12
Malpede, Karen, 225 n.10
Mandl, Bette, 14, 35 n.4, 37
Mandrell, Barbara, 220, 230
Manheim, Michael, 55 n.7
Marranca, Bonnie, 217, 218, 225 n.12
Martin, Robert A., 96 n.1, 98 n.17, 99 nn. 20 and 24, 101 n.36, 114 n.13, 144 n.4, 145 n.18
Marx, Karl, 14, 59
Mason, Jeffrey D., 15
Mauss, Marcel, 59
Melandri, Lea, 32
Meyer, Michael, 55 n.9
Meyer, Richard D., 144 n.4
Miller, Arthur, 12, 14–17, 59–145.
Plays: *After the Fall*, 15, 116, 118, 133–44, 145 n.25; *All My Sons*, 15, 103, 104, 105–6; *The Crucible*, 15, 103, 109–12, 116, 118, 119–25, 132, 133, 134, 143, 144 n.11, 145 n.13; *Death of a Salesman*, 11, 14, 15, 59–101, 103, 106–8, 109; *Timebends*, 144 n.3, 145 nn. 16, 27, and 28; *A View from the Bridge*, 15, 103, 104, 108–9, 116, 118, 125–33, 143, 144 n.11, 145 nn. 15, 21, and 22
Miller, Henry, 12
Miller, Jonathan, 27
Miller, Jordan Y., 168 n.4, 169 nn. 7 and 8
Miller, Richard, 36 n.25
Millett, Kate, 12, 19 n.6
Moi, Toril, 30–31, 36 n.18
Monroe, Marilyn, 145 n.26
Montherlant, Henri de, 12
Mozart, Wolfgang. Opera: *The Magic Flute*, 142
Mulvey, Laura, 51, 56 n.16

Nathan, George Jean, 169 n.7
Naylor, Gloria, 54. Novel: *The Women of Brewster Place*, 54
Nelson, Benjamin, 100 n.25
Nelson, Doris, 35 n.4
Nietzsche, Friedrich, 169 n.5

O'Neill, Eugene, 12, 13–14, 25–66, 63; characters of, 25–36; parents of, 49; race relations in plays of, 48; Roman Catholicism in plays of, 36 n.14. Plays: *All God's Chillun Got Wings*, 14, 48–55; *Anna Christie*, 25, 40, 47 n.9; *Desire Under the Elms*, 25, 39, 47 n.8; *Dreamy Kid*, 48; *Emperor Jones*, 48, 52, 56 n.20; *Great God Brown*, 39; *Hairy Ape*, 55 n.7; *Iceman Cometh*, 35 n.4, 37; *Ile*, 14, 41, 47 n.11; *Long Day's Journey into Night*, 13, 14, 25–36, 37, 41, 43, 47 n.10, 61; *Moon for the Misbegotten*, 25; *Mourning Becomes Electra*, 25, 35 n.13; *Strange Interlude*, 25, 27, 28, 35 n.10; *Welded*, 51, 53, 56 n.17
Open Theater, 18, 215–16

Paolucci, Anne, 202–3, 206, 207, 208, 210 nn. 18, 23, and 26
Parker, Brian, 98–99 n.19, 101 n.34
Parshley, H. M., 19
Pearlman, Mickey, 17
Perrine, Laurence, 191 n.3
Pinero, Arthur Wing. Play: *The Second Mrs. Tanqueray*, 36 n.27
Pirandello, Luigi, 219
Poe, Edgar Allan, 154
Popkin, Henry, 98 n.19
Porter, Catherine, 226 n.27
Porter, Thomas E., 98 n.15
Propp, Vladimir, 32, 36 n.21
Proust, Marcel, 29
Provincetown Playhouse, 48

Quirino, Leonard, 169 n.5

Rabelais, François, 172
Rabkin, Gerald, 225 n.12
Raleigh, John Henry, 26–28, 35 n.3, 50, 55 nn. 7 and 14
Ranald, Margaret Loftus, 48, 54, 55 n.4, 56 n.24
Redmond, James, 169 n.5
Reid, Kate, 96 n.3
Reiter, Rayna R., 66 n.1
Rich, Adrienne, 18
Riddell, Joseph N., 169 n.5
Robeson, Paul, 48
Robinson, James, 37–38, 47 n.3
Roderick, John M., 168 n.1
Rossetter, Kathy, 96 n.3
Roth, Philip, 208, 209 n.5, 210 n.28
Roudané, Matthew C., 144 n.2, 145 n.14
Roudiez, Leon S., 35 n.2
Rubin, Gayle, 14, 59–60, 65, 66 nn. 1 and 12

Sanders, Leslie Catherine, 50, 55 n.11
San Francisco Magic Theatre, 214
Schlueter, June, 170 n.12
Schneider, Daniel E., 99 n.22, 100 n.27, 101 n.30
Scholes, Robert, 170 n.11
Sedgwick, Eve Kosofsky, 14, 60, 66 nn. 5 and 7
Shakespeare, William, 32, 149, 175; characters in plays of, 179. Play: *The Tempest*, 32
Shaw, Irwin, 169 n.8
Sheaffer, Louis, 13, 34 n.1, 35 n.13, 37, 38, 39, 47 nn. 1 and 4, 49, 55 n.6
Shepard, Sam, 12, 18, 63, 213–40. Plays: *Buried Child*, 214, 219, 222; *Curse of the Starving Class*, 214, 216–17, 219, 221–22; *Fool for Love*, 18, 214, 215, 218, 219–24, 227–40, 239 n.6; *A Lie of the Mind*, 18, 214, 217–18, 227–40, 240 n.15; *Paris, Texas*, 218; *True Dylan*, 213, 224 n.1; *True West*, 214, 222
Sheppard, Sam, 214
Shewey, Don, 214, 225 n.3
Showalter, Elaine, 19 nn. 1, 2, and 8
Sievers, David W., 168 n.4
Simon, Sherry, 225 n.14
Sophocles. Play: *Oedipus the King*, 151–52
Stanton, Kay, 15
Stanton, Stephen S., 170 n.14
Stendhal, 12
Sterne, Laurence, 60, 66 n.5. Novel: *A Sentimental Journey*, 60
Strachey, James, 170 n.11
Strindberg, August, 37, 38. Play: *The Ghost Sonata*, 39, 51
Styron, Rose, 99 n.24

Taborski, Boleslaw, 56 n.18
Tandy, Jessica, 166
Tarule, Jill Mattuck, 47 n.12
Tharpe, Jac, 168 nn. 1 and 4, 169 n.5, 170 nn. 12 and 16, 179 n.3, 180 n.7
Theater Genesis, 214
Tillyard, E. M. W., 168 n.2
Timpane, John, 16–17
Tischler, Nancy M., 171, 179 n.1
Tiusanen, Timo, 35 n.7
Turner, Victor, 170 n.11
Twain, Mark, 55 n.7. Novel: *The Adventures of Huckleberry Finn*, 55 n.7
Tynan, Kenneth, 168 n.4, 171, 179 n.2

Valency, Maurice, 208–9, 210 n.29
Valgemae, Mardi, 205, 209 n.1, 210 n.22

Index

Veláquez, Diego, 229, 237. Painting: "Las Meninas," 229, 231, 237
Vidal, Gore, 170 n. 15
Vlasopolos, Anca, 16
von Szeliski, John, 114 n.4, 168 n.4

Walker, Alice, 54. Story: "Everyday Use," 54
Wasserman, Julian N., 198–201, 210 n.12
Weales, Gerald, 97 n.13, 101–2 n.37
Weissman, Philip, 169 n.7
Wilden, Anthony, 27, 35 n.6
Williams, Raymond, 150, 168 n.3
Williams, Tennessee, 12, 16–17, 149–80. Plays: *Cat on a Hot Tin Roof*, 177, 179 n.6; *The Glass Menagerie*, 171, 175; *The Milk Train Doesn't Stop Here Any More*, 171; *The Night of the Iguana*, 171, 173; *Orpheus Descending*, 175; *Small Craft Warnings*, 173, 174, 180 n.9; *A Streetcar Named Desire*, 16, 149–70; *Suddenly Last Summer*, 171, 175, 180 n.12; *Summer and Smoke*, 174, 175; *Sweet Bird of Youth*, 171. Other writings: "Note of Explanation," 179 n.6; "The Timeless World of a Play," 177–78, 180 n.11
Wilson, Ann, 239 n.8
Wilson, Robert, 215
Windham, Donald, 179 n.2
Winkler, Karen J., 239 n.2
Woods, Bob, 180 nn. 11 and 13
Wycherley, William, 60, 66 n.5. Play: *The Country Wife*, 60